Confucianism as a World Religion

Confucianism as a World Religion

CONTESTED HISTORIES AND CONTEMPORARY REALITIES

Anna Sun

PRINCETON UNIVERSITY PRESS

PRINCETON AND OXFORD

Copyright © 2013 by Princeton University Press
Published by Princeton University Press, 41 William Street,
Princeton, New Jersey 08540
In the United Kingdom: Princeton University Press, 6 Oxford Street,
Woodstock, Oxfordshire OX20 1TW

press.princeton.edu

Library of Congress Cataloging-in-Publication Data

Sun, Anna Xiao Dong, 1971–
Confucianism as a world religion : contested histories
and contemporary realities / Anna Sun.
pages cm
Includes bibliographical references and index.
ISBN 978-0-691-15557-9 (hardcover)
1. Confucianism. I. Title.
BL1853.S84 2013
299.5'12—dc23
2012036448

British Library Cataloging-in-Publication Data is available

This book has been composed in Sabon

Printed on acid-free paper. ∞

Printed in the United States of America

1 3 5 7 9 10 8 6 4 2

For YX

I use the term Confucianism as covering, first of all the ancient religion of China, and then the views of the great philosopher himself, in illustration or modification of it, his views as committed to writing by himself, or transmitted in the narratives of his disciples. The case is pretty much as when we comprehend under Christianity the records and teachings of the Old Testament as well as those of the New.

James Legge, *The Religions of China*, 1880

Confucianism is no more a religion than, say, Platonism or Aristotelianism.

Fung Yu-lan, *A Short History of Chinese Philosophy*, 1948

I have not found any formulation of a named religion earlier than the nineteenth century: "Buddhism" (1801), "Hindooism" (1829), "Taouism" (1839), "Zoroasterianism" (1854), "Confucianism" (1862). . . . We may simply observe once again that the question "Is Confucianism a religion?" is one that the West has never been able to answer, and China never able to ask.

Wilfred Cantwell Smith, *The Meaning and End of Religion*, 1963

CONTENTS

PREFACE

I REMEMBER THAT DAY WELL.[1] I was a first-year graduate student in sociology at Princeton University in the spring of 1999, full of curiosity and attending as many lectures and talks as I could, from sociology to history, from philosophy to literature. One day I saw a poster advertising a roundtable discussion on America's religious discourse. It was to take place in Richardson Auditorium, the imposing concert hall built in the late nineteenth century that has a magnificent presence on campus.

That evening, as I sat in the capacity audience that filled the ornate hall, waiting for the discussion to start, I was deeply intrigued. The roundtable had the most interesting lineup. In an article published a few days later about the event in the *Princeton Weekly Bulletin*, the speakers were described as follows:

> On April 8, the University Center for Human Values sponsored a roundtable discussion in Richardson Auditorium moderated by broadcast journalist Bill Moyers. Participants included William F. Buckley, Roman Catholic author and journalist; Rev. Dr. James Forbes, senior minister at the interdenominational Riverside Church, New York City; Rabbi Laura Geller, senior rabbi of Temple Emanuel, Beverly Hills, Calif.; Joan Halifax, Buddhist, founder of Upaya in Santa Fe, NM; Seyyed Hossein Nasr, professor of Islamic studies at George Washington University; and Tu Weiming, professor of Chinese philosophy at Harvard.[2]

For a long time I had known and admired the work of Professor Tu Weiming, a renowned scholar who was arguably the person most responsible for bringing Confucianism into the cultural mainstream in the United States in recent years, especially since the 1980s. But was Professor Tu a religious leader, the way the other panelists were? Was he representing a religion the way the senior rabbi was representing Judaism and the Zen Buddhist priest was representing Buddhism? What was the role of a "Confucianist," as Professor Tu sometimes called himself, in the company of people with clearly defined religious identities?

As someone who emigrated from Beijing to San Francisco at age nineteen, I was always deeply interested in religion. My parents were quite secular, although their secularity was more a matter of indifference than a concise decision. Not having grown up in religious households themselves, they had never given much thought to religion; their intellectual training being in French culture and literature, they emphasized the value of reason and rationality above all else. Their secular attitude was not entirely dissimilar to the Enlightenment-minded ideology of the Chinese socialist state, although unlike the state they were not against religion; they were merely not interested in it. But so many books in their library—from fiction to history—touched on religion, I realized later; they simply ignored the theme, whereas I gradually consciously searched for it. I grew up with the collective works of Hans Christian Anderson—in lyrical Chinese translation—which were often Christian tales of salvation and redemption enchantingly veiled in fairy-tale form. My diet of books gradually included Greco-Roman mythology, history of Christianity, esoteric tales of Tibetan Buddhism, and a great deal of nineteenth-century French and Russian novels, before adding Kierkegaard and Zen Buddhism to the mix in my late teenage years.

When I moved to San Francisco to be with my family and later attended the University of California, Berkeley, I was already intensely interested in the philosophy of religion and even theology, reading Tillich and Bonhoeffer while studying social theory. It was not by accident that I took a course on the sociology of religion in my final year at Berkeley. The seminar was cotaught by Professors Robert Bellah and Ann Swidler, and it profoundly changed my perspective on religion. I was very fortunate to have been there, I soon realized, for it was the last course Professor Bellah taught before his retirement.

It was in this seminar that I first read Max Weber's seminal work, *The Religion of China: Confucianism and Taoism* (1915). I found myself struggling with Weber's characterization of Confucianism as a world religion, which struck me as fundamentally problematic.[3] Isn't Confucianism a philosophy and a way of life rather than a religion, as I learned growing up in China in the 1970s and 1980s? From reading different accounts of Confucianism, I became aware of the many debates over the religious nature of Confucianism throughout history, but my impression remained that Confucianism was considered by most Chinese people to be a philosophy rather than a religion. For instance, I did not know anyone in China who would say that he or she is a believer of the "Confucian religion." The label "Confucian" normally refers to a moral or ethical outlook, or a particularly cultured or scholarly way of life.

On that day in the Richardson Auditorium at Princeton, each participant of the roundtable discussion represented a major religious tradition: Catholicism, Protestantism, Judaism, Buddhism, Islam, and, in the case of Professor Tu, Confucianism. This very much followed the commonly accepted category of "world religions" in our day; sometimes a few other religions, such as Daoism or Hinduism, are added, but the lineup on this panel was quite standard. As I later discovered, such assemblies have been taking place ever since the first World Parliament of Religions in Chicago in 1893, during which a Confucian official-scholar, Pung Kwang Yu, represented Confucianism.[4] That day at the Princeton roundtable, a little over a hundred years after the Chicago World Parliament of Religions, Professor Tu explained what it meant to be a Confucianist in our pluralistic contemporary life with his customary clarity: "My commitment to my way as a Confucian, which means learning to be human, is predicated on my ability to appreciate many different paths."[5]

But I was troubled not only by the question of whether one could speak of Confucianism as a religion, but also by the larger assumption that made this entire event possible: how did Confucianism become one of the so-called world religions?

This question led me to Firestone Library, the university library only a few hundred yards from Richardson Hall, with its fifty miles of bookstacks. I started with contemporary publications about world religions and world civilizations, of which there was a great number, most if not all mentioning Confucianism as one of the great religions of China, alongside Buddhism and Daoism. But when did the concept first come into being? A historian of China, Lionel Jensen, argued in his 1998 book *Manufacturing Confucianism* that the Jesuit missionaries of the sixteenth and seventeenth centuries were responsible for turning the ancient Confucian tradition into "Confucianism." But the Jesuits' understanding of Confucianism had only a limited impact, mostly in the missionary realm rather than in the larger social world. The way we view Confucianism as a world religion today seems to have originated in a very different source. I wondered whether it might have something to do with the globalization of the world, a historical, material, and institutional process of which the idea of "world religions" might have been an essential part.

One late night, while browsing the open stacks on the third floor of the library, looking for the earliest texts on comparative religions or world religions I could find, I discovered quite a few volumes that attracted my interest: *The Religions of China: Confucianism and Taoism Described and Compared with Christianity* by James Legge, published in 1880; *Natural Religion: The Gifford Lectures Delivered before the University of Glasgow* by Friedrich Max Müller, published in 1889; *Comparative Religion: Its Genesis and Growth* by Louis Henry Jordan, published in 1905. Then I realized that there seemed to be a pattern emerging. Many of these books were published between the late nineteenth century and early twentieth century, with quite a few printed in the 1880s and 1890s, the era that saw the convening of the first World Parliament of Religions in 1893. Eastern religions were prominent in the new classification of world religions, and many of the books included Confucianism as a world religion. Why were there so many books about world religions, especially Eastern religions, published between the 1870s and the early twentieth century? What was the story behind this sudden emergence of comparative religion scholarship as well as general interest books? And who was Friedrich Max Müller, cited in so many people's work from those years? These questions, rooted in my encounter with Weber's inclusion of Confucianism in his sociology of world religions project, eventually led to my dissertation research.[6]

I had the great good fortune of being guided throughout the dissertation process by Professor Robert Wuthnow, a sociologist of religion whose deep historical sensibility and genuine depth and clarity of thought have been my intellectual inspiration ever since.

The search for answers has taken me from Firestone Library to archives in Great Britain as well as Confucius temples in China, and from my dissertation work to subsequent research projects. My journey first took me to Oxford University, where Friedrich Max Müller and James Legge both taught in the late nineteenth century. I spent several months in the Department of Special Collections and Western Manuscripts at Bodleian Library, the place where materials related to Max Müller are stored. In the New Bodleian Reading Room, which is across the street from the splendid original limestone Bodleian Library, I went through every piece of paper in the Max Müller Archive, which filled more than eighty archival folders and boxes, examining everything from manuscripts to letters, from notebooks in Max Müller's own meticulous hand (one of which was devoted to his new project, "Sacred Books of the East") to letters and newspaper clippings saved by Max Müller himself ("Letters on Various Controversies in Which Max Müller Was Involved, 1845–91"). Through my time in the Bodleian as well as excursions into the East India Company Archive in the British Library in London and the University Archives at Oxford, Cambridge, and the University of Manchester, Max Müller's singular contribution to the making of Confucianism as a world religion became more and more apparent. It was Max Müller, the first professor of comparative religion at Oxford, who was responsible for the inclusion of Confucianism in the world religions paradigm, and he was aided by his acquaintance James Legge, the first professor of Chinese at Oxford and a former missionary in China, who was responsible for the translation of the most essential Confucian texts into English.

Other discoveries and connections were made in more serendipitous ways. During my first visit to Oxford, I stayed at Harris Manchester College, a small college with beautiful gardens and quiet quadrangles, thanks to a philosopher friend's introduction. It was very convenient, for it was only a stone's throw away from the Bodleian Library. When I consulted the college library, however, I was astonished by the sheer volume of books as well as pamphlets on comparative religions in its Carpenter Library. I later learned that it was the best collection of such texts at Oxford. The college was in fact one of the allies of the emerging field of comparative religion in the turn of the twentieth century, thanks to its status as one of only two non-Anglican colleges situated in Oxford, the other being Mansfield College, which was nearby. Leafing through the many pamphlets and books in the Carpenter Collection as well as the Library of Protestant Dissent at Harris Manchester, I discovered intellectual affinities between the German Lutheran Max Müller, one of only six Nonconformist professors at Oxford in his day, and Joseph Estlin Carpenter, the illustrious principal of Manchester College from 1914 to 1919, who was an important scholar of comparative religion and a well-known Nonconformist Protestant dissenter.

This connection allowed me to situate the making of Confucianism as a world religion in a broader historical context. It was certainly a story about missionary history in China and the British colonial production of knowledge of the East; it was clearly also a story about the institutional struggle to establish comparative religion as a progressive new discipline promoted by many Nonconformists (i.e., not members of the Church of England; non-Anglicans) in religiously conservative Anglican Oxford. These interconnected developments led to the birth of the new paradigm of world religions in the intellectual center of the British Empire, which has had lasting impacts in our contemporary world, including the classification of Confucianism as one of the great world religions. Indeed, the paradigm's ripples can still be felt today, which was what I experienced in the audience in Richardson Auditorium, astonished by the undisputed religious status of a Confucianist among religious leaders in the United States, nearly one hundred years after Max Müller's death.

But has this impact reached China? Why is Confucianism today not even one of the "Five Major Religions" recognized by the Chinese state? Are there people in China who treat Confucianism as a religion? What does it mean to be a Confucian in contemporary Chinese society in the first place? After my archival research in Oxford, which provided the main sources for my dissertation on the making of Confucianism as a world religion and the emergence of comparative religion as a discipline, I realized that these questions could be answered only through concrete fieldwork in China, through observing everyday practice and interviewing people about their religious life. This led me back to China for several years of extensive fieldwork; I traveled widely and learned firsthand about what was happening on the ground.

Between 2006 and 2009 I served as a co–principal investigator in the Templeton Foundation project "Empirical Studies of Religions in China," collaborating closely with other sociologists to study the contemporary revival of religion in Chinese society.[7] Working on a survey of 7,021 respondents in both urban and rural areas demonstrated to me the intrinsic complexity of doing survey research of religion in China; I also discovered the significant limits of the classification scheme of religions that most Western social scientists seem to take for granted. For instance, in the case of Confucianism, only 12 people out of 7,021 claimed to be "Confucians." Should we therefore draw the conclusion that Confucianism as a religion is nearly extinct in today's China?

My hunch was no, due to my awareness of the inherent methodological constraints of putting diverse Chinese religious practices into convenient yet problematic categories of "Buddhism," "Daoism," and "Confucianism." But how can we learn about the reality of Confucian religious life in China? The answer resides in Confucius temples, the sacred temple sites reserved for the veneration of Confucius and his disciples. We could learn a great deal about the present state of Confucian ritual life through studying ritual practice in these temples, whose tradition can be traced back two thousand years.

The first temple I conducted research in was the Confucius Temple in Foshan in 2000, a vibrant southern city known for its manufacturing. The experience was a revelation. From 2009 to 2011, as a participant in the "Confucian Revival in Mainland China: Forms and Meanings of Confucian Piety" international research project, I conducted fieldwork in twelve Confucius temples, including temples in Beijing, Shanghai, Hangzhou, Nanjing, Chengdu, Chongqing, Jinan, and Qufu. Along the way I interviewed people who offered prayers in Confucius temples, administrators and merchants who manage the temples and profit from the growing interest in Confucian ritual practice, as well as intellectuals involved in the current revival of Confucianism.

Indeed, the timing of this project couldn't have been better. There has been a gradual emergence of a revitalization of Confucian tradition in China in recent years, including a heated, very public intellectual debate over the religious nature of Confucianism in 2000–2004. I became one of the first social scientists to examine this revival. This has been a multifaceted revival that emphasizes, to different degrees, the cultural relevance, educational potential, ethical nature, and political prospects of Confucianism. Since 2008, around the time of the Beijing Olympics, the Chinese government has also been consciously promoting Confucianism for its own political purposes. One of the more radical developments is the formation of a small group of activists who envision Confucianism as a full-fledged state religion in China's future.[8]

The very last interview I conducted for this project was with Jiang Qing, the scholar who is an acknowledged leader in the promotion of Confucianism as the state religion of China. The interview took place in his home office in the city of Shenzhen, the so-called Chinese Silicon Valley, in December 2011. The city was a fishing town as recent as the 1970s, but at the time of my visit, I saw only innumerable glass-and-steel high-rises under a brilliant southern sky. Shenzhen's transformation is a powerful reminder of the tremendous economic growth China has undergone in the past thirty years. Designated as the first "Special Economic Zone" at the beginning of China's "Reform and Opening" policy in 1979, Shenzhen today is a major financial center and commercial port and has an extraordinary concentration of high-tech factories. Foxconn Technology, a company that manufactures products such as the iPad and iPhone for Apple, alone employs about four hundred thousand people. Foxconn started to attract international attention in 2010 when an exceptionally high number of suicides were reported at its Shenzhen factory, where workers lived in crowded dormitories and routinely worked twelve-hour shifts.[9] A series of articles in the *New York Times* in 2012 further scrutinized "the human cost" of the amazingly efficient production of state-of-the-art goods such as the iPad as well as the economic competitiveness of the Chinese labor force.

In this somber new world of relentless expansion of global capitalism, uncertainty over the future of Chinese political reform, and lament of the loss of traditional cultural meanings and ethical values, it is not surprising that, for many intellectuals, Confucianism represents the hope of stabilizing a fast-changing society with a much-needed cultural, ethical, political, and even religious foundation. A self-identified Confucian who offers a rigid interpretation of Confucian values and ideals, not unlike fundamentalists in other traditions, Jiang has been writing about the possibility of establishing Confucianism as a national religion since the 1980s. He has also made concrete efforts to revive Confucian ritual practice through supporting a small Confucian center called the Sacred Hall of Confucius in Shenzhen.[10] His proposition of adopting Confucian political philosophy to replace communist ideology has made him into a kind of political dissident; his views have been tolerated by the state, but his publications are constantly monitored and sometimes censored.[11]

The most striking aspect of Jiang's thought is his insistence on turning Confucianism into a full-blown form of religion, with rigorous religious doctrines and rituals, as well as an institutionalized clergy that has the possession of all Confucian temple properties, currently owned by the state. It is important to note that most of these ideas cannot be found in the actual history of Confucianism in China. A religious seeker who first explored Buddhism, then Christianity, Jiang is someone who believes that religion is essential to the establishment of a good and just society. In his articulation of Confucianism as a state religion, he has clearly been modeling his vision based on his own understanding of Christianity. However, although he is clearly attracted to both the ethical framework and religious depth of Christianity—in fact, he went as far as learning from a Christian friend how to pray—in his strongly nationalistic view, Confucianism would be a force against the spread of Christianity—a "foreign religion"—in a postsocialist China.

As Jiang narrated his own intellectual and religious journey over green tea in his book-lined study in one of the high-rise buildings, his gestures framed by a large window behind him through which numerous identical buildings could be seen in the distance, it suddenly dawned on me the extraordinary juxtaposition of different forces at work in this moment. Here, in a city representing the economic future of China, was an intellectual whose worldview had been shaped by the terrors of the Cultural Revolution in the 1960s and 1970s, the spiritual search for meaning experienced by many of his peers in the 1980s and 1990s, and the pride over the great strides China has made as well as the fear over the perceived threat of the domination of Western values in the 2000s. The notion of Confucianism as a religion represented for Jiang a uniquely Chinese solution to the problems of socialism and global capitalism.

Is Confucianism finally going to become a real religious force in Chinese society? The long historical shadow cast by the nineteenth-century classification of Confucianism as a world religion has grown pale in the brilliant light of the twenty-first century. As China goes through a profound economic and social transformation that makes it an increasingly vital part of the global world, the changing role Confucianism plays as a religion is unfolding at this very moment and may have a profound impact on China's future. It has been my great privilege to follow and chart Confucianism's course.

ACKNOWLEDGMENTS

IN ACKNOWLEDGING INTELLECTUAL debts acquired during a long project, there is some danger of appearing to bask in the light of great institutions and great minds. The simple truth is that the persons and institutions I wish to acknowledge are generous as well as great, and I have benefited from both these attributes.

Of the great institutions, I mention first Princeton University Press, as represented by my editor par excellence, Fred Appel, and his expert colleagues, Sarah David, Debbie Tegarden, Ali Parrington, and Joseph Dahm. I thank the editorial board of the press, and the anonymous readers who offered helpful comments. I thank the Institute for Advanced Study, which welcomed me in 2010–11; my wonderful academic home, Kenyon College; the Chiang Ching-kuo Foundation, for the collaborative project "Confucian Revival in Mainland China: Forms and Meanings of Confucian Piety" (2009–12); the John Templeton Foundation, for the research project for which I served as co–principal investigator, "The Empirical Study of Religions in China" (2006–9); the Mellon Foundation, for archival research in the United Kingdom; the Institute for Historical Research at the University of London; Harris Manchester College, Oxford; and Princeton University's Department of Sociology. I also thank the Chinese Academy of Social Sciences for many courtesies.

It must never be forgotten that libraries and archives are great institutions, too. I thank the Firestone and Gest East Asian libraries of Princeton University; the Harvard-Yenching Library; the library of the Institute for Advanced Study; and the Bodleian Library, Oxford. Among the archives at Oxford, I thank the Department of Special Collections and Western Manuscripts at the Bodleian Library, and the archives of the Taylorian Institute, Harris Manchester College, and Mansfield College. I thank the archive of Oxford University Press; the British Library's British India Office archive; the archive of the University of Manchester; the archive of the Faculty of Oriental Studies at the University of Cambridge; and the archive of the School of Oriental and African Studies at the University of London.

Some parts of this book initially appeared in edited volumes in earlier forms. I thank Koninklijke Brill NV for permission to use material from two published chapters: "The Fate of Confucianism as a Religion in Socialist China: Controversies and Paradoxes," in *State, Market, and Religions in Chinese Societies* (2005), and "The Revival of Confucian Rites in Contemporary China," in *Confucianism and Spiritual Traditions in Modern China and Beyond* (2012), both edited by Fenggang Yang and Joseph Tamney. I thank Oxford University Press for permission to use material from my chapter "To Become a Confucian" in *Oxford Handbook of Religious Conversion*, edited by Lewis Rambo (forthcoming).

As to great minds, my thanks go first to my undergraduate mentor in the sociology of religion who continues to be my intellectual inspiration, Robert Bellah, at the University of California, Berkeley, where I was fortunate to also absorb the teaching of Ann Swidler. At Princeton, my incomparable dissertation advisor was the Confucian *junzi* Robert Wuthnow. There I benefited also from the wise and rigorous instruction of Susan Naquin and the generous support of Gilbert Rozman. Michele Lamont, now of Harvard University, has been a constant intellectual guide who has inspired me to continue pursuing research on the sociology of knowledge.

I thank my distinguished collaborators in the Templeton Foundation project, Rodney Stark, Byron Johnson, Fenggang Yang, and F. Carson Mencken; and in the Chiang Ching-kuo Foundation project, Sébastien Billioud, Joël Thoraval, and Takahiro Nakajima.

Of friends made at the Institute for Advanced Study, I am particularly grateful to Joan Scott, Didier Fassin, Tomoko Masuzawa, Jeffrey Stout, Nicola Di Cosmo, and the members of the "Secularism Seminar," the "Moralities Seminar," and the Asian Studies seminar. I single out for special affection the venerable Giles Constable.

I thank colleagues who have invited me to give talks based on this project. They include Merle Goldman at Harvard Fairbank Center for Chinese Studies, Daniel Bays at Calvin College, Barry Keenan at Denison University, and Tao Jiang and On-cho Ng of the University Seminar on Neo-Confucian Studies, Columbia University. I have benefited greatly from their feedback and also from the comments made by colleagues and students who attended the talks. I also thank colleagues who have offered comments at various conferences in sociology, Asian Studies, and Religious Studies where I presented earlier versions of chapters in this book.

At Kenyon College I thank my supportive colleagues in sociology Howard Sacks, Jennifer Johnson, Marla Kohlman, Jan Thomas, John Macionis, Ric Sheffield, Nikole Hotchkiss, and Celso Villegas. Special thanks go to George McCarthy for being an inspiration in social theory. Colleagues in Asian Studies and Religious Studies who have helped my research include Joseph Adler, Ruth Dunnell, Miriam Dean-Otting, Royal Rhodes, Jianhua Bai, and Wendy Singer.

In the wider community of scholars—I wish I could mention all who have helped me—I thank Andrew Abbott, Roger Ames, Stephen Angle, Timothy Barrett, Richard Bernstein, Miranda Brown, Nicholas Bunnin, Wendy Cadge, Hsi-Yuan Chen, Heu-Yuan Chiu, Kelly Clark, John Comaroff, Paul Copp, Deborah Davis, William Theodore de Bary, Daniel Garber, Robert Harding, Kimberly Hart, Renate Holub, Becky Hsu, Chin-shing Huang, Chun-chieh Huang, Hans Joas, Sungmoon Kim, Keith Knapp, Cecile Laborde, James Z. Lee, Xun Liu, G.E.R. Lloyd, Yun-feng Lu, Richard Madsen, Martin Maw, Barry Mazur, Gretchen Mazur, Margarita Mooney, the late Frederick Mote, Diane Obenchain, Robert Pippin, Michael Puett, Lewis Rambo, Jeffrey Richey, Peter Dale Scott, Zoe Shen, Kwong-loi Shun, Fabien Simonis, William Swatos, Stephen Teiser, Michael Tian, Weiming Tu, Ezra Vogel, the late Frederic Wakeman, Ann Waltner, R. Stephen Warner, R. Bin Wong, Robert Woodberry, Chuck Wooldridge, King-to Yeung, Jiyuan Yu, Victor Yuan, Everett Zhang, and Sharon Zhu.

I am especially grateful to Fenggang Yang, P. J. Ivanhoe, Peter Perdue, and Thomas Wilson for their great insights and intellectual generosity.

These scholars have enriched the pages that follow. Responsibility for errors and misjudgments that remain is mine alone.

This book would not have been possible without the deep love, unconditional support, and daily intellectual inspiration of my husband, Yang Xiao. I dedicate this book to him, for it has been our shared journey.

Confucianism as a World Religion

Introduction

Confusions over Confucianism

THE PROBLEM I SET OUT TO SOLVE in this book is the confusions and controversies over the religious nature of Confucianism. Although Confucianism has long been commonly accepted as one of the major world religions in our popular imagination, and portrayed as the most important religion of China in introductory textbooks on world religions, it might come as a surprise to many that it is neither considered a religion by most people in China nor counted as a religion by the Chinese government. In fact, Confucianism is not included in the Chinese official classification of the Five Major Religions, which includes Buddhism, Daoism, Islam, Catholicism, and Protestantism. And although many scholars in the West have treated Confucianism as a religion since the turn of the twentieth century, such as Max Weber in his influential 1915 study *The Religion of China: Confucianism and Taoism*, intellectual disagreements among scholars over whether Confucianism is actually a religion have never ceased. Today these ongoing debates take place within many academic disciplines, including religious studies, history, anthropology, philosophy, Asian studies, sinology, and sociology.

In recent years several excellent and widely read studies of Confucianism have renewed people's interest in the life and thought of Confucius, such as *The Authentic Confucius* and *Lives of Confucius*, as well as research that draws attention to the important development of Confucianism in contemporary Chinese society, such as *China's New Confucianism*.[1] And a few studies have made major contributions to the historical and theoretical examinations of the concept of religion, from *Genealogies of Religion* to *The Invention of World Religions*.[2] This is indeed the perfect time for us to revisit the deep-seated issues involved in the confusion over the religious nature of Confucianism.

I argue that the confusions come mainly from three sources: (1) the conceptualization of Confucianism as a world religion at the end of the nineteenth century in Europe, which was a historical product of the emergence of the "world religions" paradigm in the West; (2) the problematic way in which Confucianism—and Chinese religions in general—has been studied in the social sciences, represented by survey research that often recycles existing questions, such as "Do you belong to a religious denomination?" which are based on a Judeo-Christian framework of religion that cannot capture the complexity and uniqueness of Chinese religious life; and (3) the complex and often contradictory development of Confucianism in today's China, in which Confucian rituals are currently experiencing a lively revival among ordinary people, while the state is consciously promoting Confucianism as a possible source of political ideology and social ethics in order to legitimize its rule in the twenty-first century.

In the past twenty years, there has indeed been a revival of diverse religious ritual practices in Chinese society, including Confucian ritual practice, as the country undergoes rapid technical, industrial, and economic growth. The Communist Party has been grappling with the tension between its stated atheism and the reality of China's ritual-rich religious life, and Confucianism has emerged as a possible test case for the party to modify or even reinvent its relation to religion. As an ancient, "native" tradition rather than something with a "foreign" origin, such as Christianity, Confucianism also has broad appeal to many increasingly nationalistic Chinese people, including a sizable number of intellectuals. It is indeed conceivable that Confucianism may play a significant role in China's political developments in the near future, as Daniel Bell suggested in his 2008 book *China's New Confucianism: Politics and Everyday Life in a Changing Society*.[3] However, institutionally and politically, the religious status of Confucianism in China has never been fuzzier.

In this book I set out to untangle the many tousled threads that have made the discussion of the religious nature of Confucianism particularly difficult, both in the past and in the present. In order to make sense of the many seeming contradictions in our understanding of Confucianism, we need to be aware of the epistemological, political, and social assumptions that are embedded in the discussions of its religious nature. All concepts and classifications have histories, and I contend that in the case of the controversies over Confucianism as a religion, they are never purely intellectual or scholarly disagreements; there are always complex political and social dimensions to the struggles over the classification of Confucianism.

WHY CONFUCIANISM MATTERS

What constitutes a religious life in today's world? What are the new forms of religious life for people living in the twenty-first century? I suggest that the case of Confucianism can help us see beyond the existing social scientific criteria that center on church attendance and membership, which are rooted in monotheistic definitions of religious life that are primarily influenced by the religious histories of Euro-America, and instead turn our attention to the shifting boundaries of religious life that are constantly redefined and made sense of through the richness of people's shared everyday life.

On October 23, 2009, the *New York Times* published an article titled "Globally, Religion Defies Easily Identified Patterns."[4] The article refers to the report, "Religious Change around the World," released the day before by Tom W. Smith of the National Opinion Research Center at the University of Chicago.[5] The thorough report rightfully claims to be "the most comprehensive analysis to date of global religious trends," yet for anyone looking for a definitive answer to the secularization debate, he or she is bound to be disappointed. For instance, in the case of the United States, although the report confirms that there have been declines in terms of church attendance and identification with a religion, when it comes to the frequency of praying, there have been clear increases in recent years: "Daily praying (several times a day + daily) fell from 54% in 1983 . . . then rose to a high of 59% in 2004–2006."[6] Indeed, as the report concludes,

> But this does not amount to a simple confirmation of secularization theory. The secularization hypothesis predicts a general and sweeping decline in religion. While the preponderance of evidence does show a secular shift across time, age cohorts, and levels of development, the pattern is very mixed and nuanced. Trends are not universal and vary greatly in magnitude and on how widespread they are. They differ both across and within religious traditions and geo-cultural regions. Also, there is considerable variation across different religious indicators.[7]

This report is unusually perceptive in its emphasis on the variations across different religious indicators. And it also points to how different indicators—whether we examine church attendance, membership identification, or frequency of prayers—will give us vastly different understandings of the state of religious life in a given society.[8] A recent essay in the *New York Review of Books*, "China Gets Religion!," makes a great case for broadening our conceptual frameworks about religion in order to discover the vibrant religious life being lived in Chinese society.[9]

These conclusions resonate clearly with my own research on the reemergence of religious life in contemporary China in general, and the revival of Confucian rituals in particular. However, there are two main difficulties in describing Confucianism in the traditional language of religion. The first lies in the fact that it is hard to define membership in Confucianism because there are no definitive conversion rites in Confucianism, such as baptism in Christianity, which is a necessary rite for many Christians, or the rite of *guiyi* in Buddhism, which is an elective rite for the most devout Buddhists rather than for all Buddhists. There is nothing that is the equivalent in the Confucian tradition, even though there have been recent attempts to create such rituals for Confucianism, including efforts made at the Sacred Confucius Hall in Shenzhen, which remain isolated attempts, still too obscure for most people to even be aware of.

The second comes from the fact that there are no official religious organizations in contemporary Confucianism, such as churches or mosques, nor is there an official priesthood or clergy. Although there are still many Confucian temples available for ritual practice in China, they are officially cultural institutions, under the auspices of the State Administration of Cultural Heritage (*guojia wenwu ju*), an agency that is part of the Ministry of Culture.[10] Even the two most ardent promoters of Confucianism as a religion today, the Hong Kong Confucianity Academy (established in 1930) and the Sacred Hall of Confucius in Shenzhen (established in 2009), are not registered as religious organizations; the former is an educational and cultural institution with no campus of its own, and the latter is a cultural venue sharing space with an art gallery in a large public park.

As Confucianism lacks a conversion rite, official religious organizations, and a clergy, it is indeed difficult to speak of membership in Confucianism in general, since the social foundation of Confucianism is not religious institutions but diverse and interconnected social and cultural systems. As a result, to become a Confucian is a gradual process that involves ritual practices, moral self-cultivation, as well as participation in certain Confucian cultural and social institutions. Moreover, to be a Confucian has meant very different things in different historical periods and different cultural contexts in China. Indeed, to be a Confucian is to have one of the most fluid identities, hence the traditional religious indicators cannot be applied to Confucianism straightforwardly.

What makes the case of Confucianism representative of certain characteristics of contemporary religious life might be its "diffused" rather than "institutional" nature, as C. K. Yang first suggested in 1961.[11] In the case of institutional religion, we find churches or mosques with a clear institutional structure, organized clergy, and definitive membership affiliations. In the case of diffused religion, the religious activities are conducted in a wide range of settings, such as the family, and there is often a fluid sense of belonging—rather than the more visible institutional ties of membership—shared by people who participate in common ritual practices. Sociologists such as Nancy Ammerman and Lynn Davidman have been studying religions outside of the often confining framework of organized institutions; for instance, by focusing on the everyday practices of Judaism as "lived religion" or "everyday religion," they show how people creatively "live out" their religious identities in everyday life, instead of trying to define them through their memberships or beliefs.[12]

My study shares similar concerns. I believe we should respect the primacy of the everyday practice of religion, and I agree with the critical insight that it is us, scholars of religion, who should try to adjust our conceptualizations and definitions of religion in order to accurately represent the rich, diverse social reality of practice through our research. It should not be the other way around. This is indeed the approach taken by several excellent recent empirical studies of religion in contemporary China, from Adam Chau's 2006 ethnographic study *Miraculous Response: Doing Popular Religion in Contemporary China* to Vincent Goossaert and David Palmer's 2011 comprehensive analysis *The Religious Question in Modern China*, which examines the development of China's multiple religious modernities.[13] Other notable examples—both historical and contemporary research—include recent work by Richard Madsen, Mayfair Yang, Xun Liu, and Rebecca Nedostup.[14]

Does this mean that a more diffused religious tradition such as Confucianism is as *legitimate* a religion—conceptually—as the ones that are centered on institutionalized practice, such as congregational life? Should we pay as much attention to personal worship and other noninstitutional forms of rituals, such as private prayers, as to more institutionalized forms of religious action, such as church attendance? One might suggest that we can find many forms of prayers and prayerfulness in Confucian life, from communal prayers in Confucius temples during formal ceremonies to private prayers to Confucius, to meditative practices such as the reading of classical texts from the Confucian canon, which is a tradition that is similar to *lectio divina*.[15]

Furthermore, we see over and again in both survey research and ethnographic fieldwork that a Chinese person may routinely worship at different religious sites belonging to "different religions"—"different" according to our classification—concurrently, from a temple devoted to Confucius to another devoted to the *guanyin* bodhisattva, from a shrine for the God of Wealth to the shrine for one's ancestor spirits, sometimes on the same day or in the same week. Should we argue that it is wrong to conclude that this person's practice is deviant from the perceived standard behavior of religious life, which assumes that one should follow the practice of only a single religious tradition at a given time?

I argue that the answers have to be yes to such questions, for it is of utmost importance for us to take seriously forms of religious life that are fundamentally different from the monotheistic model that has been the unacknowledged norm in the history of the scientific study of religions. Instead of treating the differences between the actual Chinese religious practices and our existing intellectual framework as denoting something abnormal, exceptional, or impure, we need to reevaluate our own conceptual schemes and treat the actual practice in everyday life in China as normal and legitimate, no matter how novel it might seem to us.

This new emphasis on the uniqueness of religious life rather than its perceived commonness (the kind of questions asked in religion surveys around the world, including belief, membership, church attendance) will allow us to do better justice to the rich, imaginative, and creative nature of religious practice as lived by people in different societies. Indeed, in societies not dominated by Judeo-Christian or Muslim traditions, such as China, non-monotheistic religious life has been the more familiar form of practice. We might discover that Chinese religious life has more in common with Greek and Roman religions before the rise of Christianity than with contemporary America, where the main mold and logic of religious practice has been monotheistic.[16]

By focusing on the uniqueness of Confucianism in this study, I hope we will arrive at a more complete account of the fate of religion in our increasingly rationalized, scientifically advanced, yet still often miraculously enchanted twenty-first-century life. By critically examining the historically conditioned theoretical categorization of Confucianism as world religion, as well as its implication in the social scientific research about Confucianism and Chinese religions in general, we can allow ourselves to focus on the empirical reality of Confucianism through conceptual lenses that are informed by our historical sensibility, methodological reflection, and an openness about the meaning of the very notion of "religion" itself in our global contemporary life.

THE MOST PRESSING QUESTIONS

For every scholarly project, there are at least one or two hard-hitting questions that touch on the deepest concerns of that particular intellectual enterprise. They might take the form of a question from the audience after a public presentation of the project or the form of a written response from a colleague who has thought about the same issues long and hard. They might even take the form of a nagging concern that refuses to go away as one tries to formulate a systematic solution to the problem at hand. Such questions are necessary for the integrity of the project; one has to deal with them with as much clarity as possible, either implicitly in one's thinking about the fundamental issues or explicitly in one's answers to critics. Such questions keep us honest.

For this project, the most hard-hitting question seems to be the following: although great efforts seem to have been made to historicize the concept of religion and especially the concept of Confucianism as a religion, the question remains whether there is a hidden definition of religion that is being used in discussions of the contemporary revival of Confucianism. In other words, is there a "minimal" definition of religion—Durkheimian perhaps—being implicitly adopted, since this study has an emphasis on the revival of Confucian rituals? Is this project committing to an unacknowledged normative understanding of religion as ritual practice?[17]

Indeed, why do we emphasize ritual practice in Confucianism? In *Ritual and Its Consequences*, Seligman et al. argue that they are more interested in what rituals do than what they are. Their insight on the performative aspect of rituals resonates with my research. They state that ritual "creates and re-creates a world of social convention and authority beyond the inner will of any individual," and they argue that this understanding of ritual is central to many traditions, especially Judaism and Confucianism: "[S]uch traditions understand the world as fundamentally fractured and discontinuous, with ritual allowing us to live in it by creating temporary order through the construction of a performative, subjunctive world. Each ritual rebuilds the world 'as if' it were so, as one of many possible worlds."[18]

I believe that ritual in the Confucian tradition has indeed been helping create "a world of social convention and authority" for people who practice them, and ritual has been the fundamental element that holds this tradition together through thousands of years of fractions and discontinuities. Ritual practice in Confucianism has been essential, continuous, as well as creative. Regardless of how we define Confucianism and whether we call it a "religion," Confucian rituals have been and will possibly remain the most salient component of this complex tradition, from the time of Confucius's teaching to the dawn of the twenty-first century. Instead of trying to understand the changing landscape of Confucianism only through decoding Confucian thoughts, it is time for us to pay close attention to the actual ritual actions carried out by ordinary people. These actions represent a link with the past, as well as a bridge to the future.

Although I do not attempt a substantive definition of religion in this study, as a sociologist I do believe that it is important for us to stay value-neutral regarding whether Confucianism is a religion. In his invigorating book *Religion in China: Survival and Revival under Communist Rule*, Fenggang Yang suggests that "there are three major social forces contending to define religion: scholars, believers, and the government."[19] This is indeed the case, and it is especially true in contested situations such as Confucianism. In his book Yang does offer a substantive definition of religion; he believes that it is our obligation as social scientists—both to be "socially responsible" and to "engage in scientific endeavor"—to strive to define religion in our research.[20]

My response is to emphasize the uniqueness of my sociological project, which is an in-depth analysis of the processes through which the state and other social actors—including scholars of Confucianism, social scientists, Confucian practitioners, and other activists—contest, negotiate, and construct Confucianism. In this project I am not offering an analytical and substantive definition of religion as a scholar because it is essentially irrelevant to my subject matter. What I am studying is not whether Confucianism *is* a religion but whether and how Confucianism has been constructed and contested as a religion by various social forces.

More specifically, this is what I mean by my value-neutral position. Because of the late nineteenth-century formulation of the "world religions" paradigm, it has already become a *social fact* that Confucianism has been understood as a world religion for over a century, both in our popular imagination and in our academic knowledge production. It exists independent of what competing definitions of religion we as scholars use. The truth is that we can no longer go back to the time when Confucianism was not seen as a world religion; we are living with the very concrete legacy of this historical classification and its lasting legacy. As scholars we must closely examine this social fact of "Confucianism as a world religion" through concrete, historical, and empirical analysis.

And this social fact is not unchanging. The classification of Confucianism is what the philosopher of science Ian Hacking calls an "interactive kind." In *The Social Construction of What?*, Hacking argues that "ways of classifying human beings interact with the human beings who are classified":

> There are all sorts of reasons for this. People think of themselves as of a kind, perhaps, or reject the classification. . . . Moreover, classifications do not exist only in the empty space of language but in institutions, practices, material interactions with things and other people. . . . Interactions do not just happen. They happen within matrices, which include many obvious social elements and many obvious material ones. . . . Inanimate things are, by definition, not aware of themselves in the same way. Take the extremes, women refugees and quarks. A woman refugee may learn that she is a certain kind of person and act accordingly. Quarks do not learn that they are a certain kind of entity and act accordingly.[21]

Indeed, the classification of Confucianism as a world religion exists not only in language but also in institutions, practices, and material and social interactions. The classification has been made use of by Western comparative religions scholars since the 1870s, Chinese political activists since the 1910s, social scientists since the turn of the twentieth century, and potentially the Chinese state in the near future. These social actors have tried to modify, challenge, negotiate, or redefine the content and meaning of the classification, and the classification also affects the actual practice and identification of people who are subjected to it. As a matter of fact, this particular classification has been having this interactive, "looping effect" for over a hundred years, and my research aims to show the matrices through which the interactions take place.

In doing so, I examine the ways in which Confucianism is employed by different people and groups—as a religion or not as a religion—without agreeing with one side of the debate or the other. In other words, as a sociologist, I focus on the observation, analysis, and unpacking of the social factors related to the different positions, such as the concrete ways in which people engage with the debate, rather than offering an open-and-shut definition of religion.

This also allows me to stay open-minded in examining future possibilities of the development of Confucianism. For instance, if Confucianism were to be classified as a religion by the Chinese government in the near future, I would be studying what effects this change might have on the ways people practice Confucian rituals and ethics, and what effects this might have on people with other religious identities. Would Confucianism acquire new forms of conversion process? Would a Chinese Christian still feel comfortable considering herself or himself Confucian? An analytical strategy of distinguishing "use" and "mention" is indeed sometimes useful in this context; I often do not "use" religion as a category in my analysis—that is, according to a normative, universal definition—but I do "mention" and pay close attention to the myriad ways people make use of the category of religion throughout my historical and ethnographic work.[22] As a result, I can examine the diverse cultural, political, and institutional processes underlining debates and conflicts without holding a specific position regarding whether Confucianism is a religion.

In other words, my engagement with religion—what is claimed to be or contested to be religion in social life—is fundamentally historical, acknowledging both the historical nature of its changing developments in social reality and the historical nature of the changing categories we use as scholars in understanding them. This means that the intellectual concepts and heuristic tools available to us in this particular given historical moment also condition my attempt at a value-neutral analysis, the way all humanistic scholarship is. Rather than trying to offer an ahistorical definition of religion, I follow Nietzsche's insight in *On the Genealogy of Morality*: "Only something which has no history can be defined."[23]

UNDERSTANDING CONFUCIANISM EMPIRICALLY

The three themes of this book—the historical process of the making of concepts and classifications regarding Confucianism in the nineteenth century, the problems with social science methodology in our study of

Confucianism in the twentieth century, the multifaceted realities of the revival of Confucianism in contemporary China in the twenty-first century—constitute the three parts of this book. Part I, "The Puzzle of Classification: How Did Confucianism Become a World Religion?" has three chapters. In chapter 1, "Four Controversies over the Religious Nature of Confucianism: A Brief History of Confucianism," I briefly introduce the four major controversies in the past five centuries over whether Confucianism is a religion: The first is the Chinese Rites and Term Controversy (1579–1724), which involved Jesuit missionaries in China. The second is what I call the Term Controversy (1877–91); it involved missionaries in China as well as scholars in the newly emerging intellectual discipline "comparative religion." (This controversy is examined in full in chapter 2.) The third is the Confucianity Movement (*kongjiao yundong*) (1911–20), which was a failed movement to make Confucianity (*kongjiao*) into China's state religion. The fourth is the latest debate over the religious nature of Confucianism, the so-called Confucianism as a Religion Controversy (*rujiao shijiao zhizheng*), which took place in China between 2000 and 2004. (This debate is examined in full in chapter 3.)

Chapter 2, "The Making of a World Religion," examines the connection between the making of Confucianism as a religion and the emergence of comparative religion as a discipline in Grant Britain in the late nineteenth century, based primarily on extensive archival research I conducted in the Max Müller Archive at Bodleian Library in Oxford, the British India Office Archive at the British Library, and the Archive at the Oxford University Press. I show that by allying himself with Max Müller and the emerging discipline, former missionary and the first professor of Chinese at Oxford James Legge moved the controversy over the religious nature of Confucianism from the small circle of missionaries in China to a new arena, which was the emerging field of comparative religious studies, and both the settlement of the so-called Term Controversy and the legitimation of Confucianism as a world religion were facilitated by the new discipline. Through innovative boundary work, Max Müller and Legge helped establish a legitimate intellectual field to promote the discourse of world religions of which Confucianism was an essential part.

Chapter 3, "The Confucianism as a Religion Controversy in Contemporary China," analyzes the contemporary debate in China over whether Confucianism should be classified as a religion. I first introduce the formation of the official religious classification, the Five Major Religions in the 1950s in socialist China; I then focus on the contemporary Confucianism as a religion controversy in 2000–2004, an important debate among Chinese intellectuals with significant academic, social, and political implications.

The next part of the book, part II, is titled "The Problem of Methodology: Who Are the Confucians in China?" and contains three chapters devoted to the difficulty of studying Confucianism in empirical research. Chapter 4, "Confucianism as a World Religion: The Legitimation of a New Paradigm," is an overview of how Confucianism has been classified as a world religion in both popular and academic texts in the past one hundred years. Through an analysis of popular as well as scholarly publications, academic associations, and academic curriculum since the turn of the twentieth century, I suggest that this classification has had a lasting impact on both our popular imagination and academic institutions.

Chapter 5, "Counting Confucians through Social Scientific Research," discusses the long-standing problem of identifying Confucians in China (and East Asia in general) through social science research methods, a problem deeply rooted in the nineteenth-century conceptualization of Confucianism and the overall classification of Chinese religions. In this chapter, as someone who has had experience designing a major survey of Chinese religious life in 2007, I argue that we need to fundamentally change the way we frame our research questions in order to gain a real sense of the diversity and vitality of Chinese religious practice.

Chapter 6, "To Become a Confucian: A New Conceptual Framework," offers a new conceptual framework for addressing the empirical question of who the Confucians are in China, suggesting a three-tier definition that takes into consideration Confucian religious ritual practice such as Confucius worship and ancestral worship, as well as Confucian spiritual exercise and social rituals. In this conceptualization, we might be able to make the distinction among a ritual Confucian, a spiritual Confucian, and a cultural Confucian in the context of contemporary life.

The last part of the book, part III, is titled "The Reality of Practices: Is Confucianism a Religion in China Today?" It can be argued that there have been several important stages in the recent endorsement of Confucianism by the Chinese state. I suggest that these developments can be divided into five steps, each signified by concrete and noteworthy events:

1. *The Political Ideology Step*
   This critical step was signified by the use of the "harmonious society" (*hexie shehui*) slogan, explicitly borrowed from Confucian political philosophy, by President Hu Jintao on September 19, 2004, at the Sixteenth Chinese Communist Party Congress. It has become the central political idea of the Hu Jintao–Wen Jiabao administration; the party has been using the slogan consistently since then.[24]

2. *The State Ritual Step*
   The first official veneration of Confucius in the Qufu Confucius Temple on September 28, 2004, marked the beginning of this development. The annual formal ceremony has been broadcast

on Chinese national television since 2005. Since then, numerous formal ceremonies honoring the birthday of Confucius have taken place in Qufu and Beijing, as well as many provincial cities and towns with newly renovated Confucius temples.

3. *The Culture Step*
The culture step has at least two parts. The first aspect is the overseas one, represented by the founding of the first Confucius Institute on November 21, 2004, in Seoul, South Korea, which launched a global project supported by state funding in the amount of two billion yuan. By the end of August 2011, there were already 353 Confucius Institutes and 473 Confucius Classrooms in 104 countries and regions in the world.[25] Indeed, now one can find a Confucius Institute "from Paris Diderot University to Penn State University, and from Argentina to Zimbabwe."[26] They not only promote the name of Confucius as a Chinese cultural brand but also attempt to recast contemporary China as synonymous with Confucianism. The second aspect is domestic, represented by the October 2006 broadcast of Yu Dan's widely popular seven-part television lecture series on the *Analects* of Confucius, aired on a state-owned, prime Chinese television station. Her book on the *Analects* based on the series has sold several million copies.

4. *The Confucian Symbol Step*
This refers to the emphasis of China's Confucian heritage through symbolic means, such as images, texts, and artworks. The opening ceremony of the Beijing Olympics on August 8, 2008, with its numerous references to Confucius and Confucianism, was the first major event that attempted to link China's recent rapid economic growth—displayed in the cutting-edge stadiums and the high-tech capability of the Beijing Olympic Games—with its Confucian past. The latest example might be the erection of the giant bronze statue of Confucius near Tiananmen Square in January 2011, which was mysterious taken down a few months later, on April 21, 2011.[27]

5. *The International Politics Step*
This is a new development in the state's promotion of Confucianism. One might argue that the award of the first Confucius Peace Prize on December 8, 2010, possibly a response to the 2010 Nobel Peace Prize, is one of the first exercises in using Confucius as an explicit political tool on the stage of international politics.

As we can see, 2004 marked the turning point of the official revival of Confucianism in ideological, ritualistic, and cultural terms. Explicitly symbolic and political uses of Confucianism on the international stage soon followed and have increasingly intensified.

In my study, I focus on personal rituals performed in Confucius temples rather than formal ceremonies, such as the annual veneration and worship of Confucius taking place on his birthday on September 28, which so far have been mostly organized and conducted by central or local government officials.[28] Although such ceremonies certainly contain religious elements, they tell us more about the way in which the state mobilizes symbolic resources for its own political purposes than the less noticeable, yet arguably more resilient revival of Confucian rituals practiced by ordinary people.

Chapter 7, "The Emerging Voices of Women in the Revival of Confucianism," examines the role of women in the current revival of Confucianism, from their participation in intellectual debates regarding Confucianism, to their promotion of Confucian thoughts in popular culture, to their participation in ancestral worship rituals.

Chapter 8, "The Contemporary Revival and Reinvention of Confucian Ritual Practices," is based on my fieldwork from 2000 to 2010, primarily interviews and participant observations in a dozen Confucius temples throughout China. I suggest that there is a noteworthy revival as well as reinvention of religious ritual practices in Confucius temple settings, and there is also a revival of Confucian social rituals in today's China.

Chapter 9, "The Politics of the Future of Confucianism," touches on the possible future developments of Confucianism in Chinese society: as cultural identity, political ideology, ethical outlook, ritual practice, symbolic tool in politics, and even the foundation for the civil religion of China. Will Confucianism evolve into a full-fledged "religion" in the current social and political climate? Will there be tension between a "Confucian religion" and other religious traditions? This chapter addresses these important issues regarding the future of Confucianism.

PART I

THE PUZZLE OF CLASSIFICATION

How Did Confucianism Become a World Religion?

CHAPTER 1

Four Controversies over the Religious Nature of Confucianism

A Brief History of Confucianism

"The Master Said": Confucius and His Disciples

ACCORDING TO THE ARCHAEOLOGIST Lothar von Falkenhausen, the "age of Confucius" started five hundred years before Confucius's birth and lasted till the end of China's great Late Bronze Age (ca. 1000–250 BCE).[1] This coincided with the Zhou dynasty (ca. 1046–256 BCE), the longest dynasty in Chinese history. Von Falkenhausen suggests that it was during this "age of Confucius" that the foundation of Confucianism was established. The so-called Five Classics were written during this period—the *Odes*, *Documents*, *Rites*, *Changes*, and *Spring and Autumn Annals*—which later became part of the Confucian classical canon. It was also during this period that the traditional ritual system was stabilized and instituted, which included the worship of ancestral spirits.

The Zhou dynasty is divided into two parts: the Western Zhou dynasty (1046–771 BCE) and the Eastern Zhou dynasty (770–256 BCE). The Eastern Zhou dynasty consisted of the Spring and Autumn period and the Warring States period. During the Spring and Autumn period, the many small states that carved up China were in constant warfare with one another, with 1,219 wars over about 250 years, until one state, Qin, conquered the rest.[2] In 221 BCE, the so-called First Emperor finally consolidated all the states and established the Qin dynasty, which was the first unification of China.

Confucius (ca. 551–479 BCE) lived through this tumultuous period of constant warfare between patrimonial states, and the experience greatly shaped his ethical and political thought. Confucius was born in the state of Lu and was orphaned at a young age. The sinologist D. C. Lau notes that we know little of Confucius's youth except that he was poor and fond of learning; Confucius once remarked that "at fifteen I set my heart on learning" (*Analects*, 2.4).[3] Renowned for his erudite mind and virtuous character, Confucius eventually became a much-revered teacher, although he always wanted to be a trusted advisor to a powerful ruler, a desire shared by many scholars of his time, in order to help create a peaceful and well-ordered society, governed not by brutal physical force but by the virtue of benevolence (*Analects*, 12.19).

Finally, at the age of fifty, Confucius was appointed to be the minister of crime of Lu. However, his advice was not followed, and he decided to leave the state in 497 BCE with some of his disciples. Confucius did not return to Lu for thirteen years; during his exile he visited different states and offered advice to rulers who cared to listen. He returned to Lu when he was sixty-eight, and he devoted the remaining years of his life to teaching until his death at seventy-two. Legend has it that Confucius had three thousand disciples during his lifetime, and this number was repeated in the first century BCE historical text *Records of the Grand Historian*. Among the disciples, twelve are mentioned frequently in the *Analects*, which is a collection of sayings and anecdotes of Confucius edited by his disciples and the students of his disciples. Confucius and his followers always looked back to the founders of the Zhou dynasty, the Sage Kings, as moral and political exemplars, particularly as the dynasty was reaching its final stage, marked by disorder.

Confucius famously said that he was "a transmitter, not a creator" (*Analects*, 7.1). Von Falkenhausen points out that Confucius gave clear philosophical expressions to gradual changes in society that had been ongoing long before his time, such as the emphasis of living community rather than divine ancestors in ritual practice, the stress on honest reverence rather than sanctimonious display, and, most important, the valuing of virtues, which can be obtained through self-cultivation, over noble lineage. Indeed, for Confucius, to be a *junzi*, originally meaning being a prince, was no longer a birthright but was achieved. Because of Confucius's teaching, *junzi* came to mean a virtuous person, regardless of one's birth or social status.

Although Confucius notably stated that he preferred not to address matters related to gods and spirits (*Analects*, 7.21), there were many discussions about the proper performance of rituals in the *Analects*, and the importance of ritual practice to Confucius cannot be underestimated. Confucius spoke of *tian*, literally meaning the sky, or the heaven above, frequently; there are fifty-one mentions of this in the *Analects*. According to the philosopher P. J. Ivanhoe, Confucius believed that heaven had a concrete plan for human beings, and that he had been chosen to play a special role in the realization of this plan toward a peaceful, just, and harmonious society; the proper way to achieve this ideal world is the *dao* (the way).[4] Ivanhoe also points out that Confucius demonstrated a dynamic view of worship, especially regarding sacrifice and prayer. For Confucius, reverence on the part of those participating in worship is important; he expressed little interest in prayers for supplication, and he considered that he had been praying throughout his life by following the *dao* (*Analects*, 7.35).

The so-called Cult of Confucius, which venerated Confucius's spirit after his death, did not start until the Han dynasty (206 BCE–220 CE), after the fall of the short-lived Qin dynasty (221–207 BCE). The first mention of a cult of Confucius was in the late Han dynasty, when an emperor sent a surrogate to venerate the spirit of Confucius at Confucius's grave. Several Han emperors followed his example by offering sacrifices at Confucius's family ancestral temple in Qufu. Subsequent emperors of different dynasties carried out this ritual practice, and Confucius temples—temples devoted to the veneration of Confucius and his disciples—also flourished in major cities and prosperous towns throughout Chinese history. According to the historian Thomas Wilson, in the imperial pantheon of gods and spirits that dominated Chinese temple life, the temples devoted to the veneration of Confucius occupied a notable place in the hierarchy, and they have been an important part of Chinese religious life.[5]

In the Tang dynasty (618–907), a liturgy for the worship in Confucius temples was constructed based on canonical texts on rituals, and these codes for sacrifices were used throughout imperial China, with modifications along the way. Wilson notes that the Tang codes required the first offering be presented by the crown prince, the second and the third by the two top officials of the Directorate of Education; in the Ming dynasty (1368–1644), the ritual sacrifices were supervised by senior officials from the Court of Imperial Sacrifices, the Directorate of Education, and the Ministry of Rites.[6]

Besides such public and state performances of rituals, another important component of Confucian ritual practices was the personal worship of ancestral spirits. Although ancestral worship existed in China long before the rise of Confucianism, it has been appropriated by disciples of Confucius as an essential ritual. When the Jesuit missionaries in China were forced to deal with the issue of the Chinese Rites in the seventeenth century, which became the so-called Chinese Rites and Term Controversy, the heart of the matter was Franciscan and Dominican missionaries'— and later the Vatican's—objection over Chinese converts' participation in Confucian ritual ceremonies, as well as their practice of keeping ancestral shrines at home, with tablets inscribed with their ancestors' names.

THE CONFUCIAN CANON AND THE CIVIL SERVICE EXAMINATION SYSTEM

The centrality of Confucianism in the social, cultural, and political life of China is closely related to the centrality of the civil examination system in the long history of imperial China, which started with the first unified dynasty in 221 BCE and ended with the demise of the last dynasty in 1911. Although the origin of the examinations can be traced back to the Han dynasty, it was Emperor Yang of the Sui dynasty (581–618) who established the first civil service examinations in 605, selecting officials for the court by testing their knowledge of literary subjects. Throughout the Tang and Song dynasties (650–1250), the examinations, which focused on the Confucian canon, were greatly expanded and methodically institutionalized. By the Song dynasty, exams were held at the local, provincial, and national levels every three years, with candidates going through tests that took from twenty-four to seventy-two hours to finish in complete isolation in specially built exam cells (the historical site of the large provincial civil examination complex, in the southern city of Nanjing, at one point housed twenty thousand exam cells). It was through this rigorous and rigid examination of knowledge of Confucian learning that officials were selected, which solidified the incorporation of the Confucian canon into the foundation of state cultural and political ideology.

According to the historian Benjamin Elman in his definitive analysis of the civil examination system, *A Cultural History of Civil Examinations in Late Imperial China*, the system was the institutional link that connected three important aspects of Chinese political, social, and cultural life: (1) the imperial dynasties used the rigorous civil service examinations to select officials to fill the most important positions within the dynastic government; (2) the gentry-literati elites (selected members of the gentry who maintained their elite social and cultural status through classical scholarship as well as knowledge of lineage rituals) utilized the examinations to gain political positions and economic assets; and (3) classical studies, which formed the core content of the examinations, flourished because of the examinations, yet they were also reconstructed through the complex interactions between imperial bureaucracy and elite gentry-literati groups.[7]

Classical studies in China had traditionally been the studies of the Confucian canon, yet the canon never stayed exactly the same. The classical Confucian curriculum was constantly adjusted and reinterpreted, especially in the late imperial period, namely, the Ming (1368–1644) and Qing (1644–1911) dynasties. Elman argues that late imperial examinations made "Dao learning," which is often translated as Neo-Confucian learning, the orthodoxy in official life as well as in literati culture.

THE FOUR BOOKS: THE LEGITIMATION
OF THE NEO-CONFUCIAN ORTHODOXY

Beginning in the Han dynasty and throughout the early years of the Song dynasty, the Confucian canon consisted of the Thirteen Classics, which included the early texts, the Five Classics, as well as later texts such as the *Analects*, the *Mencius*, and *The Classic of Filial Piety*. Even as the canon was expanding, the Five Classics remained the essential texts on how to achieve an ideal society as well as how to become a virtuous person, and they were used as the foundation of the civil service examinations. However, by the fourteenth century, the emphasis of the Five Classics in examinations was replaced by a new grouping of Confucian texts, the so-called Four Books, and this shift in the classical curriculum marked an important moment in the development and transformation of Confucianism in China.

This change reflected the great impact of a new school of Confucian thought and practice that started in the Song dynasty, which is what we now call Neo-Confucianism. It was Zhu Xi (1130–1200), a leading Neo-Confucian philosopher, who was one of the first to advance the idea of the Four Books, which included the *Analects*, the *Mencius*, the *Great Learning*, and the *Doctrine of the Mean*. As the historian Daniel Gardner points out, this moving away from the Five Classics points to an "inward shift" toward morality that is governed not by social conventions or rituals but by inner sources of personal morality.[8] Zhu viewed the newly grouped Four Books, texts that advocated the idea of self-cultivation through both philosophical and spiritual exercises such as contemplation and reading, as the most significant parts of Confucian texts. By doing so, he de-emphasized the complex historical lessons put forth by the Five Classics, the old set of selections from the Confucian past.

The civil examinations in effect instituted the Song Neo-Confucian moral philosophy as the orthodox of Confucian thought in the fourteenth century, and as a result the Neo-Confucian interpretation of Confucianism became the orthodoxy throughout late imperial China, until the end of the examination system in 1905, a few years before the fall of the Qing dynasty in 1911.

CONFUCIANISM AS A RELIGION IN MODERN CHINA

Not long before the Chinese Republican Revolution in 1911, during which the Qing dynasty was overthrown, there were intellectuals who felt that China needed a national religion in order to strengthen its cultural and political identity on the world stage. In 1895, Kang Youwei

(1858–1927), an eminent scholar and a leader in the political reform movement, campaigned for the establishment of Confucianism as a state religion. Kang believed that this could be China's answer to the challenges of the modern age, in which each nation had its own identity on the world stage; the modern Western powers claimed Christianity as their spiritual guiding force, and Confucianism could be made into a key piece in his reform and modernization plan for China. However, this attempt failed both politically and socially by 1916.[9]

A few years later, in 1919, the anti-imperialist and modernizing May Fourth Movement began its deep transformation of Chinese social and political culture. It gave birth to the New Culture Movement, which had its heyday in the 1920s and advocated both democracy and science for a new, modern China. During this period, traditional values and practices were treated as defective and backward, preventing China from becoming part of the modern world, and Confucianism began to be seen as the source of all social and political ills of China. Hu Shih (1891–1962), a leading intellectual in the May Fourth Movement, famously said in 1921, "Down with Confucianism!," which soon became a slogan.[10] It was an attitude shared by many Chinese communists.

During the Cultural Revolution (1966–76), Confucianism was again vilified as the foundation of malevolent traditional "feudal" values and was constantly condemned. The anti-Confucian sentiment reached its height when Confucius himself was singled out in the "Criticize Lin Biao, Criticize Confucius" (*pilin pikong*) political campaign (1973–76), initiated by Mao Zedong as a political strategy to denounce Mao's former designated successor and deceased rival Lin Biao and his followers, and this "last-ditch struggle" became "the Cultural Revolution's last hurrah."[11]

Shortly after the Communists took power in 1949, the government announced their official classification system of religions, which is still in effect in China today. According to this Five Major Religions (*wuda zongjiao*) classification, there are five officially recognized religions in China: Buddhism, Daoism, Catholicism, Protestantism, and Islam. This classification scheme was the product of a particular set of political and social concerns of the Chinese government in the 1950s, which is addressed in more detail in chapter 3.

CLARIFICATION OF TERMS

Before we start investigating some of the key controversies over Confucianism as a religion throughout history, we need to first clarify the different usages and meanings of the term "Confucianism," both in English and in Chinese.

Although the word "Confucius," the Latinized name of Kong Fuzi, was first used by Jesuit missionaries in China in the late sixteenth century, the English word "Confucianism" didn't come into existence until the nineteenth century. According to the *Oxford English Dictionary*, the term "Confucianism" was first used in a passage mentioning "Confucianism, the state and national creed" in 1862.[12] However, the real usage of the word as referring to a religion wasn't until 1877, in James Legge's pamphlet *Confucianism in Relation to Christianity*. In a later text, Legge elaborated on the meaning of the word "Confucianism":

> I use the term Confucianism as covering, first of all the ancient religion of China, and then the views of the great philosopher himself, in illustration or modification of it, his views as committed to writing by himself, or transmitted in the narratives of his disciples. The case is pretty much as when we comprehend under Christianity the records and teachings of the Old Testament as well as those of the New.[13]

Today "Confucianism" in English refers to both the philosophical teaching of Confucius and the religion associated with Confucius.

In Chinese, however, it is difficult to find the exact equivalent of the English word "Confucianism." One might say that the English term "Confucianism" as referring to a religion is both a translation and an invention. The closest Chinese term might be *rujiao*, "the Confucian religion," but the word *jiao* doesn't always mean "religion" in Chinese. Indeed, a great number of confusions about Chinese religions are related to equating the Chinese word *jiao* with the English word "religion" without further qualifications. In fact, the term *jiao* did not acquire its current usage as "religion" until the turn of the twentieth century.[14]

For instance, Buddhism, Daoism, and Confucianism are commonly referred to in Chinese as *sanjiao*, a phrase that first appeared in ninth-century China, but the term meant "three teachings" at the time, rather than "three religions." The literal meaning of *jiao* is "teaching," and the contemporary usage of *jiao* as "religion" didn't start until the beginning of the twentieth century, when the word *jiao* became part of a newly coined term *zongjiao*, which does explicitly mean "religion." T. H. Barrett and Francesca Tarocco suggest that the two words, *zong* and *jiao*, have in fact been "brought together in the sixth century by one or two scholar-monks who differentiated strands in Buddhist thought as different 'principle-teaching,' combining the two terms, though other similar terms were also current."[15] The "slightly *ad hoc*" combination eventually found its way to Japan among the Buddhist clergy, and it was "reintroduced to China as *zongjiao* towards the end of the nineteenth century."[16]

In fact, the modern meaning of the word in Japanese was a fairly recent creation as well, which was first used in treaties between Japan and the West, as Sarah Thal states:

During the nineteenth century, as European and American ships repeatedly sought and finally gained entry to Japanese ports, a nativist movement gained vigor in part by reviving attacks on Buddhism and Christianity as foreign forms of worship. Thus, when the term *religion* (translated as *shukyo*, "sectarian teachings") was introduced into Japanese in the 1860s as part of treaties guaranteeing the rights of resident foreigners, the concept quickly became associated with "evil, foreign teachings" antagonistic to native tradition and subversive of native authority.[17]

In other words, the ad hoc classical Chinese term *zongjiao* acquired new usage in Japan in its encounter with the West and produced a new category with its own social and political connotations.

When the term was reintroduced to China in the turn of the twentieth century, it was politicized in a different way in the Chinese context, as the historian Rebecca Nedostup remarks:

The upshot of this act of triangulated translation was that the Japanese reintroduced to China an already familiar term, *zongjiao*, but in a newly unfamiliar sense—a "return graphic loan," in Lydia Liu's phrase. The prior existence of *zongjiao* as a compound referring to Buddhism, Anthony C. Yu writes, may well have influenced Japanese translations (and the Chinese officials and scholars of subsequent decades who followed them), but the discourse in which *shukyo/zongjiao* applied was now much broader. In fact, even before the redefined term *zongjiao* was popularized in China, the modern sense of religion as national characteristic and evangelistic instrument of social Darwinian competition had crept into the thought of politicians such as Kang Youwei; in essence, then, *jiao* (teaching) had taken on the characteristics of *zongjiao avant le nom*. It was these qualities—as well as the notion of separating religion from politics, education, science, and so on—that distinguished the realm of modern religion, *zongjiao*, from the categorization of *jiao* that had preceded it, much in the way the post-Reformation secularist calculus of religion had created that category anew on the bed of earlier conceptions of European religious life.[18]

This new concept of religion has had many profound implications. For instance, one of the subsequent assumptions about religion is that when we speak of "three religions" rather than "three teachings," we are referring to three distinct religions that are mutually exclusive. This distinction among "religions" is a new development. According to Xun Liu, a historian of Daoism, many Daoists have seen the "three teachings" as complementary to one another rather than contradictory. Chen Yingning (1880–1969), "arguably the most influential theoretician and practitioner of the Daoist self-cultivation practice known as 'inner alchemy,'" was representative of this view:

[Chen] argued that the three teachings of Confucianism, Buddhism, and Dao-ism must not be perceived as mutually exclusive. From his own experience of having studied all three, he did not see any barriers among them.[19]

Indeed, this was a position shared by Confucian literati as well as practitioners of Buddhist and Daoist teachings throughout the history of imperial China.

In the contemporary Chinese debates over the religious nature of Confucianism, scholars have followed the following unspoken rule of distinguishing often confusing terms: *rujia* (the school of Confucian teaching) and *ruxue* (Confucian learning) are usually used to refer to Confucianism as a philosophy or school of thought, whereas *rujiao* (the Confucian *jiao*, or the Confucian religion) is used to refer to Confucianism as a religion. In this book, I translate *rujia* and *ruxue* as "Confucianism as a philosophy" or "Confucian thought" and *rujiao* as "Confucianism as a religion" or the "Confucian religion."

The Key Positions Regarding the Religious Status of Confucianism in Contemporary Scholarship

Confucianism as Philosophy

The Chinese term *zhexue* (philosophy) did not come into existence until the 1880s. Nishi Amane (1829–87), a Japanese scholar who studied in the Netherlands, invented the term on the basis of two Chinese characters to translate the Dutch term *filosofie*.[20] The first book-length history of Chinese philosophy was by Hu Shi (1891–1962), titled *The Outline of Chinese Philosophy*, with the first volume appearing in 1919. This history of the beginning of modern Chinese philosophy is important because it shows that, just like the category of religion, philosophy as a category in China is also an early twentieth-century invention.

The first landmark book that treated Confucianism primarily as a philosophy was the two-volume history by Feng Youlan (1895–1990), *A History of Chinese Philosophy*, translated into English by Derk Bodde in 1952 and still in print today.[21] The second was the influential and authoritative anthology by Wing-Tsit Chan (1901–94), *A Source Book in Chinese Philosophy*, written in English and published in 1963 (there is now a Chinese translation).[22]

Chan famously attributed "humanism" to Confucius; the following passage is from a section called "The Humanism of Confucius":

[T]he humanistic tendency had been in evidence long before his time, but it was Confucius who turned it into the strongest force in Chinese philosophy. He did not care to talk about spiritual beings or even about life after death.[23]

New generations of philosophers working on Chinese philosophy in America often teach in philosophy departments, such as David Wong, P. J. Ivanhoe, Roger Ames, Bryan van Norden, Eric Hutton, Chenyang Li, Li-Hsiang Lisa Rosenlee, and JeeLoo Liu. They are now teaching in philosophy departments and tend to read Chinese thinkers primarily as philosophers; their work focuses largely on conceptual analysis and reconstruction of arguments.[24]

Confucianism as Thought

Scholars of intellectual history tend to resist using "Chinese philosophy" as a label for Confucianism; instead, they prefer the phrase "Chinese thought." We can find this approach in some of the best intellectual historians of China, such as Benjamin Schwartz, Frederick W. Mote, Hoyt Cleveland Tillman, Peter Bol, Willard Peterson, and Yu Ying-shi. The most comprehensive history of schools of thought in early China is arguably Schwartz's *The World of Thought in Ancient China*, which treated Confucianism less as a philosophy in Plato's sense than as a system of thought that deals with the self, politics, and society.[25]

Wing-Tsit Chan and his collaborator William Theodore de Bary both emphasized the metaphysical and philosophical content of Confucianism. Many scholars who treat Confucianism as thought, such as Hoyt Cleveland Tillman and Peter Bol, have argued that Chan overemphasizes metaphysics and philosophy in Neo-Confucianism, overlooking its social and political aspects.[26] Yu Ying-shi has recently argued that *daoxue* (the Dao learning, usually translated as Neo-Confucianism) should be understood primarily as a political movement and political thought.[27]

Confucianism as Social and Political Ethos

Social scientists have long been interested in the role of Confucianism in the development of modern Asia. Following the publication of Weber's *Religion of China: Confucianism and Taoism*, especially its English translation in 1951, many have connected Confucian values with the so-called "modernization process" in Asian countries such as China, Japan, Korea, and Singapore. For instance, the sociologist Gilbert Rozman's volume *The East Asian Region: Confucian Heritage and Its Modern Adaptation* deals with the social implications of Confucian values in premodern and modern times in what he calls Confucian East Asia. In their volume *Modernization, Globalization, and Confucianism in Chinese Societies*, sociologists Joseph B. Tamney and Linda Hsueh-Ling Chiang examine the impact of modernization and globalization on Confucianism in Mainland China, Taiwan, and Singapore.[28]

Scholars who are interested in the so-called "Asian Values versus Human Rights" debate, or the political and social issues in contemporary China in general, such as democracy, human rights, family, and gender, often treat Confucianism more as a social and political philosophy than as a religion. The Asian Values versus Human Rights debate was an international event, especially in the 1990s; politicians and heads of states made declarations, and many academics joined in the discussion.

A prominent scholar in the debate was Daniel A. Bell, a Canadian-born philosopher who has been teaching political philosophy at Qing Hua University in China. He views Confucianism largely as a communitarian philosophy that connects the self, family, community, and the state, and his 2008 book *China's New Confucianism: Politics and Everyday Life in a Changing Society* is a major contribution to the discussion of Confucianism as social and political ethos in contemporary China.[29]

Confucianism as Religiosity and Spirituality

There are also scholars who treat Confucianism as both social-political philosophy and religious tradition, such as William Theodore de Bary, Tu Weiming, and Irena Bloom.[30] Tu Weiming's earliest argument for Confucian religiosity can be traced back to his 1976 book *Centrality and Commonality: An Essay on Chung-Yung*.[31] The Chinese translation of the book has a different title, *The Religiosity of Confucianism: Modern Interpretation of Zhongyong*, which stresses the central theme of the book, namely Confucian religiosity.[32] Tu sometimes also uses the term "spirituality" instead of "religiosity."

The phrase "Boston Confucians" originated in 1991, at the Second Confucian-Christian Dialogue Conference in Berkeley. Three participants from Boston—Robert Neville, John H. Berthrong, and Chung Chai-sik—shared similar views regarding Confucianism, treating it as a tradition with strong elements of religiosity.[33] Robert Neville, a theologian and longtime dean of Boston University Divinity School, and John Berthrong, professor of comparative theology at Boston University, have been Boston Confucianism's most significant advocates.[34]

Confucianism as Rituals and Practices

The religious studies scholar Rodney L. Taylor is often regarded as having done "perhaps the most extensive analysis of Confucianism as a religion."[35] He has published extensively on the religious dimensions of Confucianism, such as *The Cultivation of Sagehood as a Religious Goal in Neo-Confucianism* (1978), *The Way of Heaven: An Introduction to the Confucian Religious Life* (1986), and *The Religious Dimensions of*

Confucianism (1990).[36] The historian Thomas Wilson has arguably done the most exemplary historical work on the ritual aspect of Confucianism; his studies of the ritual formation of Confucian orthodoxy and the Confucian family and state cults are widely admired and cited.[37]

Now let us turn to two scholars whose views regarding Confucianism are even more difficult to categorize, yet both are central to a nuanced understanding of the divergences among scholars in Confucian studies today. The historian Benjamin Elman agrees with Wilson that Confucianism is not purely a system of social and ethical philosophy:

> The previous tendency to conceive of literati thought (*Ruxue*) in imperial China purely as a system of social and ethical philosophy certainly overlooked liturgical practices, such as the public and private expressions of imperial and literati respect for Confucius demonstrated by performing sacrifices in temples directly honoring the sage and his disciples.[38]

However, Elman still emphasizes the nonritualistic aspect of Confucianism and views the elite literati's practice as the essential aspect of Confucianism:

> It's best to think about Confucianism as a kind of classical learning. It is a largely secular tradition focusing on politics, government, and society—how human beings should live, what's the best way to organize a society and a state, how morality should inform a society. It's somewhat analogous to the classical traditions of Greece and Rome that Europeans valued so highly.[39]

This is reflected in his suggestion that *ru* should be translated as "classicism," a view shared by the historian Michael Nylan.[40]

The religious studies scholar Stephen Teiser's take is similar to Elman's in some respects. In his introduction to *Religions of China in Practice*, titled "The Spirits of Chinese Religion," Teiser observes that in the Han dynasty, the term *ru*, which he calls Confucianism, covered at least the following three things:

1. Books: Confucianism amounted to a set of books that were mostly written before Confucius lived, but the later tradition associated these books with his name.
2. Ritual apparatus: Confucianism had a complex ritual apparatus, an empire-wide network of shrines patronized by government authorities.
3. Conceptual scheme: Confucianism was a conceptual scheme, a fluid synthesis of some of Confucius's ideals and the various cosmologies popular well after Confucius lived.[41]

Although this is a typology of the Han dynasty beliefs and practices, it can still be used to point to the diverse intellectual approaches in the study of *ru* today. The focus on the ritual apparatus can be seen as an indicator of one's affinity with a more religion-oriented understanding of Confucianism; for instance, the historian Susan Naquin includes Confucian temples in her definitive study of Peking temples, and the anthropologist Jun Jing centers on the rebuilding of a Confucian temple in a rural village in his ethnography.[42]

If we put together recent works by Taylor, Wilson, Elman, Teiser, and many others, a consensus seems to emerge about the extremely diverse, nuanced, history-specific, and practice-specific aspects of Confucianism, and some of these aspects are "ritualistic" or "religious."

As G.E.R. Lloyd has argued in *Disciplines in the Making: Cross-Cultural Perspectives on Elites, Learning, and Innovation*, the distinctions between realms of knowledge that we today take for granted, such as philosophy, history, art, religion, and science, are in fact historical products of discipline making by learned elites in institutions of education, which should not be assumed to "correspond to well-defined areas of social and human experiences."[43] The many differing views on the nature of Confucianism—as philosophy, thought, social and political ethos, spirituality, or religion—is a good example of this discrepancy between disciplinary knowledge and concrete historical and social reality.

Interestingly, these contrasting—sometimes even contradictory—scholarly views do not necessarily lead to intellectual conflicts today, for academic scholars in general tend to engage in discussions only in one's own disciplinary field, which has a clear and often strict boundary, such as history, philosophy, and sociology. Only in the occasional interdisciplinary settings, such as conferences that include people from different disciplines, do these differences become pronounced, such as the divergence between a philosopher's take on Confucianism and a sociologist's. Despite the existing intellectual disagreements, however, such exchanges are in general very congenial, for the competitions take place mostly within one's discipline, rather than across disciplines.

But there have been fierce conflicts over the nature of Confucianism in history, when the issue at stake was not merely intellectual but theological, political, and social as well. These controversies have crossed the boundaries of not only intellectual fields but also political and social institutions.

Four Historical Controversies over the Religious Nature of Confucianism

Throughout history, there have been several rounds of major conflicts over the religious nature of Confucianism. I argue that there have been four major controversies: (1) the Chinese Rites and Term Controversy, 1579–1724; (2) the Term Controversy, 1877–91; (3) the Confucianity

TABLE 1.1. Major Controversies over Confucianism

	The Chinese Rites and Term Controversy 1579–1724	The Term Controversy 1877–91	The Confucianity Movement 1911–20	The Confucianism as a Religion Controversy 2000–2004
Main issues in the debate	**The Term** Whether "Deus" should be translated as *shang-ti*. **The Rites** Whether Chinese Catholic converts could worship/venerate their ancestors and Confucius.	**The Term** Whether "Deus" or "God" should be translated as *shang-ti*; whether Confucianism, or "the cult of Confucius," should be considered a religion (the term "Confucianism" was invented in 1862).	**The Term** Whether *kongjiao* (Confucianity) should become *guojiao* (state religion) in China after the Republican Revolution in 1911.	The religious nature of Confucianism in China.
Main participants	Jesuit, Franciscan, and Dominican missionaries; Chinese Catholic converts; the Vatican; the Qing imperial court.	Protestant Missionaries in China; Western sinologists; Western comparative religion scholars; colonial institutions that supported the publication of key texts that settled the controversy.	Confucianity organizations such as the Association of Confucianity (*kongjiaohui*); public intellectuals; politicians.	Public intellectuals with political agendas; scholars of Chinese classicism, history, and philosophy; activists in the emerging movements that promote Confucianism as a religion.

| Settlements | The Jesuit mission was terminated by Emperor Yongzheng in 1724. In 1939, Pope Pius XII finally lifted the prohibition on the veneration of ancestors. | Confucianism was included in the classification of eight major world religions by Max Müller in 1891 and is part of the *Sacred Books of the East* seminal series. | The Confucianity Movement faded away after it was used to justify a failed attempt to establish a new monarchy. | Not yet settled. |

Movement Controversy, 1911–20; and (4) the Confucianism as a Religion Controversy, 2000–2004. (The Term Controversy and the Confucianism as a Religion Controversy are discussed in depth in the two following chapters.)

Although these controversies differ greatly in historical details, they in fact share striking structural similarities. For instance, they share the same objective, which is to define Confucianism vis-à-vis the concept of religion; they also share a similar mixture of participants, including individual actors, religious organizations, scholars and academics, and the Chinese state. Among the controversies, three have more or less been settled historically, although the settlements had little to do with the authority of intellectual persuasions or arguments; they were settled because of the larger social and political forces at work. The future settlement of the one remaining controversy over the religious nature of Confucianism will also be the result of various cultural, social, and political power struggles. Here is a comparative overview of the four controversies:

The First Controversy: The Chinese Rites and Term Controversy, 1579–1724

The first major controversy over Confucianism started with Jesuit missionaries in China.[44] The Jesuit China Mission was founded by Francis Xavier (1506–52), who went as far as Japan but did not reach China. The most prominent Jesuit missionary in China was Matteo Ricci (1552–1610), who arrived in Macau in 1582, lived in various parts of China, and died in Beijing in 1610. By the time of his death, he had translated the Four Books, then considered essential reading in the Confucian canon, into Latin. He had also translated Epictetus's *Handbook* into Chinese, composed songs for the emperor's court, and converted several eminent Chinese literati.[45]

Jonathan Spence tells us how legendary Ricci still is in contemporary China:

> From the first moment I went to China as a student, the one Chinese name of a Westerner that I found recognized by everyone was Li Madou, Matteo Ricci. To say I was interested in Li Madou evoked smiles and nods all over China. This Italian Jesuit, who went to China in 1583, has a kind of special resonance in the hearts of the Chinese even now in the 1990s, a remarkable tribute to one particular missionary.[46]

Ricci was celebrated for his linguistic abilities and extraordinary memory, among other accomplishments. According to Spence, "Ricci wrote quite casually in 1595 of running through a list of four to five hundred random Chinese ideograms and then repeating the list in reverse order, while Chinese friends described him as being able to recite volumes of the Chinese classics after scanning them only once."[47] In the beginning Ricci wore a Buddhist's robe in order to appear more Chinese, but after spending a dozen years in China, he discovered that he should emulate the influential Chinese literati in his appearance in order to "gain greater status" and to be taken seriously, and he began to dress as a Confucian scholar.[48] These are indeed telling details, for they show how Ricci was willing to adapt to Chinese culture in many different ways and that his missionary work was as much about accommodation as conversion.

Around 1600 Ricci began formulating his famous "accommodation policy," which had two parts. First, he argued that the Chinese ritual practices of veneration of ancestors and of Confucius were not based on a theory or doctrine that the ancestors' ghosts existed or that Confucius was a god, hence Chinese converts should be allowed to practice these rites. Second, he believed *Deus* (God) should be translated by using the existing Chinese term *shang-ti*. D. E. Mungello, a leading historian of Jesuit missions in China, offers a rich account of Ricci's Confucian-Christian synthesis in his meticulous study of the Jesuit accommodation policy:

> The term "accommodation" applies to the setting in China where Jesuit missionaries accommodated Western learning to the Chinese cultural scene and attempted to achieve the acceptance of Chinese literati through the Confucian-Christian synthesis. Ricci noted that the Confucian scholar-officials even denied that they belonged to a religious sect, but rather constituted an academy devoted to good government and the welfare of the empire, with an emphasis upon keeping an ordered and peaceful society. . . . Ricci stated that the Confucian precepts were in conformity with the innate light of reason and Christian faith. . . . Ricci prepared the ground for his Confucian-Christian synthesis by stating: "The teachings of the academy, save in some few instance, are so far from being contrary to Christian principles, that such an institution could derive great benefit from Christianity and might be developed and perfected by it."[49]

Ricci's strategies were representative of Jesuit missionaries in China. However, not long after Ricci's death in 1610, the Jesuits faced severe setbacks. Here is Mungello's brief account of the so-called Chinese Rites Controversy:

> In 1692 when the Kangxi Emperor [of the Qing dynasty] issued the Edict of Toleration for Christianity, the glory and hope surrounding that ruling were already undermined by the Chinese Rites and Term Controversy (abbreviated hereafter as "Rites Controversy"). . . . The Chinese names for God as well as the rituals used to honor ancestors and Confucius were at the core of this

bitter 17th century debate. On one side of this controversy stood accommodative Jesuits who argued that the indigenous Chinese terminology for God did not taint the Christian God with pagan associations. While there was some difference of opinion among the Jesuits on the question of terminology, they were nearly unanimous in arguing that most Chinese rites to ancestors were not idolatrous. They believed that the rites to ancestors had an essential social and moral significance which did not violate the monotheistic nature of the Christian God.[50]

In other words, there were three issues at the heart of the debate. Here is a summary given by Ray R. Noll in a volume on the controversy published by the Ricci Institute for Chinese-Western Cultural History:

> The expression "Chinese Rites" as it came to be used in the missionary circles of the Far East and at Rome encompassed three specific areas: (1) the periodic ceremonies held in honor of Confucius, generally but not exclusively by the scholar class in halls or temples dedicated to this great national philosophical master; (2) the special ritual honors paid to one's ancestors, modes of tribute and filial piety that were part of the very social fiber of China, and still are today; finally, (3) the semantic search for the most appropriate term(s) in Chinese to speak of and to the Christian God. This latter is usually treated separately from the first two and designated the "Term Question" or the "Term Issue."[51]

The Jesuit missionaries allowed the rituals because they believed that these were civil rather than religious rites, and they felt that it was important to "accommodate" Chinese cultural practices. The Jesuits had forged a warm relationship with the Kangxi Emperor, an exceedingly erudite ruler who was curious about Western science and culture. The emperor favored the Jesuits partly because of their intellectual character, and he in fact supported the Jesuits' attempt to gain the Vatican's approval of their "accommodation policy" of Chinese Catholic converts. According to the religion scholar Li Tiangang, a document was drafted in China in 1701 by Jesuit missionaries who had long-standing familiarity with the emperor, such as Claudio Grimaldi (1638–1712), an Italian Jesuit who became the bishop in the Chinese capital in 1694 (his friendship with Leibniz had greatly affected Leibniz's view on China), who had joined the emperor twice in his northern frontier hunting excursions; Tome Pereira (1645–1708), a Portuguese Jesuit who had been in the emperor's court for thirty years; and Antoine Thomas (1644–1709), a Belgian Jesuit who had taught the emperor mathematics.[52] In "Brevis Relatio eorum, quae spectant ad Declarationem Sinarum Imperatoris Kam Hi, Peking, 1701," they stated,

> In our opinion, we believe that the worship (bai) of Confucius is to pay respect to him as an exemplary teacher of virtuous conducts; it was not to ask for

good fortune, nor blessing in intelligence, social status, or material wealth. The ritual worship (*jisi*) of ancestors comes from one's love for one's family . . . ; even though there is a wooden tablet representing the ancestors, it is not the case that [people believe] the actual spirit of the ancestors resides on the tablets.[53]

The Kangxi Emperor commented on the document, "This is well-articulated, following the direction of the great Dao. . . . There is nothing that needs to be corrected." With these handwritten comments, Kangxi explicitly supported the view that Confucian practices such as the veneration of ancestral sprits and Confucius's spirit is not religious.

As the comparative religion scholar Guy Stroumsa points out in *A New Science: The Discovery of Religion in the Age of Reason*, the Jesuits' position is in some ways a paradox:

> [T]he Jesuits had sought to find deep religious feelings even in the weirdest and wildest pagan rituals and beliefs of the native peoples of America. As we shall see here, their brethren who embarked on a mission to evangelize China developed a highly different approach. They soon found themselves arguing that the rituals of the Chinese elites, of which they thought highly, and which they sought to respect, reflected all but true religiosity. The Chinese rituals, according to them, rather reflected deep morality and political sense. There is a paradox here that demands explaining: it was precisely the high level of culture shown by the Chinese, a culture that the Jesuits found comparable to that of Europe, that brought them to deny the Chinese, or at least their intellectual elites, any real religiosity.[54]

But their view encountered strong opposition, among other missionary orders both in China and in Rome:

> In opposition to the Jesuit position stood a large array of groups including the Franciscan, Dominican and Augustinian orders. . . . They argued that the native Chinese terminology for God and the Chinese rites to ancestors and Confucius did violate the teachings of Christianity. . . . Impelled by powerful cultural and political forces arrayed against the Jesuits, the papacy ruled against accommodation. An extensive investigation by the Holy Office led to the decree of 1704 which was followed in 1707 by the Nanjing Decree of the papal legate de Tournon. The 1704 ruling served as the basis of the Papal decrees of 1715 and 1742 which banned the Chinese Rites and prohibited further debate.[55]

Although the Kangxi Emperor had issued the Edict of Toleration for Christianity in 1692, he was greatly annoyed by the 1704 papal decree that ruled against Chinese rites.[56] In 1706, the Kangxi Emperor issued an edict banishing all missionaries without official *piao*, "the certificate by which they promised to follow the practices of Matteo Ricci and to remain in China all their lives."[57] In 1724, a year after Kangxi's death, his son, the Yongzheng Emperor, "issued an edict which ordered all missionaries—except those with skill in astronomy, who were to serve in the bureau of astronomy—to be banished to Marco."[58] During the period 1724–36, a great number of missionaries in China were expelled, even though many remained in the capital, and Christianity survived only in underground churches, until the return of missionaries—most of whom were Protestants at this time—in the nineteenth century.

It is understandable why the Chinese Rites and Term Controversy is sometimes called the longest global religious conflict. And because of its complexity, it is difficult to say exactly when it ended. As Spence puts it, "the Rites Controversy is almost impossible to date," although it's feasible to use the dates of the Jesuit mission in China (1579–1724) as historical markers.[59] Stroumsa remarks,

> The polemic known as "la Querelle des Rites" reached its peak in 1700 in the Sorbonne with the condemnation of the Jesuits' efforts at accommodation and Rome's confirmation of that condemnation. It became one of the most significant affairs in the modern history of the Catholic Church. The enemies of the Jesuits seemingly won the day within the Church. But in a deeper sense, the Jesuits prevailed, as they had launched, much beyond the Catholic hierarchy, the deep and long-standing attraction to all *chinoiseries* among European intellectuals that would be so evident throughout the eighteenth century and would lead to the birth of sinology.[60]

Indeed, many leading intellectuals of the European Enlightenment, including Leibniz, Spinoza, and Voltaire, were fascinated by the Jesuits' idealized view of China.[61]

The prohibition of the veneration of ancestors was finally lifted in 1939, when Pope Pius XII issued decrees of toleration regarding the veneration of ancestors. The "Rites" part, which is essentially a question regarding the religious nature of Confucianism (the worship of ancestors and Confucius), was finally settled when Pope Pius XII approved the following statements:

> Everyone knows that some ceremonies in Oriental countries, although in earlier times they were tied in with pagan rites, now that customs and minds have changed with the flow of the centuries, merely preserve civil expression of devotion toward ancestors, or of patriotism, or of respect for fellow countrymen. . . . Bowing the head and other tokens of civil honor before the deceased or images of the deceased, and even before a tablet of a deceased person, inscribed with nothing but the person's name, should be regarded as permissible and proper.[62]

As we will see later in this study, the revival of rituals venerating ancestral spirits and Confucius in China today poses a new challenge to this view of Confucian rituals as "civil expressions."

On October 24, 2001, Pope John Paul II sent a historic message to an international conference held in Rome called "Matteo Ricci: For a Dialogue between China and the West," celebrating the fourth centenary of Ricci's arrival in China. The pope paid tribute to Ricci in the following way:

> From his first contacts with the Chinese, Father Ricci based his entire scientific and apostolic methodology upon two pillars, to which he remained faithful until his death, despite many difficulties and misunderstandings, both internal and external: first, Chinese neophytes, in embracing Christianity, did not in any way have to renounce loyalty to their country; second, the Christian revelation of the mystery of God in no way destroyed but in fact enriched and complemented everything beautiful and good, just and holy, in what had been produced and handed down by the ancient Chinese tradition. And just as the Fathers of the Church had done centuries before in the encounter between the Gospel of Jesus Christ and Greco-Roman culture, Father Ricci made this insight the basis of his patient and far-sighted work of inculturation of the faith in China, in the constant search for a common ground of understanding with the intellectuals of that great land. . . . Father Ricci's merit lay above all in the realm of inculturation. Father Ricci forged a Chinese terminology for Catholic theology and liturgy, and thus created the conditions for making Christ known and for incarnating the Gospel message and the Church within Chinese culture.[63]

If we take Pope John Paul II's words as the final authority, he seemed to be conceding on the "Term" part of the controversy when he stated, "Father Ricci forged a Chinese terminology for Catholic theology and liturgy."

Although the English term "Confucianism" didn't come into existence until 1862, the historian Lionel Jensen has argued that "Confucius," the Latinized name of Kong Fuzi, was "translated"—or, more accurately, invented—by Jesuit missionaries.[64] In his much discussed, thought-provoking 1998 book *Manufacturing Confucianism*, Jensen claims that "Confucianism is largely a Western invention" by Jesuit missionaries, reflecting how Westerners understood, or wished to understand, themselves.[65] He remarks,

> And it is with the work of this missionary community that the intertwined tales of Confucius the hero and Confucianism the religion begin, for it was from this community's mission among the Chinese that the man and the religion were made.[66]

The legacy of the Jesuits is no doubt complex. Were they in fact responsible for the formulation of Confucianism as a religion? In a review of

Jensen's book, the sinologist Nicolas Standaert tells us the difference between *lex* or *secta*, terms used by the Jesuits to describe *ru*, commonly translated today as "Confucians,"[67] and *secta Idolatrorum*, which was used for Buddhism:

> By considering *ru* as *lex* or *secta* of the literati, the Jesuits invented *ru* as not idolatrous. The implication of this was that *ru* was a non-religious group in the modern sense of the word, and the Jesuits even insisted that its ritual practices were "political" and "civil" (something any anthropologist today would deny). This invention was taken over and reformulated by eighteenth century European thinkers who, among others, took China as a place where "religion" was not needed. This birth of non-religion led to the birth of the modern category of religion (as opposed to science, rationality, etc.). In the nineteenth century, possibly parallel to the development of the academic study of religion, the "three sects" of China started to be translated as "three religions" and also the "sect of literati" was manufactured as "Confucianism." . . . All this deserves more investigation.[68]

As we'll see in the next section, Standaert's doubt about the Jesuits' role in the manufacturing of Confucianism and his insight about the importance of the development of the "academic study of religion" in the making of Confucianism as a religion can indeed be supported by historical investigation.

The Second Controversy: The Term Controversy, 1877–1891

According to the second edition of the *Oxford English Dictionary* (1989), the terms "Confucius," "Confucian," and "Confucianism" appeared for the first time in the following order:

> Confucius: Latinized from the Chinese Kung Fu Tsze. A translation of three of the Chinese Classics, by four of the Roman Catholic missionaries, was published at Paris in 1687, under the title *Confucius Sinarum Philosophus, sive Scientia Sinensis Latine exposita*. (Prof. J. Legge.)
>   Confucian: A. *adj*. Of or relating to the Chinese philosopher Confucius, or his teaching, or followers. B. *n*. A follower of Confucius.
>   1837 *Penny Cycl*. VII. 447/1 Nor have the true Confucians ever represented the *Great First Cause* under any image or personification whatever. 1847 MEDHURST *Theol. Chinese* 4 The Confucian Age was tolerably free from idolatry. 1877 J. E. CARPENTER *Tiele's Hist. Relig* 35 The canonical books of the Confucians. 1878 J. H. GRAY *China* I. iv. 94 Confucian temples are occasionally used as colleges.
>   Hence Confucianism, the doctrines or system of Confucius and his followers; Confucianist, an adherent of Confucianism; also *attrib*. or *adj*.

1846 WORCESTER cites *Q. Rev.* for *Confucianist.* 1862 R. H. PATTER-SON *Ess. Hist. & Art* 406 Confucianism, the State and national creed, ignores idol worship altogether. 1878 J. H. GRAY *China* I. iv. 97 Even Confucianists yielded to the fashionable mania. 1880 LEGGE *Relig. China* 4, I use the term *Confucianism* as covering, first of all the ancient religion of China, and then the views of the great philosopher himself in illustration or modification of it. 1884 *Athenæum* 23 Feb. 244/1 The Confucianist philosophy.

Although the year 1862 is therefore often referred to by sinologists as the year of the birth of the word "Confucianism" (with the word "Confucianist" appearing earlier, in 1846), W. C. Smith points out that the first significant usage of "Confucianism" was in fact with James Legge's *Confucianism in Relation to Christianity*, published in Shanghai in 1877. He remarks on the title of Legge's book,

> The full title of this particular book is instructive, illustrating as it does the obvious and yet important point that the concepts being fashioned to present the Chinese religious situation to the West were (naturally) fashioned "in relation to" the concepts already in use for the Western situation.[69]

Legge's book—or, to be more accurate, pamphlet—was the printed version of a paper he had presented in absentia at the Missionary Conference in Shanghai on May 11, 1877, "a general meeting of all Protestant missionaries in China."[70]

The Shanghai Missionary Conference marked the beginning of the second controversy, which I shall call the Term Controversy. Although the debate started in missionary circles, it was moved to the new arena of comparative study of religions in the 1880s and 1890s. James Legge was the central figure in this controversy, and his victory came in the form of the inclusion of Confucian texts in the landmark publication *Sacred Books of the East*, the fifty-volume series from Oxford University Press, for which Legge contributed six volumes. The series is still used by scholars and students today.

James Legge (1815–97) was a Scottish missionary who spent thirty-four years in China. In Norman J. Girardot's excellent biography of Legge, *The Victorian Translation of China: James Legge's Oriental Pilgrimage*, we learn that Legge discovered his missionary calling early on:

> The fulfillment of his desire to become a "true Christian" came about only in his subsequent decision to study for the Congregationalist ministry and to join the ranks of missionaries being sent out to the far reaches of the world by the London Missionary Society.[71]

At the time, Protestant missions to China were beginning to flourish, after Robert Morrison (1782–1834) became the first successful Protestant missionary in 1807. The London Missionary Society, "the principle missionary vehicle for evangelical dissenters in the first half of the nineteenth century," was established in 1795, and James Hudson Taylor (1832–1905), the missionary who founded the China Inland Mission, arrived in China in 1854.[72] In 1839, at age twenty-four, Legge sailed for Malacca, "working assiduously on his Chinese lessons."[73]

Legge eventually spent thirty-four years as a missionary: in Malacca from 1839 to 1843 and Hong Kong from 1843 to 1873. Besides missionary work, Legge became interested in the translation of Chinese classics, often with the assistance of Chinese intellectuals such as Wang Tao (1828–97). After Legge's retirement from missionary work in 1873, he returned to England, having already achieved the status of one of the first and best translators of Chinese classics. In 1875 Legge was awarded the first Prix Stanislas Julien for sinology, and in 1876 he became the first professor of Chinese at Oxford. He taught courses in Chinese language and literature at Oxford and stayed there until his death in 1897.

In his twenty years at Oxford, Legge secured his reputation as the most illustrious translator of Chinese classics through his voluminous translations of the Confucian canon, many of which published as part of the series *Sacred Books of the East*. Legge's extensive and occasionally opinionated commentary demonstrates his profound knowledge of the Chinese classics and the commentary tradition; some of his translations are still being reprinted and used by sinologists today.[74] Indeed, his influence was such that Girardot called the period from Legge's arrival in Oxford to the end of the nineteenth century "the Leggian epoch of sinology."[75]

Legge was certainly the person responsible for the extended usage of the term "Confucianism," which first appeared in his 1877 paper delivered at the Missionary Conference in Shanghai. He stated clearly in his 1880 book *Religions of China: Confucianism and Taoism Described and Compared with Christianity* that he used "Confucianism" to indicate that it is a religion. But many missionaries who had worked in China did not share his view. The most contentious disagreement was the "term" question inherited from the Jesuits' Chinese Rites and Term Controversy, which had been debated among Protestant missionaries since the 1840s.

Here is a concise summary of the controversy offered by the historian Donald W. Treadgold:

> The "term controversy" continued for decades, and developed an aspect it had not had among the earlier Roman Catholics. They had debated how to translate the name of God into Chinese, but the converse question had not been agitated because they had not engaged in any such enterprise as Legge's translation of the Chinese classics into a Western language. Legge wished to

render "God" as *Shang-ti* in the Chinese Bible; he proceeded to render *Shang-ti* as "God" in translating the classics. In 1877, at the first national Missionary Conference in Shanghai, he held that Confucianism was "defective rather than antagonistic" to Christianity; ... contended that Confucius, like Moses, neither teaches nor denies immortality; ... and reiterated his "well-known conviction" that *Shang-ti* in the classics refers to God. ... Legge's paper was read for him, since he was in Oxford. It gave such thorough offence that the Conference voted to exclude the paper from its printed record, "in deference to the wishes of those who regarded it as taking one side" in the term controversy. One writer called this decision a blot on the conference, especially since several American papers touched on the term question (presumably opposing *Shang-ti*); the horror of Confucianism shown at the conference "fell little short of madness"; no sooner was the doctrine mentioned that someone, usually an American, rose to denounce it.[76]

In this atmosphere that "fell little short of madness," the Shanghai Missionary Conference seemed to have succeeded in silencing Legge and his "too intellectual, too eclectic, too tolerant, too secular, too universal, and too comparative" attitude toward missionary work.[77] Treadgold sums up what was really at stake for the missionaries in China:

> The term controversy continued a while longer; it was never clearly decided. ... Nevertheless one computation shows that 90% of the Protestant books printed in 1892 employed *Shang-ti*, which may simply have meant that those among the missionaries who wrote books followed Legge but were greatly outnumbered by their less scholarly colleagues. The "term controversy" no doubt occupied more of the Protestant missionaries' time than it might if they had had more than a very few converts to instruct and churches to help organize. However, it was no empty debate about the meaning of the words; it involved the whole questions of whether the ancient Chinese had been monotheistic and the related question of whether Chinese culture had elements Christians ought to respect or whether it should simply be attacked and destroyed. Legge left no doubt of his conversion to the belief that classical Confucianism had been monotheistic, and demonstrated it by removing his shoes on entering the Altar of Heaven in Peking and declaring, "This is holy ground," to the horror of his fellow evangelicals. He did not accept the argument that the God of the Chinese was not "the same being" as the God of the Christians; there was but one God.[78]

However, although Legge's position seemed to have been defeated at the 1877 Shanghai Missionary Conference, at the 1893 World Parliament of Religions in Chicago, Confucianism was officially inducted into the hall of fame of leading world religions, along with Christianity, Islam, and Buddhism. In chapter 2, we will find out how and why the Term

Controversy was settled in Legge's favor, how Confucianism became one of the world religions, and how it became an indispensible component of the emerging field of comparative religious studies.

The Third Controversy: The Confucianity Movement, 1911–1920

If we are not going to accept Jensen's idea that Confucianism is simply "a critical symbol among the contemporary community of Western interpreters,"[79] then we need to look at how Confucianism is understood in China. In this brief overview, I sketch out the so-called Confucianity Movement (*kongjiao yundong*) that took place in the 1910s and 1920s, which I view as the third major controversy over Confucianism.

Although *rujiao* (Confucianism as a religion) cannot be found in the religion category in Qing dynasty local gazettes, where one can often discover estimates of the numbers of Buddhists, Daoists, and Catholics in a given town or county, there are occasional mentions of Confucians in other contexts, such as in the discussion of religion in governmental regulations. In a national regulation of foreign missionaries issued in 1871 (the tenth year of the *Tongzhi* reign), presumably authorized by the Tongzhi Emperor, the phrase *rujiao renshi* (the followers of Confucianism) was constantly utilized in connection with the conduct of missionaries. The first mandate begins with the following imperative: "Missionaries should obey Chinese customs, following the examples set by the followers of *rujiao*."[80] The fifth mandate starts with the following description: "Catholics don't worship the gods, nor the ancestors, unlike the Confucians."[81] However, there was no official classification given by the Qing imperial state regarding the religious nature of *rujiao*.

The desire for a state religion arose even before the 1911 Republican Revolution that overturned the Qing dynasty and marked the end of imperial China. Kang Youwei was the first to advocate for the establishment of *kongjiao*, *kong* being the surname of Confucius, meaning the religion of Confucius. The most accurate translation of the term is "Confucianity," since it is clearly modeled after the term "Christianity." In 1898 Kang spoke of "the territory of the state (*guodi*), the citizens of the state (*guomin*), the religion of the state (*guojiao*)"; this was the first significant use of the term "state religion."[82]

In October 1911, after the success of the Republican Revolution, Sun Yat-sen (1866–1925) became the first president of the Republic of China. The new government first forbade the study of the Confucian canon in schools in order to draw a clear break with the past, but this policy encountered great resistance. From 1912 to 1913, there were dozens of "Associations of Confucianity" established all over the country, set up by Kang and his supporters.[83] On August 15, 1913, several prominent scholars including Liang Qichao (1873–1929), a leading social and political philosopher and a student of Kang's, and Yan Fu (1854–1921), a leading translator of Western thought, petitioned to make Confucianity China's state religion in the new constitution. This marked the climax of the so-called Confucianity Movement.[84]

A year later, when the military strongman Yuan Shikai (1859–1916) declared himself the second president of the Republic, he revived imperial Confucian state rituals in order to gain legitimacy for his government. However, when he made himself the emperor of China in 1915, supporters of the Confucianity Movement began to see how Confucianism was used to justify reactionary goals. Yuan's short-lived reign ended with his death in 1916. When another coup to establish a new monarchy failed in 1917, with Kang Youwei supporting the supposedly parliamentary monarchy, the Confucianity Movement suffered another fatal blow.[85]

In the late 1920s, the Republican government ordered the Confucianity associations to change their name from *kongjiao hui* (Association of Confucianity) to *kongxue hui* (Association of Confucian Learning). This change of a single word is indeed a crucial one; *jiao* already denoted religion in the 1920s, whereas *xue* clearly marked learning or education.

Although the movement to reinvent Confucianism as a religion faded quickly after that, some of the followers of Kang did continue to advance his ideas. For example, a Confucianity Academy was established in Hong Kong in 1930 by Chen Huanzhang, who had been active in the Confucianity Movement, and there were also attempts to make Confucianism a state religion in Taiwan in the 1920s and 1930s when Taiwan was under Japanese rule. (Today Confucianism is classified as a religion in Indonesia and Hong Kong but not in Taiwan.)

As Vincent Goossaert and David A. Palmer noted, "[T]he failure of the Confucian religion project in Republican China was due more to the political context than to inherent defects; the promoters of Confucianism would find other outlets for the dissemination of their values and ideals."[86] By "other outlets" they mean the so-called redemptive societies, which were "national modern-style associations that registered with the state as religious, philanthropic, or public interest associations." These redemptive societies "attempted to modernize the traditional notion of the union of the Three Teachings with the aid of a more modern, academic language and by incorporating Christianity and Islam into the traditional Union of the Three Teachings."[87] They flourished in the Republic of China, such as Yiguandao, but they were eliminated after the Communists took power in Mainland China in 1949.[88]

The Fourth Controversy: The Confucianism as a Religion Controversy in China, 2000–2004

Shortly after the establishment of the People's Republic of China in 1949, the government announced its official classification system of religions, which is still in effect in China today. According to this Five Major Religions classification, there are five officially and legally recognized religions: Buddhism, Daoism, Catholicism, Protestantism, and Islam. This classification scheme is the product of particular political and social concerns of the Chinese state in the 1950s, and scholars in China have challenged this classification openly in recent years.

In 2000, a full-fledged controversy broke out among Chinese intellectuals over the religious nature of Confucianism. Named the Confucianism as a Religion Controversy by the participants, it remains unsettled today, and there are intellectual, cultural, as well as political stakes over its settlement. This controversy is discussed in depth in chapter 3.

CHAPTER 2

The Making of a World Religion

Confucianism and the Emergence of Comparative Religion as a Discipline in the Nineteenth Century

SINCE THE END OF THE NINETEENTH CENTURY Confucianism has been considered by many to be one of the major world religions, and the place of Confucianism in the world religions paradigm today has been institutionalized through academic and popular texts, academic curricula, as well as scholarly departments and associations. How did this happen, after the turbulent history of the Chinese Rites and Term Controversy? When Legge followed Ricci's accommodation rules and pronounced that one should translate the term *shang-ti* in Chinese classics into "God" at the 1877 Shanghai Missionary Conference, his paper was excluded from the official proceedings.[1]

It was in Legge's paper for this conference that the word "Confucianism" was first used to refer to "the religion of the Chinese," and the resistance of the missionaries attending the conference came from their realization that by comparing Confucianism with Christianity, Legge was trying to find "various 'relations' or 'parallels' with Christian tradition."[2] This comparative approach, elevating Confucianism to a position that made it possible to be compared to Christianity, was unacceptable to most Protestant missionaries in China at the time; it was too liberal a view among theologically conservative missionaries. There were intense debates in the *Chinese Recorder and Missionary Journal* after the conference; according to Legge's biographer Girardot, one missionary thought that "Legge's views were extremely dangerous and could 'cause trouble.'"[3] But the controversy was eventually settled in Legge's favor, with a resolution that is still very much with us today, which is the view of Confucianism not only as an ancient Chinese religion, but also as one of the great world religions. How did this settlement take place?

In this chapter, I argue that the Term Controversy was settled in Legge's favor because it was not settled in the Chinese missionary circle, where it had originated and where much of the Jesuit Rites and Term Controversy took place in previous centuries. It was settled in the newly emerged field of the "science of religion," also called comparative religion. By collaborating with Friedrich Max Müller, a fellow Oxford don, shortly after the Shanghai Missionary Conference, Legge took the dispute out of the confines of the missionary community, where the Term Controversy had a long and complicated history, and brought it into the new arena of the science of religion and the emerging discipline of comparative religion. It was here that the controversy was finally settled, and its legacy is still relevant to our understanding of Confucianism today.

Max Müller, a larger-than-life figure accustomed to controversies of his own, wanted to establish his authority in the new field of comparative religion, a goal he eventually archived; today he is remembered as a founder of the discipline:

> There are perhaps only two serious contenders for the title "the father of comparative religion"—the Dutch Egyptologist C. P. Tiele and the great philologist, German by birth, British by adoption, Friedrich Max Müller (1823–1900). In choosing to give the accolade to the latter, we have no wish to minimize Tiele's outstanding work. But Max Müller was the more universal figure. . . . [W]e have already quoted him on two occasions: from what we have presumed to identify as the foundation document of comparative religion, his *Introduction to the Science of Religion* (1873), and from the slightly earlier preface to *Chips from a German Workshop*. In both we see him not only as the scholar, but also as the advocate of the new science—and it is for his advocacy we select him. Far more effectively than any other among his contemporaries, he was able to convince the Western world that in matters of religion, as in matters of language, "he who knows one, knows none."[4]

Yet Max Müller knew nothing about Chinese language, nor Chinese religion; Legge was Max Müller's only informant. The depth of Legge's knowledge in both the Chinese language and religion, as well as the prestige of Legge's position as the first professor of Chinese at Oxford, made Legge invaluable to the establishment and legitimation of the new discourse that Max Müller sought to promote.

The intellectual affiliation of the two men is no doubt significant, but the significance of their association also lies in the timing of the meeting of their minds. It occurred at the end of the nineteenth century and the height of the British Empire; with a general public eager to understand the world beyond their horizon, the pluralistic and comparative approach of Max Müller and Legge marked the beginning of a new era in the history of the study of religion. The 1893 World Parliament of Religions symbolized the beginning of a religious pluralism that presented a Christian version of the universal, in which Confucianism occupied a notable space; it is remarkable that this happened only sixteen years after the first real use of the term "Confucianism" appeared at the Shanghai Missionary Conference. Both Legge and Max Müller were crucial figures in the dawn of the new century of world religions, and they were indeed pioneers in the emerging field of comparative religion, which is now, as religious studies, a vibrant academic discipline and an essential part of liberal arts education.

In the rest of this chapter, I first introduce the concepts of "controversy" and "boundary work" from the perspectives of sociology of scientific knowledge and sociology of professions. I then offer a sketch of the extraordinary career of Max Müller, highlighting his frequently failed quests for academic authority throughout his academic life. I then focus on the collaborations between Max Müller and Legge, which led to the settlement of the Term Controversy. I show that the success of their collaboration depended on the innovative boundary work performed by both Legge and Max Müller. This chapter ends with a general analysis of the early institutionalization of the world religions discourse.

THE SETTLEMENT OF SCIENTIFIC CONTROVERSIES

The issue at the heart of what I call the Term Controversy was an issue of religious knowledge: Legge and his missionary opponents disagreed over the "true meaning" of the Chinese term *shang-ti* as well as whether it was "right" to compare Confucianism to Christianity. If their disagreement was simply a dispute over knowledge claims—I have the truth, you do not—then shouldn't they have been able to settle the controversy simply by proving their own cases with evidence? Indeed, as Max Müller claimed as early as 1870, the study of religion was a "science," and a "man of science's first allegiance" was to "truth":

> In these our days it is almost impossible to speak of religion without giving offense either on the right or on the left. With some, religion seems too sacred a subject for scientific treatment; with others it stands on a level with alchemy and astrology, a mere tissue of errors or hallucinations, far beneath the notice of the man of science. In a certain sense, I accept both these views. Religion is a sacred subject, and whether in its most perfect or in its most imperfect form, it has a right to our highest reverence. . . . But true reverence does not consist in declaring a subject, because it is dear to us, to be unfit for free and honest inquiry; far from it! True reverence is shown in treating every subject, however sacred, however dear to us, with perfect confidence; without fear and without

favor; with tenderness and love, by all means, but, before all, with an unflinching and uncompromising loyalty to truth.[5]

If we view the Term Controversy as a controversy over truth claims, and if we take seriously Max Müller's declaration about the nature of the study of religion, then the settlement of the controversy should indeed be about "an unflinching and uncompromising loyalty to truth." Was this how the controversy was settled?

Our commonsensical understanding of knowledge appears to have a dualist nature: there is society on the one hand, with external factors such as culture, politics, and economics that could have an impact on our intellectual life; on the other hand there is thought or knowledge, which is supposed to be free of these external factors. Hence we speak of the problematic scholarship that is polluted by certain historical conditions or ideology (such as Orientalist scholarship), or the sham scientific knowledge that in fact serves malicious political agendas (such as Nazi eugenics). The sociologist of science Steven Shapin puts it in the following way:

> The "social" was taken as that which was "external" to science, and it was persistently debated by what means authentic science kept "the social" at bay, how and to what extent "social influences" infiltrated science without deleterious effects, or how what seems to be properly scientific knowledge was "in fact" socially marked ideology.[6]

This is the view represented by traditional sociology of knowledge; in the 1970s and 1980s, a new view emerged among scholars who promoted the so-called sociology of scientific knowledge (SSK). As Shapin, one of the leading sociology of scientific knowledge theorists, points out, their radicalness comes from their belief that knowledge is intrinsically social:

> While traditional sociology of knowledge asked how, and to what extent, "social factors" might influence the products of the mind, SSK sought to show that knowledge was constitutively social, and in so doing, it raised fundamental questions about taken-for-granted divisions between "social versus cognitive, or natural, factors."[7]

For the sociologist of science Bruno Latour, the very formation and production of knowledge is a social process, and there is no distinction between the social versus the cognitive or the natural. In his study of the production of scientific and technological knowledge, *Science in Action: How to Follow Scientists and Engineers through Society*, Latour states that "the construction of facts and machines is a collective process,"[8] and that the settlement of scientific controversies is an inherently social and political process, which always involves social networks of power:

When we approach the places where facts and machines are made, we get into the midst of controversies. The closer we are, the more controversial they become. When we go from "daily life" to scientific activity, from the man in the street to the men in the laboratory, from politics to expert opinion, we do not go from noise to quiet, from passion to reason, from heat to cold. We go from controversies to fiercer controversies.[9]

Latour gives us the following hypothetical example. Assume that Mr. Anybody and Mr. Somebody have a scientific dispute. How does Mr. Anybody win the dispute? He would bring in articles that are authored by and with references to notable specialists in the field, Nobel Prize winners or people who have received significant grants from important institutions such as the National Science Foundation. This "appeal to higher and more numerous allies" is called "the argument from authority," which is one of the strategies used in settling controversies.[10] By allying himself with powerful actors and institutions in the specific scientific field through referencing the scientific literature, Mr. Anybody is no longer alone in his argument. Latour concludes that "although it sounds counter-intuitive at first, the more technical and specialized a literature is, the more 'social' it becomes."[11]

In his study of the institutionalization of pasteurization, *The Pasteurization of France*, Latour expends his argument about the social nature of knowledge by showing that it was not the sheer power of scientific innovation and knowledge that transformed Pasteur's discoveries into the social reality of pasteurization; rather, it was through the working of a complex set of factors, including the public hygiene movement in France, the formation of the medical professions, colonial interests, as well as Pasteur's personal ambition and political abilities, that the pasteurization of France was achieved.[12]

What bearing does this have on the Term Controversy? As I will argue, the settlement of the Legge controversy was a thoroughly social process. I have mentioned how both Legge and Max Müller made use of the strategy of forming alliances with authority in legitimizing their own ideas. Another of their strategies was to take the controversy from one field (the missionary circle) to another (the new science of religion/comparative religion field), which is a form of boundary work. This helped Legge achieve and secure his victory. The boundary work exercised by Legge is a strategy that has not been discussed by sociologists of controversies; for instance, in Ruth Macklin's article "The Forms and Norms of Closure," she discusses two classification schemes of closure of controversies: the first suggested by Tom L. Beauchamp (sound argument, consensus, procedural closure, negotiation closure, natural death), the second suggested by Ernan McMullin (resolution, closure, abandonment), neither of which is well suited to explain the closure of the Legge controversy.[13]

BOUNDARY WORK IN THE FORMATION OF DISCIPLINES

The idea of boundary work was introduced by the sociologist of science Thomas Gieryn in 1983. In his article "Boundary-Work and the Demarcation of Science from Non-Science: Strains and Interests in Professional Interests of Scientists," Gieryn defines it the following way:

> "Boundary-work" describes an ideological style found in scientists' attempts to create a public image for science by contrasting it favorably to non-scientific intellectual or technical activities.[14]

By defining a boundary between science and non-science, scientists benefit from this demarcation in various ways, from the legitimation of their intellectual authority to the pursuit of individual career opportunities. Gieryn sees boundary work as a crucial strategy in establishing intellectual authority and legitimacy; as Lamont and Molnár put it, Gieryn "stresses the power (flexibility and often arbitrariness) of interpretative strategies in constructing a space for 'science' in pursuit of epistemic authority."[15]

Although the idea of boundary work was first introduced to study the professional ideology of scientists, boundary work can be seen in any field of knowledge production, and the concept has been used to study humanistic disciplines. For instance, Mario Small examines the boundary work performed in the legitimation of two African American studies departments at Temple University and Harvard University.[16]

Max Müller's boundary work consisted of his effort of erecting a boundary between the new "science of religion" and the other existing approaches to the study of religion (such as theology and history of religion), and by doing so he became a founder of the newly defined intellectual arena of science of religion. His participation in the boundary-building process allowed him to define the goals and nature of the emerging discipline; his own ideas became the measuring stick according to which future work in the field was to be assessed. As a result, he was free from the often harsh evaluation process that he was subjected to in other more established disciplines, such as Sanskrit and Vedic studies; within the new discipline, his work was emulated rather than judged.

James Legge also achieved a new level of intellectual authority by allying himself with the new discipline. His boundary work consisted of his participation in the *Sacred Books of the East* project; he presented his view on Chinese religions as part of the science of religion project through the *Sacred Books of the East*, and the implicit boundary erected between his work and the work of other missionary sinologists gave his ideas a new life. By bringing his ideas about Chinese religion, particularly his contested understanding of Confucianism as an ancient Chinese religion, into the new intellectual arena, he became one of the founding architects of the world religions discourse, and his views were revered rather than challenged in the new discipline. Despite the fact that his position was nearly defeated in the term controversy by his fellow missionaries, Legge eventually successfully settled the controversy by moving his views on Confucianism into the new discipline of science of religion.

In other words, Max Müller's boundary work brought him lasting fame and a luminous reputation as the founder of a discipline, whereas Legge's boundary work secured his interpretation of Confucianism as part of the world religion discourse.

THE EXTRAORDINARY CAREER OF FRIEDRICH MAX MÜLLER

In any historical account of the intellectual discipline of the science of religion, the nineteenth-century Sanskrit scholar and comparative philologist Max Müller must occupy a central place. Today, his *Introduction to the Science of Religion* (1870) is considered "the foundation document of comparative religion [the science of religion] in the English-speaking world,"[17] and he is commonly remembered as the founder of the discipline, by both historians and scholars of religion.[18] In *Manufacturing Religion*, Russell T. McCutcheon offers the following assessment:

> Of particular interest is that Müller, like Eliade after him, was instrumental in establishing and promoting the "independent yet reverent study of the ancient religions." It is commonly acknowledged that it was Müller who was, according to Jacques Waardenburg, the "first scholar who lucidly and imperatively envisaged and proclaimed an autonomous 'science of religion.'"[19]

As a prolific scholar who had published dozens of volumes in his lifetime, as an Oxford professor who was known as a charismatic speaker, as the editor of the influential Oxford University Press series *Sacred Books of the East*, and as the president of the 1893 World Parliament of Religions and various other associations for the science of religion, Max Müller was an immensely influential figure in the short history of the discipline, both as a scholar and as its leading field builder.[20]

One might even argue that he was a "founder of discursivity," without whom we would not have the language to talk about comparative religion at all. Foucault calls Freud and Marx "founders of discursivity," who are "unique in that they are not just the authors of their own works. They have produced something else: the possibilities and the rules for the formation of other texts."[21] These words can indeed be used to describe Max Müller, who has arguably also "established an endless possibility of discourse" through his world religions project.[22]

Max Müller was born in Dessau, Germany, in 1823, the son of Romantic poet Wilhelm Müller (1794–1827), whose poems were used for Schubert's two famous song cycles *Die schöne Müllerin* and *Die*

Winterreise. Max Müller began his academic training at University of Leipzig, studying classics, philosophy, and several oriental languages, including Arabic and Sanskrit. The first chair in Sanskrit at University of Leipzig was established in 1841, the year Max Müller began his education there, and he studied under the first professor of Sanskrit, Hermann Brockhaus (1806–77). At the time the romantic allure of ancient Indian civilization had been casting spells over many German intellectuals, from the poet Johann Wolfgang von Goethe (1749–1832) and the critic Friedrich Schlegel (1772–1829) in the older generation to Max Müller in the younger generation.[23]

After Max Müller received his doctorate in 1843, with a dissertation on Spinoza, he continued his Sanskrit studies in Berlin in 1844. In Berlin he also studied with Franz Bopp (1791–1867), arguably the founder of comparative philology, and the philosopher Friedrich von Schelling (1775–1854). In 1845 he went to Paris for the purpose of attending the lectures on the *Rig Veda* of French Sanskritist Eugene Burnouf (1801–52). It was in Paris where Max Müller became interested in producing a critical edition of the Sanskrit text of the *Rig Veda*, the oldest scripture of the Hindus; he wanted to be the one to complete this painstaking and colossal task.

Two important early supporters of Max Müller, Baron Christian von Bunsen (1791–1860), the Prussian ambassador to Britain, and Horace Hayman Wilson (1786–1860), the famed Sanskritist who was the first Boden Professor of Sanskrit at Oxford, together persuaded the East India Company to pay for the cost of publishing Max Müller's edition of the *Rig Veda* by Oxford University Press. Max Müller went to London in 1846 to work on the complete set of manuscripts, which was held at the London archive of the East India Company.[24] The first volume of Max Müller's edition of *Rig Veda* was published in 1849, the last one in 1874.[25]

Max Müller moved to Oxford from London in 1848 to supervise the printing process. This was the beginning of his years in Oxford, where he stayed until his death in 1900. Although he did pay short visits to Germany after he moved to Britain, he never lived in Germany again, nor did he ever visit India, although much of his career was to be devoted to the study of Indian language and religion.[26]

In 1850, two years after he arrived in Oxford, Max Müller was offered the chance to teach comparative philology as a replacement at the Taylorian Institute at Oxford, a language-teaching institution. The Taylorian Professorship was held by the linguist Francis Henry Trithen (1820–54), who "soon after his appointment began to go out of his mind, and could not deliver all the lectures."[27] Max Müller applied for and was granted the Taylorian Professorship after Trithen's death in 1854, but it was not a professorship of the university, hence it was not as prestigious. In 1858, however, Max Müller was elected a fellow at All Souls College, which made him a lifetime member of the university, and he was becoming a popular and well-connected figure in the university community. A brief sketch from *The Oxford University Press: An Informal History* sums up Max Müller's reputation at Oxford well:

> He was very illustrious in his day, the equivalent of the twentieth-century "television don." He lectured to packed halls up and down the country on Aryan roots and the origins of religion, once giving a royal command performance before Queen Victoria on the Isle of Wight. He had come to England from Germany in 1846 at the age of 23, seeing his fortune in Sanskrit rather than in the over-worked field of the European classics.[28]

Despite his enormous popularity, however, one of the defining events in Max Müller's life was his failure to obtain the Boden Professorship of Sanskrit. It was a chair established in 1832 by Lieutenant Colonel Joseph Boden of the East India Company, who was "being of opinion that a more general knowledge and critical knowledge of the Sanskrit language will be a means of enabling his countrymen to proceed in the conversion of the Natives of India to the Christian Religion, by disseminating a knowledge of the sacred scriptures amongst them, more effectually than all other means whatever."[29] It had been vacated after the first Boden Professor Horace Hayman Wilson's death on May 8, 1860. Arthur Anthony Macdonell (1854–1930) describes the election of the professorship for the *Dictionary of National Biography* of 1901:

> [Max Müller] was opposed by (Sir) Monier Monier-Williams, an old member of Balliol and University Colleges, who had been professor of Sanskrit at the East India College at Haileybury till it was closed in 1858. The election being in the hands of convocation—a body consisting of all masters of arts who keep their names on the books of the university—came to turn on the political and religious opinions of the candidates rather than on their merits as Sanskrit scholars. Party feeling ran high. His broad theological views, as well as the fact of his being a foreigner, told against Max Müller, especially in the eyes of the country clergy, who came up to Oxford in large numbers to record their votes. The election took place on 7 Dec. 1860, when Monier-Williams won the day with a majority of 223, the votes in his favour being 833 against 610 for Max Müller.[30]

In *Scholar Extraordinary*, a biography of Max Müller, a slightly different account is offered:

> Max Müller's next attempt to secure a higher income and position at Oxford, by obtaining the Boden Professorship of Sanskrit, ended in a complete failure. This was a decisive turning point in his scholarly and intellectual life, and for this reason the episode has to be narrated fully. But the story also illustrates the

dark and bright Oxford which had become the setting of his life. The election to this Professorship of Monier Williams instead of Max Müller in December 1860 was an incident in the long struggle between the academic reformers and conservatives, in which the latter, after being defeated over the wider question of remodeling the university, won a startling incidental victory. . . .

The supporters of Monier Williams equaled in number those of Müller, and included many Bengali pundits, but they were not so distinguished. For six months and more a vigorous election campaign was carried on, with manifestos, handbills, letters to newspapers and, above all, personal canvassing by means of letters and word of mouth. Müller had his committee, and Monier Williams has two, one at Oxford and the other in London.[31]

Monier-Williams, a leading Sanskrit scholar and the author of a much-used Sanskrit dictionary, was appointed, and he held the professorship from 1860 to 1899, a year before Max Müller's death in 1900.

In the Bodleian Max Müller files, a few souvenirs from the election can still be found among Max Müller's papers. One of them is a "List of Testimonials: In Favour of Max Müller, Fellow of All Souls College, M.A. Christ Church," which is a list of thirty-five names and organizations, from the late H. H. Wilson and Dr. A. Weber, professor of Sanskrit in Berlin, to a "List of Missionary Societies which have applied for copies of the *Rig-Veda*."[32]

In the same file there is also a contentious flier titled "Boden Sanskrit Professorship" that indirectly attacked Max Müller's candidacy; it was dated December 1, 1860, a week before the election took place:

A Sacred Trust has been committed to the University of Oxford by the last COLONEL BODEN. . . .

By general Consent one is pronounced a Scholar of world-wide reputation, the other a Scholar well known to his Friends and Pupils.

But one of them is specially and earnestly recommended to Convocation by a vast majority of our own Professors, by a great number of our Countrymen in India itself, including the Bishop of Calcutta, and "all to who he has spoken on the subject in that country," by the Native Teachers, and by all the Scholars of Europe. . . .

They know the man,—they know the Natives,—they are in daily communication with them,—they know the Language, they know the Sacred Books to which the Natives appeal.

Is it wise to disregard their opinion? No.

The Professorship is not for Oxford, or for England alone.

It is for Christendom.

It *is* for India.

It *is* for Christianity.

Let us then Vote for the man who is well known and admired in India, who even by the voice of his opponents is declared to be a trustworthy depositary of the Christian interests of a Christian Foundation, and who, by the general testimony of Sanskrit Scholars throughout the world, is incomparably the fittest Candidate for this the highest post of Sanskrit Learning.[33]

The flier was signed by a "D.D.," and it was clearly the manifesto of a supporter of Monier-Williams. The implicit message was that Max Müller was not the one "who is well known and admired in India," and he was not "a trustworthy depositary of the Christian interests of a Christian Foundation." What this flier makes clear is also the strong connection between the endorsement of the study of Sanskrit (or any so-called Oriental language) and Christian missionary work in the nineteenth century, which very much parallels the development of sinology in the same period, as we have seen in the case of Legge.[34]

Max Müller's failure to obtain the Boden Professorship was a serious blow to him. Although a professorship of comparative philology was founded on his behalf in 1868, it could not make up for the bitter disappointment he suffered; he resigned from teaching duties as professor of comparative philology in 1875, although he held the chair until his death. Macdonell, who became the third Boden Professor of Sanskrit in 1899, believes that this resulted in the dramatic change of direction in Max Müller's career as a scholar:

> There can be little doubt that this defeat was a bitter disappointment to Max Müller, and exercised a very decided influence on his subsequent career as a scholar. Sanskrit studies had formed the main interest of his intellectual life for almost twenty years. Had he been successful in the contest, his activity would probably have been almost entirely limited to his favorite subject, and, though he would in that case have been less famous, he would doubtless have produced, during the latter half of his life, works of more permanent value in the domain of research.
>
> His marvellous industry was now largely deflected into other channels. He began to pay considerable attention to comparative philology, delivering two series of lectures on the science of language at the Royal Institution in 1861 and 1863. . . . Max Müller was not only the introducer of comparative philology into England; he also became a pioneer in this country of the science of comparative mythology. . . .
>
> Allied to his mythological researches was his work on the comparative study of religions, which was far more important and enduring. Here, too, he was a pioneer; and the literary activity of the last thirty years of his life was largely devoted to this subject.[35]

The "last thirty years of his life" began in 1870, when Max Müller delivered four lectures on the "Science of Religion" at the Royal Institute.[36] This indeed marked the beginning of the second stage of his intellectual life, and it was during this time that his collaboration with Legge took place.

But before we move on to the next stage of Max Müller's life, when he became known as the founder of comparative religion, it is important to note that the Boden Professorship was far from being the only major setback in Max Müller's academic career. In 1876, two years after Max Müller's edition of the *Rig Veda* was finally completed, the American Sanskritist William Dwight Whitney (1827–94), a Yale professor and the first president of the American Philological Association, published a very critical review of the translation:

> Hardly another literary enterprise of the present century has become more widely known than M. Müller's publication of the Rig-Veda and its native commentary. Both in itself and in virtue of what it has led to, it has pressed itself in extraordinary degree upon men's attention. When it was begun, more than a quarter of a century ago, its author was an obscure young German student; when it is finished, he is one of the most noted men of the age. . . . He has had his reward. No man was ever before so lavishly paid, in money and in fame, for even the most unexceptionable performance of such a task. For personal gratitude in addition, there is not the slightest call. If Müller had never put hand to the Veda, his fellow-students would have had the material they needed perhaps ten years earlier, and Vedic study would be at the present moment proportionately advanced.[37]

Here I do not give a detailed analysis of the complex issues involved in the "Müller vs. Whitney Controversy," which is how the *New England Journal of Education* reported it on February 26, 1876. It suffices to say that Whitney's challenge to Max Müller became an international drama in the 1870s; years later, Henry Adams remarked, "[I]n the combative days of Whitney and Max Müller, I had more than enough to do in merely trying to keep out of the range of weapons."[38] It is important to note, however, that there was more at stake than merely scholarly reputation or rivalries; as Stephen Alter puts it, "[T]he Whitney-Müller controversy thus brought to a dramatic climax the Victorian era's interweaving of linguistics and natural science."[39]

What is relevant to us in this controversy was Whitney's relentless criticism of Max Müller's Sanskrit scholarship, and this seems to be a criticism still shared by scholars today: "[I]t is Müller's presence in pursuit of a comprehensive study of religion which has lasting importance; for, in the end, his substantive contribution to . . . Vedic study were short-lived, disappointing and dismal."[40]

Throughout Max Müller's life, there were various controversies, both scholarly and nonscholarly, that challenged his authority and power. For instance, there was the Sub-Librarianship of the Bodleian Library controversy in 1865; an open letter from "A Member of Convocation" spoke of "the threatened opposition to Professor Max Müller's appointment as

Sub-Librarian to the Bodleian Library."[41] In fact, in the Max Müller Papers Archive in the Bodleian Library, an entire archival box is filed under "Letters on Various Controversies in Which Müller Was Involved, 1845–91, including Letters to Georgina Max Müller [wife of Max Müller] and Printed Articles and Pamphlets."[42]

How did Max Müller secure his intellectual reputation and authority while facing so many challenges? In order to regain his intellectual authority after 1860, Max Müller devoted more and more energy to his work—not his work in Sanskrit and Vedic study, but his work as a pioneer of the scientific study of language and religion. By moving out of Sanskrit studies, Max Müller shifted the site of evaluation of his work to a new location, where he could participate in the very construction of standards of evaluation, that is, what it meant to be producing works of significance. Max Müller rescued his intellectual reputation and authority by investing and participating in a new discipline; through drawing boundaries for the emerging field of the science of religion, he legitimized his position of power and left behind a lasting reputation.

The Settlement of the Term Controversy: The Collaboration of Max Müller and Legge

I bracket the period of the settlement of the Term Controversy between 1877 and 1891 for the simple reason that 1877 marked the beginning of the controversy at the Missionary Conference in Shanghai and 1891 marked the year that Legge contributed his last volume of translation to the series *Sacred Books of the East*. In this section, I show that the intellectual collaboration of Max Müller and Legge was beneficial to both parties: Max Müller's comparative work offered Legge what Latour calls "the argument from authority" in the ongoing debate over the translation of the term *shang-ti*, and Legge's interpretation of Confucianism provided Max Müller with the missing piece in his articulation of the world religions discourse. Their further collaboration resulted in Legge's contributing five volumes to the *Sacred Books of the East* series, edited by Max Müller, which is Max Müller's most enduring legacy. The rest of this section is devoted to a detailed analysis of the publication of the *Sacred Books of the East*.

In 1875, a year before Legge was to receive his appointment as the first professor of Chinese at Oxford, Max Müller reached out to Legge, who had been living in Oxford. It was clear that Max Müller viewed Legge as a potential collaborator from the beginning. According to Legge's biographer Girardot,

> It started with a letter sent on February 13, 1875, in which Müller praises Legge's *Chinese Classics*, mentions his plans for an anthology of sacred books,

and invites Legge to meet him in Oxford on Friday. We have no record of the actual meeting but may assume that they discussed the prospects of a Chinese chair at Oxford and Legge's contribution to the *Sacred Books of the East* series, still pending approval at the university and press.[43]

In his letter, Max Müller told Legge, "I have long wished . . . to tell you how much I admire your magnificent edition of the *Chinese Classics*."[44] Max Müller was interested in Legge's work, he said, because the general lack of textual knowledge of Chinese religions represented a gap in his project of world religions; as early as 1870 Max Müller had lamented, in his "The Science of Religion: Lecture One," the fact that there were not enough translations of sacred texts from China:

> We possess the whole sacred canon of the Buddhists in various languages, in Pali, in Sanskrit, in Burmese, Siamese, Tibetan, Mongolian, and Chinese, and it is our fault entirely, if as yet there is no complete translation in any European tongue of this important collection of sacred books. The ancient religions of China again, that of Confucius and that of Lao-tse, may now be studied in excellent translations of their sacred books by anybody interested in the ancient faith of mankind.[45]

After their acquaintance, Legge's work on Chinese religions began to supply supporting evidence for Max Müller's own comparative religion projects, from the 1870s until 1900. Like almost every interested scholar in Europe at the time, Max Müller had relied on Legge's translation of Chinese classics to learn about the Confucian tradition. In 1900, when Max Müller wrote the essay "The Religions of China" shortly before his death, he invoked Legge in his own argument for the existence of the concept of God in China, and the essay reads very much like something Legge would have written. He also gave Legge full credit for introducing the connection between religion and the Chinese language:

> How closely the fundamental ideas of the Chinese religion are connected with language has been shown for the first time by Professor Legge. He has laid bare a whole stratum of language and religion in China of which we had formerly no idea, and it is owing to our ignorance the Chinese religion has so often been represented as unconnected with Nature-worship as we find in all Aryan religions; as without any mythology—nay, as without God.[46]

Legge was indeed the person responsible for the first extended application of the name "Confucianism."[47] He also strongly believed in the religious nature of Confucianism:

> I use the term Confucianism as covering, first of all the ancient religion of China, and then the views of the great philosopher himself, in illustration or modification of it, his views as committed to writing by himself, or transmitted

in the narratives of his disciples. The case is pretty much as when we comprehend under Christianity the records and teachings of the Old Testament as well as those of the New.[48]

Legge's view was certainly not shared by everyone, as we have seen regarding the 1877 Missionary Conference in Shanghai.

In 1880, Legge gave the Spring Lectures of the Presbyterian Church of England on Chinese religions, delivered at Presbyterian College in London. These lectures became his most comprehensive treatise on Confucianism and were published as a book in the same year under the title *The Religions of China: Confucianism and Taoism Described and Compared with Christianity*. At the time of his lectures, he was under so many attacks that he felt the need to defend his position once and for all:

> The questions have often been put to me, "But is Confucianism really a religion? Was it anything more than a system of morals intended for the government of human society?" The most extended expression of this sentiment is given in a recent number of *The China Review*, where the writer says, "Confucianism pure and simple is in our opinion no religion at all. The essence of Confucianism is an antiquarian adherence to traditional forms of etiquette—taking the place of ethics; a sceptic denial of any relation between man and a living God—taking the place of religion; while there is encouraged a sort of worship of human genius, combined with a set of despotic political theories. But who can honestly call this a religion?" Certainly if this were a fair account of all there is in Confucianism, I would not call it a religion. But the representation is absurdly unfair.[49]

Legge then gave the audience at Presbyterian College a presentation of Confucianism that specifically evoked the authority of Max Müller's comparative philology and mythology:

> I will now give a view of some of the religious thoughts of the fathers of the Chinese people, the fruits of which are found in the beliefs of their descendants down to the present day. In doing this, I will go back to a period long anterior to the composition of the most ancient Chinese books, and glance with you at some of the primitive written characters. . . . We shall be in the position of the Aryan philologists, who, from the root-words of Sanskrit and other kindred languages, try to give us pictures of the earliest Aryan life, as, for instance . . . Professor Max Müller, in his "Essay on Comparative Mythology."[50]

Legge's first example was the character *t'ien*, literally meaning "sky," which he took to be the symbol of heaven:

> Our first example shall be the character *t'ien*, the symbol of heaven. Its application must have been first to the visible sky, but, all along the course of history, it has also been used as we use Heaven, when we intend the ruling Power,

whose providence embraces all. . . . Professor Max Müller says: "In Chinese, *t'ien* denoted sky or day, and the same word, like the Aryan dyu, is recognized as the name of God."[51]

Legge clearly counted on Max Müller's theoretical framework to bolster his own argument for the religious nature of Confucianism; it does not matter that Max Müller did not know a word of Chinese. In order to settle the term controversy, Legge tried to shift the debate from the old context of missionary and sinological communities to the new context of comparative philology and comparative religion; such boundary work made it possible for him to settle the score without confronting real opposition.

The Birth of the Sacred Books of the East

Max Müller's most significant legacy is arguably the fifty-volume *Sacred Books of the East*.[52] The making of the series coincided with the emergence of comparative religion as a discipline in England, as well as in other parts of Europe.[53] Max Müller was the key architect of the series; after his resignation from his chair as professor of comparative philosophy in 1875, he devoted a great deal of time and energy to the project. He recruited leading philologists and translators of his day to contribute to this grand project, including T. W. Rhys Davids (1843–1922), an esteemed scholar of Buddhism who founded the Pali Text Society, as well as Legge. It was through Legge's interpretation of Confucianism as an ancient religion of China that Confucianism came to be seen as one of the great world religions. With the involvement of some of the most well-known scholars of Eastern languages and cultures in Europe, *Sacred Books of the East* became a canonical series, as well as Max Müller's most lasting contribution to the discipline of comparative religion.

The religions represented in the *Sacred Books of the East* reflect Max Müller's taxonomy of religions. He indeed took the classification of religions seriously; the religion scholar Jonathan Z. Smith recounts,

> One hundred and twenty-six years ago [in 1870], F. Max Müller, considered by some historians to be the progenitor of our field, in a lecture delivered at the Royal Institution in London and subsequently dedicated to Ralph Waldo Emerson, challenged religious studies with what is, in essence, a wager: "All real science rests on classification, and only in the case we cannot succeed in classifying the various dialects of faith, should we have to confess that a science of religion is really an impossibility."[54]

Before we turn to Müller's classification, it is necessary to note that the notion of "universal religions" or "world religions" was first invented by Cornelis Petrus Tiele (1830–1902), the other important figure responsible for the rise of comparative religion as a discipline. In his influential monograph *Outline of the History of Religion to the Spread of Universal Religions*, which was published in Dutch in 1876 and in English in 1877, he elaborated on the distinction between "religions of the world" or universalistic religions, which can cross national and ethnic boundaries, and "national religions," which are confined to certain ethnic groups or geographical regions.[55]

In her brilliant and pioneering study of the birth of the world religions discourse *The Invention of World Religions: Or, How European Universalism Was Preserved in the Language of Pluralism*, Tomoko Masuzawa discusses the history of the categories:

> Whatever the precise definition and value individual scholars ascribed to the category, those who rendered these texts into English understood the sense of the term well enough that, almost in all instances, [Dutch] *Wereldgodsdiensten*, as well as [German] *Weltreligionen*, was translated as "universal religions," or what Tiele preferred, "universalistic religions." . . . Only Tiele, writing in English for the *Encyclopedia Britannica*, explicitly specifies "world religions" as a synonym for "universalistic religious communities," and he dwells on the problem of the category itself at some length.[56]

In Tiele's entry on "Religions" in the *Encyclopedia Britannica*, he classified Confucianism (along with Taoism) as "national" religions, rather than "universalistic" religions or world religions.[57] For Tiele, there were only three world religions: Christianity, Buddhism, and Islam.

Max Müller had a different classification system in mind when he planned the *Sacred Books of the East* series. In his preface, composed in October 1876, he wrote,

> Leaving out of consideration the Jewish and Christian Scriptures, it appears that the only great and original religions which profess to be founded on Sacred Books, and have preserved them in manuscript, are:
>
> > The religion of the Brahmas.
> > The religion of the followers of Buddha.
> > The religion of the followers of Zarathustra.
> > The religion of the followers of Kung-fu-tze [Confucius].
> > The religion of the followers of Lao-tze.
> > The religion of the followers of Mohammed.[58]

Unlike Tiele, Max Müller added Vedic religion (or Hinduism), Zarathustrianism, Confucianism, and Taoism to the list of world religions. This classification scheme is the same as the one he later discussed in his Gifford Lectures in 1889; he then stated that that there were eight major religions in the world, with no distinction between the "national" ones and "universalistic" ones:

> The Eight Religions: Though the bulk of the *Sacred Books of the East* is enormous, yet we have seen that they represent no more than eight religions: (1) the Vedic, both ancient and modern; (2) Buddhism, Northern and Southern, and Gainism; (3) the Zoroastrian religion of the Avesta; (4) Confucianism; (5) Taoism; (6) the Jewish; (7) the Christian; and (8) Mohammedan religions.[59]

This classification system was the foundation of the *Sacred Books of the East* project, which in turn influenced generations of comparative religion scholars as well as countless social scientists.

On January 28, 1876, the Board of Delegates of the Oxford University Press, which through its many incarnations had had a history nearly as long as the university itself, met for a regular business meeting in the Clarendon Building, home of the press since the eighteenth century. The Press Delegacy, consisting of the vice chancellor of the university and two proctors, as well as five appointed delegates, was in charge of overseeing the business operation of the press and the selection of manuscripts for publication. Among the seven members of the Board of Delegates who attended this particular meeting were the vice chancellor of the university James E. Sewell; Henry G. Liddell, a former vice chancellor (and the father of the girl who inspired *Alice in Wonderland*); George G. Bradley, master of the university who later became Dean of Westminster; and Friedrich Max Müller, professor of comparative philology who had been a delegate for six years.

On that day the routine item on their agenda was the assessment of several book proposals. It was somewhat unusual, however, to receive a proposal from a fellow delegate. Max Müller was proposing to produce a "translation into English of a selection of the Sacred Books of the five great Oriental Religions," and the delegates decided that the proposal should be considered at a later date.

Less than a week later, on February 3, 1876, with Max Müller still in attendance, the delegates reached the conclusion that the proposal "was generally accepted, and Dr. Liddell was requested to communicate further with the India Office with the view of obtaining assistance towards the work."[60] Although the delegates originally approved only twenty-four volumes of translations, from 1879 to 1910, Oxford University Press eventually published forty-nine volumes of translations (plus one volume of index) of classical texts from the so-called "Great World Religions," including texts from diverse traditions such as Buddhism, Hinduism, Islam, Daoism, and Confucianism.

Dated October 19, 1877, the official agreement between the Clarendon Press and Max Müller finally allowed Max Müller to start what would become his magnum opus:

> The said Friedrich Max Müller agrees that he will prepare or procure to be prepared by competent scholars for publication by the Delegates translations

of the Books or parts of the Books to be selected by the Editor from the Sacred Books of the Brahmans, of the Followers of Buddha, of the Followers of Zarathustra, of the Followers of Kung-fu-tze, of the Followers of Lao-tze and of the Followers of Mohammed in accordance as nearly as may be within the scheme, prepared by the Editor of which a printed copy is annexed hereto subject to such variations as the Delegates and the Editor may from time to time agree upon.[61]

The agreement also offered Max Müller £300 a year as "the editor," plus an additional fee as "a translator." Max Müller had already submitted his resignation of his professorship to the vice chancellor on December 1, 1875; at the age of fifty-two, he became professor emeritus for £600 a year (half of his usual salary), in addition to his income of £300 a year as the editor of the series.

But the passing of the proposal of the *Sacred Books of the East* very much relied on the support of the India Office (also called the Council of India):

Max Müller's grand design . . . was approved by the Delegates in 1875 [*sic*], after he had enlisted the help of Lord Salisbury, at one time Secretary of State for India, Sir Henry Maine, and perhaps most importantly Dean Liddell, to whom he had confided his intention of going to Vienna and publishing the books there if Oxford were not interested. The expenses of production were to be shared equally between the Press and the Government of India.[62]

In a letter that the secretary of Oxford University Press submitted to the under secretary of state for India, the following was stated:

The Council of India will pay a sum of £150 per annum towards the salary of Professor Max Müller for a period not exceeding eight years. . . . The Council of India will pay £2 per sheet for not more than 90 sheets a year, provided the work translated belong to the ancient literature held to be of religious or legal authority by some considerable portion of Indian society and be written in some Aryan or Semitic language, provided that a translation of such work be required, and provided the selection of the work to be translated be previously approved by the Secretary of State in Council.[63]

Interestingly, the secretary of state for India, Lord Salisbury, played a supporting role not only in the arrangement between the Oxford University Press and Max Müller for the publication of the *Sacred Books of the East*, but also in securing Max Müller's position as professor emeritus at Oxford. After Max Müller submitted his resignation on December 1, 1875, citing his desire to complete his translations ("the most ancient and most important monument of Sanskrit Literature, which, if life and health are spared, I should like to finish"),[64] there were attempts "to relieve him of the burden of lecturing on Comparative Philology by giving him a Deputy who would do that work, and to give him the status of a Professor Emeritus," and Lord Salisbury was an enthusiastic supporter of the idea:

> Even Lord Salisbury, as Secretary of State for India, took up the matter, and on January 27 [1876] Liddell wrote to Müller: "I have just received a 'private' letter from Lord Salisbury, in which he expressed a warm desire on the part both of himself and of the India Council that you may be induced to remain at Oxford and in which he says that there 'seems to be no objection in principle to the India Council co-operating with the University to incur the cost of publishing the "Indian Works" which are mentioned in your list.'"[65]

The matter was brought to the convocation in the form of a decree and was approved on February 15, 1876, less than two weeks after the delegates of the Oxford University Press approved Max Müller's proposal for the *Sacred Books of the East*.[66] It would not be an overstatement to say that the continuing support from the colonial secretary of state for India and the India Council was indeed significant in the making of Max Müller's personal career and intellectual legacy.

This fifty-volume collection consisted of translations of the "sacred writings" of "the six so-called 'Book-religions'":[67] the "Religions of the Brahmans"; the "Religion of the followers of Buddha"; the "Religion of the followers of Zarathustra"; the "Religion of the followers of Kun-fu-tze"; the "Religion of the followers of Lao-tze"; and the "Religion of the followers of Mohammed."[68] There were forty-nine volumes of translated texts in the *SBE*, published between 1879 and 1894, plus one volume of "General Index" of SBE names and subject matters, published in 1910.

There were four volumes covering Confucianism in the total of six volumes devoted to the "Sacred Books of China," all of which were selected and translated by James Legge:

1879—Volume 3:

Part I of the Texts of Confucianism: The Shû King. The religions portions of the Shih King. The Hsiâo King.

1882—Volume 16:

Part II of the Texts of Confucianism: The Yi King.

1885—Volume 27:

Part III of the Texts of Confucianism. The Lî Kî, I–X.

1886—Volume 28:
Part IV of the Texts of Confucianism. The Lî Kî, XI–XLVI.

It is clear that Confucianism occupied a central place in the world religions in the *SBE* project. After the publication of the volumes, the teachings of Confucianism became much more accessible to scholars as well as the general public who were increasingly interested in Eastern religions. The authority and popularity of the series were such that, in the decades following its publication, quite a few pirated versions, as well as books simply "borrowing" the celebrated "Sacred Books of the East" name, appeared.[69]

"The White Elephant": Oxford University Press and the Sacred Books of the East

Among the eventual fifty volumes of translations in the *Sacred Books of the East*, or the *SBE* as the people at the press called it in the 1880s and 1890s, twenty-one volumes were devoted to Hinduism, twelve to Jainism and Buddhism, eight to Zoroastrianism, six to Chinese classics, and two to Islam. The author of a history of the Oxford University Press remarked in 1978,

> It's a massive, even startling achievement, and by no means as unprofitable in the end as had once been feared. Forty years after the inception of the series sales were still going up.[70]

But this had not always been the case. Martin Maw, the current archivist at Oxford University Press, has divulged that, indeed, for many years the *SBE* was the "white elephant" for the press: precious, expensive, yet rather "useless."[71] After the arrangement with the India Office ended according to their agreement, the press felt the financial pressure of producing the additional *SBE* volumes, for the foreign language in the texts was expensive to reproduce, and "Chinese characters do not allow of very thin paper" (memo from a Mr. Milford regarding "Legge: Chinese Classics," May 9, 1928, lamenting that "it seems hopeless" to cut costs).[72] It was simply too costly to print the volumes, and there were not enough people to buy them to turn a profit.

Although the press had to bear the "heavy losses incurred by publishing the five folio volumes of the Septuagint in 1798, and the many other great works that had followed, including the *Sacred Books of the East* under the editorship of Max Müller,"[73] starting in the 1920s there were frequent queries about the out-of-print volumes, especially James Legge's translations of the Chinese classics, coming from places such as Boston, Shanghai, and New York. In one letter, dated June 14, 1927, the OUP China Branch representative in Shanghai, Mr. McNeely, alerted his colleagues in Oxford that there was a suspicious book from a "Commercial Press," which seemed to be a "photographic reproduction of the Vols. I and II of Legge's *Chinese Classics*."[74]

In a letter dated November 28, 1932, McNeely wrote again, asking whether OUP should consider reprinting Legge's Confucian *Classics*, since "[t]he authorities here have started a 'Back to Confucius' movement," making the Confucian texts available in government schools and repairing "all Confucian temples."[75]

Although the financial burden of publishing the *SBE* didn't ease until later years, there was a deeper reason why Oxford University Press undertook the project in the first place. It had to do with the history of the press and the importance of the printing of "sacred texts" as part of its identity. The first book the press had ever printed was an exposition of the Apostles' Creed by St. Jerome, published in 1468.[76] Starting in the seventeenth century, the bible-printing branch, the Bible Press, kept the press commercially successful, and it was much larger than the academic printing branch. In 1814, for instance, the scholarly side of the press, the Learned Press, paid only £1,003 for paper, whereas the Bible Press paid £19,073.[77]

In other words, the survival and the success of Oxford University Press had always been dependent on printing sacred texts, not surprising given the original purpose of the university itself, which was to produce clergy. This might explain why Oxford University Press was determined to keep the *SBE* in print: its scholarly reputation as well as its identity as the preeminent publisher of sacred texts.

"For the Internationally Religious": The Emergence of a New Discipline

In an Oxford University Press memo titled "SBE Cheap Editions," dated February 20, 1908, there was a query from the management:

> Shall we have them [the volumes] ready for the Internationally Religious people who meet at Oxford this summer? . . . I suppose the Koran is much the most likely to be popular, so I suggest reducing its price most.[78]

The "Internationally Religious people" were the scholars attending the Third Congress of the International Congress for the History of Religion. The first meeting of the Congress took place in Paris in 1900, with Tiele and Max Müller as copresidents. The second was at the University of Basel in Switzerland in 1904. Max Müller died in 1900; had he been alive in 1904, he would probably have been very pleased to know that Oxford was finally ready to open its door to such an event.

And he would not have been wrong if he had believed that his passion for the study of world religions was an inspiration for this entire generation of scholars. They relied on his books on the science of language and religion, and they also counted on his *Sacred Books of the East* to learn about the different religious traditions that they wanted to comprehend.

Although many volumes of the *Sacred Books of the East* are flawed in different ways, people had an insatiable desire for knowledge about other religions and cultures that were opened up to them through the ambivalent legacy of the British Empire.

As we will see in chapter 5, in the years between 1860 and 1940, thousands of books on world religions appeared in the marketplace, with many being pirated editions of existing texts. Max Müller and his associates seized upon the opportunity to direct the curiosity of the public in the early stages of the development of the world religions discourse; they invented an intellectual space for future discussions, even though their own views might have been problematic, such as Max Müller's Christianized reading of other religions, not to mention his theological or even missionary intentions.[79]

In the publication of the *Sacred Books of the East*, the marketplace has indeed acted as the intersection of colonial political agenda, the politics of intellectual prestige, and the genuine need of a society that was eager to understand the changing landscape of its world at the dawn of globalization. Max Müller used the series to achieve goals that he otherwise wouldn't have been able to accomplish. By identifying the increasing popular interest in world religions, and by realizing the great potential of the growing publishing marketplace as the ideal venue for public recognition, Max Müller allied himself with the forces of modernity and globalization and gained legitimacy for his emerging discipline in the process.

INSTITUTIONALIZING PLURALISM: CONFUCIANISM AND COMPARATIVE RELIGION

Masuzawa makes the following remark on the history of the world religions discourse:

> The principle objective is a genealogy of a particular discursive practice, namely, "world religions" as a category and as a conceptual framework initially developed in the European academy, which quickly became an effective means of differentiating, variegating, consolidating, and totalizing a large potion of the social, cultural, and political practices observable among the inhabitants of religions elsewhere in the world.[80]

What Masuzawa has done in her remarkable book is indeed a genealogy, tracing the "pre-history of present-day world religions discourse," which has become "instrumental in generating the new classification regime that is now ours."[81] The term "genealogy" points to the profound affinity between her work and Foucault's and Said's, and her analysis of the universalizing impulse demonstrates convincingly that "it has become exigent that the discourse on religion(s) be viewed as an essential component, that is, as a vital operating system within the colonial discourse of Orientalism."[82]

Masuzawa is very much aware of the concrete social processes through which the knowledge of "world religions" was conditioned, shaped, and legitimized:

> In effect, the individual sections comprising chapter 8 identify various events and domains that might warrant further investigation in the future: (1) the historical significance and influence of preeminent publication projects, most importantly, the *Sacred Books of the East*; (2) the preconditions and the aftermath of the World's Parliament of Religions, held in Chicago in 1893; (3) the role played by various private individuals and foundations in promoting the new scholarship on religion, or what was more likely called "natural theology" in the nineteenth century and "history of religion(s)" in the twentieth.[83]

My focus in this section is precisely on the social conditions under which the discourse of world religions was invented, cherished, and commercially produced. Here the focal point is not "world religions" or comparative religion as a discourse in general, but rather the social and institutional processes through which the notion of Confucianism as a major world religion became possible.

As Adrian Cunningham suggested in his 1990 account of religious studies in British universities, if we are looking for individuals in universities who have created the field, then "one would obviously look to Friedrich Max Müller as an outstanding example." He goes on to remark briefly on the early history of religious studies in England:

> If one thinks of courses for students under the actual title of comparative religion, then one would look to Unitarian and Congregationalist theological colleges with John Estlin Carpenter in 1876 at Manchester College (then in London) and A. M. Fairbairn at Mansfield College in Oxford in 1886.
>
> If, however, one is thinking of university departments, then 1904 is the key date with the Manchester Department of Comparative Religion. Once again, a free church influence, in this case Methodist, was significant.[84]

Here we are going to examine both the beginning of the teaching of "comparative religion" and the beginning of the building of the institution of "religious studies" in Britain, since both are important for comparative religion in becoming a mature academic paradigm. More specifically, our focus is on the following two aspects of discipline building: the support of the dissenting academies (such as Manchester College and Mansfield College) and the Free Church foundations (such as the Gifford and Hibbert Trusts) as well as the organization of associations and conferences in the shaping of the new discipline of comparative religion.

The Dissenting Academies, the Gifford Lectures, and the Hibbert Trust: Allies for a New Understanding of Religion

Much had happened in the world during the thirty-one years (1879–1910) it took for all the volumes of the *Sacred Books of the East* to be published. By 1910, there were noticeable changes even at tradition-bound Oxford. Parliament had passed the "Universities Tests Act" in 1871, which abolished communion tests that were used to prevent Catholics, Nonconformist Protestants, and members of other religions to attend Oxford and Cambridge. By 1883 Oxford had about ten Roman Catholic undergraduates, and "there were estimated to be some 200 Nonconformist undergraduates and a handful of dons."[85]

And there were two Nonconformist colleges in Oxford too: Manchester College, which moved to Oxford in 1889, following the other Nonconformist academy Mansfield College, which moved to Oxford in 1886.[86] It is worth noting how fundamentally different the dissenting academies were from the other colleges in Oxford in the late nineteenth century. Neither Manchester College nor Mansfield College was part of the University of Oxford, even though both of them occupied central locations in the town of Oxford. The radical difference came from their religious affiliations: Manchester and Mansfield were both Nonconformist, whereas Oxford had been the bedrock of Anglicanism for many centuries.

Originally founded in 1757 by Nonconformist Protestants, Manchester College was one of the so-called "dissenting academies" that provided higher education to non-Anglican students at a time when only Anglican students could attend Oxford or Cambridge (these "dissenters" included Nonconformist Protestants as well as Catholics and Jews). Although Manchester College intended to join the University of Oxford with the move, it wasn't until 1990 that it was accepted into the Oxford University system, renamed "Harris Manchester" to reflect the donation of Lord Harris and his family. A historian of Manchester College remarks,

> The basic reason for the formation of Dissenting Academies was, after all, the exclusion, since Restoration times, of Dissenters from the two English universities of Oxford and Cambridge. In order to obtain higher education Dissenters had either to go to universities in Germany, Holland or Scotland, . . . or to provide institutions of their own.[87]

When Manchester College moved to Oxford in 1889, fifty years after the beginning of the conservative Oxford Movement in 1833, it was understandable that J. E. Carpenter, who was a Unitarian theologian and "Professor of Ecclesiastical History, Comparative Religion and Hebrew" at Manchester College, worried about the move. But the situation at Oxford had changed for the better:

> [T]he new discipline of Comparative Religion had already secured a niche in the University, thanks to the pioneering activities of Max Müller, who has been described as being "among the most learned and popular figures in post-Tractarian Oxford," and who was later to become one of Estlin Carpenter's closest friends.[88]

Carpenter joined the new discipline of comparative religion right away; he started reading the Buddhist scriptures in the original Pali with the help of Rhys Davids, one of the translators for the *Sacred Books of the East*, and he eventually amassed one of the best collections of books on Eastern religions.

In this gradually more relaxing atmosphere, the Oxford Society of Historical Theology was founded in the early 1890s. The word "historical" was "intended to declare that there were to be no dogmatic preconditions," so the society could concern itself with "religion" rather than "Christian theology."[89] Max Müller was president of the society in 1893 and 1894. He was also a firm supporter of the dissenting academies in Oxford and befriended the principals of both Manchester College and Mansfield College.

It should not be surprising that the Nonconformist academies such as Manchester College were some of the first institutions to support the new discipline. Carpenter was one of the earliest members of the Oxford Society of Historical Theology, and he also invited Max Müller to be a lecturer at Manchester College from 1895 to 1900, the last five years of Max Müller's life. At the 1908 Third International Congress of the History of Religions in Oxford, Carpenter was the organizing secretary. Their shared purpose of studying religions without the constraints of Anglican theology and their shared efforts in gaining respect and legitimacy against the indifference of the establishment connected them.

The legendary Gifford Lectures began in 1888, with Max Müller as the very first lecturer, from 1888 to 1892. Under the 1885 will of Adam Gifford, or Lord Gifford (1820–87), £80,000 was bequeathed to four Scottish universities (the universities of Edinburgh, Aberdeen, Glasgow, and St. Andrews) for the establishment of a series of lectures that deal with the topic of "natural religion." Lord Gifford's intention was to discuss theology as a science, "without reference to or reliance upon any special exceptional or so-called miraculous revelation." In his will he declared,

> The lecturers shall be subjected to no test of any kind, and shall not be required to take any oath, or to emit or subscribe any declaration of belief, or to make any promise of any kind; they may be of any denomination whatever, or of no denomination at all (and many earnest and high-minded men prefer to

belong to no ecclesiastical denomination); they may be of any religion or way of thinking, or, as is sometimes said, they may be of no religion, or they may be so-called sceptics or agnostics or free-thinkers, provided that the "Patrons" will use diligence to secure that they be able, reverent men, true thinkers, sincere lovers and earnest inquirers after truth.[90]

According to Chaudhuri, Max Müller "called the lectureships a sign, and a very important sign, of the times."[91] Max Müller has indeed left a lasting influence on the Gifford Lectures; in an edited volume celebrating the centenary Gifford Lectures, *Humanity, Environment and God*, short excerpts from Max Müller's various writings are used as thematic threads to connect the essays on different areas of scholarship throughout the book.[92] Since Max Müller's inaugural lectures, the organizers of the Gifford Lectures have invited many luminous—and religiously liberal— speakers, such as William James, who lectured on "The Varieties of Religious Experience" in 1900–1902; James Frazer, who discussed nature worship in 1911–13; and, in recent years, A. J. Ayer, Richard Dawkins, and Edward Said (who died shortly before his scheduled lectures).

Another important series of lectures, the Hibbert Lectures, have been funded by the Hibbert Trust for over one hundred years. The trust was founded in 1847 under the will of Robert Hibbert, a merchant who made his fortune in Jamaica. A Unitarian, Hibbert set up the trust to encourage the spread of "Christianity in its most simple and intelligible form," and to uphold "the unfettered exercise of the right of private judgment in matters of religion."[93] Besides the financial support of the Hibbert Lectures and book series, the Hibbert Trust has also been supporting Unitarian ministers and lay scholars since its founding; students at Manchester College have received many scholarships from the trust. The first series of Hibbert Lectures in 1878 was also given by Max Müller, published as *Lectures on the Origin and Growth of Religion, As Illustrated by the Religions of India* in the same year.[94] The first lecture was so well received that for the next lectures organizers received fourteen hundred ticket applications for seats in a hall that could hold only six hundred people.[95]

For people who were interested in world religions, it was indeed a very significant moment when the World Parliament of Religions, organized by the Unitarians and Universalists of the Free Religious Association, was held in Chicago in 1893. But in Britain, the most noteworthy conference was the Third International Congress of the History of Religions, held in Oxford in September 1908. It "appears to have provided the opportunity for an exchange of ideas between anthropologists, archaeologists, philologists, Orientalists, and theologians: theology was ceasing to be a protected discipline."[96] One of the organizers was J. E. Carpenter, the principal of Manchester College from 1914 to 1919. This was the conference for the "Internationally Religious People" described in the Oxford

University Press memo; this was also the conference that anticipated the rapid growth of comparative religion as a discipline.

At the Oxford conference, Louis Henry Jordan, author of the important 1905 volume *Comparative Religion: Its Genesis and Growth*, gave a paper titled "Comparative Religion: Its Method and Scope." He first summarized the various methods being used in the comparative study of religions, then moved on to far more urgent issues:

> The time has fully come when definitely constructive work ought to be undertaken in the interest of Comparative Religion. Many lines of advance are already open and inviting, but two at least must be emphasized in the present connexion.
>
> 1. An adequate and uniform definition of comparative religion. A more exact connotation must be attached, and without further postponement, to the name of this new science. Its office designation is at present being used in the most vague and confusing way. . . . No general agreement has yet been reached touching the limits respectively of the History of Religion and Comparative Religion. . . . A brief definition of Comparative Religion, accepted and adhered to by all responsible teachers, would render immense service towards differentiating these two departments of research, each of which would then be restricted to an express and distinctive task.
> 2. The systematic training of men who aspire to leadership in this field. . . . The necessity of making provision for the express training of men who desire to devote themselves to the promotion of Comparative Religion brings under view a timely and extremely important subject. It demands our serious attention. I propose to devote to it, accordingly, the remainder of this Paper.[97]

Jordan's paper was an overview of the fledging field as well as a plan for what was to be done. A religion scholar with a keen sociological instinct, Jordan proceeded to make three recommendations:

> 1. Special Professorships. . . .
> 2. Separate University Department. . . .
> 3. A Centrally-situated Training Institution. . . . Instead of founding a few (more or less isolated) Chairs in a number of selected universities, why should not an effort be made to establish—in the chief national capitals—a central and well-endowed Institution, in which the work of scientific research in religion could be prosecuted in a broad and thoroughly scholarly manner?[98]

Now, more than one hundred years later, we can see that the "internationally religious people" did indeed get what they wished for. Today we have religious studies departments in most of the major North American and European universities, not to mention the many endowed Chairs in comparative religion. We also have training institutions in "chief national capitals," such as the Harvard Center for the Study of World Religions near Boston, the Interdisciplinary Centre for Religious Studies at the University of Leuven, and the Institute of World Religions at the Chinese Academy of Social Sciences in Beijing.

With a grand yet clear vision inherited from the founding father of the field, Jordan predicted the emergence of a new discipline, which is something Max Müller had dreamed of. In 1870, thirty-eight years before Jordan's anticipation of the institutionalization of comparative religion, Max Müller spoke of the goals of science of religion in his first lecture on "The Science of Religion" at the Royal Institution:

> A Science of Religion, based on an impartial and truly scientific comparison of all, or at all events, of the most important religions of mankind, is now only a question of time. It is demanded by those whose voice cannot be disregarded. Its title, though implying as yet a promise rather than a fulfillment, has become more or less familiar in Germany, France and America; its great problems have attracted the eyes of many inquirers, and its results have been anticipated either with fear or with delight. It becomes therefore the duty of those who have devoted their life to the study of the principle of religions of the world in their original documents, and who value religion and reverence it in whatever form it may present itself, to take possession of this new territory in the name of true science.[99]

The Establishment of a New Discipline in Great Britain and Beyond

The second half of the nineteenth century and the beginning of the twentieth century were crucial to the establishment of most of today's social science disciplines, such as psychology, economics, political science, geography, anthropology, and sociology.[100] For instance, anthropological institutions became well established in the 1880s, and courses in anthropology were widely offered in universities in Britain, France, Germany, and the United States.[101] Academic sociology developed rapidly in France at the turn of the twentieth century, with Durkheim creating the first program of sociology at the University of Bordeaux in 1887, founding Année sociologique, the first social science journal in France, in 1898, and holding the first chair in sociology ("science in education and sociology") in 1913. Sociology grew equally swiftly in America, with the first department of sociology created at the University of Chicago in 1892 under Albion Small and the second at Columbia University 1894 under Franklin Giddings.[102]

In 1904, four years after Max Müller's death, the first Department of Comparative Religion was established at the University of Manchester, with T. W. Rhys Davids, a scholar for whom Max Müller had written many letters of support, as the first chair. There was again a Free Church influence, Methodist in this case, and the University of Manchester became "the first theological faculty in Europe to require every student to take at least one course in comparative religion."[103] Cambridge finally changed its "Theological Tripos" to the "Theology and Religions Studies Tripos" in 1975, and at King's College, London, a Department of Theology and Religious Studies was founded in 1984.[104] Indeed, now there are departments of religious studies everywhere in England. However, Oxford still doesn't have a comparative religion faculty; if students of the Faculty of Theology are interested in comparative religion, they have to take courses in Oriental studies.

Here we can only briefly mention the development of religious studies in North America. It shouldn't come as a surprise that Chicago, the site of the 1893 World Parliament of Religions, was the first city in America to have lectureships on comparative religion. In 1892, George Stephen Goodspeed established the Department of Comparative Religion at the University of Chicago's Division of Humanities. William Rainey Harper, the founder of the University of Chicago, and John Henry Barrows, the pastor of the First Presbyterian Church and chairman of the World Parliament of Religions, were instrumental in promoting comparative religious studies in Chicago. And their efforts were greatly aided by a generous donor, Mrs. Caroline Haskell, who donated $40,000 in 1894 to endow two programs at the University of Chicago, the Haskell Lectureship and the Barrows Lectureship on Comparative Religion, and $100,000 also in 1894 to establish the Haskell Oriental Museum on the university campus. She wanted the lectureships to encourage studies of "Eastern religions" in America, and she wanted the Barrows Lectureship to be delivered in India, where the lectures could present the "great questions of the truths of Christianity, its harmonies with the truths of other religions, its rightful claims, and the best methods of setting them forth" to the "scholarly and thoughtful people of India."[105]

As early as 1872 Harvard Divinity School had started to offer courses on Eastern religion; the first course was called "East Asiatic Religions," taught by Charles Carroll Everett. In 1891, "The American Lectureships on the History of Religion" was established, which was founded to support both lectures and a book series (it is currently administrated by the American Academy of Religion). Some of the notable early lectures include T. W. Rhys Davids's lectures on Buddhism in 1894–95 and J.J.M. De Groot's lecture on "The Development of Religion in China" in 1910–11, later published as *Religion in China: Universism: A Key to the State of*

Taoism and Confucianism, which was cited extensively by Max Weber.[106] These efforts of field building have produced lasting results; today we can find a department of religion or religious studies in almost every college or university in America. This is exactly what Jordan predicted at the 1908 Oxford conference:

> But—lying outside of the historian's domain, and employing a method fitted to meet an entirely different demand—there stretches that field in which Comparative Religion is at work, and in which it is winning its reward. . . . To have attained skill and confident progress in such an undertaking is to have passed beyond the frontier of the History of Religions. Consciously or unconsciously, one has already entered the territory of another science.[107]

Jordan was keenly aware of the boundaries of the new discipline; these are visionary words indeed.

Edward Said speaks of Orientalism as "something more historically and materially defined," rather than just a ghostly ideology.[108] This is certainly true of the discourse of world religions. It was created in a particular moment in history; the financial involvement of the colonial British India Office, the religious tension among the theologians and the more liberal religion scholars in the academy, the intellectual struggles for academic legitimacy of the key architects of the new discipline, the missionary impulse of some of the early donors of lectureships and chairs in comparative religion, and the marketability of popular interests in the mystic Eastern religions all played important roles in the making of the world religions discourse. The discourse might have been conceived in the long line of thought presupposing Europe as the sole possessor of universal history and universal religion, but, as the sociologist Randall Collins has argued, ideas cannot beget ideas,[109] and the birth and growth of the idea of world religion was facilitated by many institutional and material factors, factors that had as much to do with the contingent and messy working of the political and social life as the logic of universalistic truth.

THE FULL DISCIPLINARITY OF COMPARATIVE RELIGION

In this chapter, through examining the career trajectory of Max Müller and the collaboration of Max Müller and Legge, we have seen how their shared strategy of boundary work helped settle the Term Controversy for Legge as well as established Max Müller's reputation as the founder of comparative religion. Through an analysis of the institutionalization of comparative religion in the early stages of its emergence as a new discipline, we learned that the establishment of the new field of comparative religion took more than the invention of an Orientalist discourse.

Has the science of religion/comparative religion/religious studies finally established itself as a legitimate discipline today? According to Andrew Abbot, there is an indicative sign of full disciplinarity:

> [T]here is one central social structure signifying full disciplinarity. That is reciprocity in acceptance of Ph.D. faculty. Border fields often employ faculty of diverse disciplines. We can think of them as having become true disciplines in the social structural sense once they hire mainly Ph.D.s in their own field. . . . This test of social structural disciplinarity is much like the intergroup fertility standard used to define biological species.[110]

Based on this test, religious studies has indeed established itself as a full discipline. Departments of religious studies (or departments of religion) today produce PhDs in universities all over North America and Europe; in the case of the United States, most faculty members in religious studies departments hold PhDs in their own field. In other words, there is already a solid institutional social structure in place in the discipline of religious studies.

In Abbott's analysis, academic disciplines have both a social structure and a cultural structure. The cultural structure refers to "an ensemble of research practices, evidentiary conventions, rhetorical strategies, genres, canonical works, and the like."[111] Another important aspect of the disciplinary cultural structure is what Abbott calls "a discipline's axis of cohesion":

> Disciplines often possess strong cultural axes, which we consider to be their central principles. Political science, we say, is about power, economics about choice, anthropology about ethnography, and so on. . . . But in the social sciences and humanities, axes of cohesion are not aligned. As my examples show, anthropology is largely organized around a method, political science around a type of relationship, and economics around a theory of action.[112]

One might say that the discipline of religious studies, as first envisioned by Max Müller and his associates, is organized around the principle of comparative methods. By consciously separating itself from history and theology, by adopting an explicitly comparative method, and by taking on a pluralistic outlook on religion, these scholars firmly established the axis of cohesion in the field of comparative religion through the implementation of the discourse of world religions.

CHAPTER 3

The Confucianism as a Religion Controversy in Contemporary China

THERE ARE ESSENTIALLY THREE POSITIONS concerning Confucianism as a religion in China since 1949, the beginning of the socialist state: (1) Confucian is not a religion; (2) Confucianism is a religion, and as such has a negative impact, for religion itself is intrinsically a negative force in society; (3) Confucianism is a religion, and it has a positive or neutral impact, for religion is either a positive force in society or a neutral one. The first position is easy to distinguish, but the other two are often conflated with each other, for they differ only in their value judgments. In today's China, the second position is based on the Marxist denouncement of religion in general, whereas the third one comes from either a favorable or a nonjudgmental view of religious life. The state has been taking the first position, denying Confucianism the status of religion; among the scholars of Confucianism all three positions can be found, and the opposing value judgments between them have become the primary cause of the most recent intellectual debates.

In this chapter I focus on how the different combinations of the three positions interact with one another, and how such interactions shape the categorization of Confucianism in China. To some extent this study touches on the larger issue of articulation, which refers to "the ways in which ideas are shaped by their social situations and yet manage to disengage from these situations."[1] Although this chapter centers on how ideas are shaped by their social situations, I emphasize that the ideas about Confucianism, like many other bodies of knowledge, "were shaped by and yet succeeded in transcending their specific environments of origin."[2] Although I am not going to examine how the knowledge of Confucianism transcends its social environments here, it is important to have this broad understanding in mind when we look at how certain views triumph over others in a particular historical moment.

Here I first outline the process of the construction in the 1950s of the official religious classification, the Five Major Religions, including Catholicism, Protestantism, Buddhism, Daoism, and Islam, but not Confucianism. Next I discuss the contemporary controversy over the religious nature of Confucianism, an important ongoing intellectual debate with potential political implications that hasn't previously been studied by social scientists. It can be traced back to the 1970s and the work of Ren Jiyu (1916–2009), a leading scholar of the history of Chinese philosophy and religions, who was also a high-ranking administrator in state-controlled academic institutions. The current controversy took place in 2000–2004, with several dozens of participants publishing progressively more heated articles in various academic journals and on much-browsed scholarly websites. The remaining parts of this chapter focus on an analysis of this controversy and its potential political impacts.

This chapter draws on interviews with officials from the State Administration of Religious Affairs, the past and current members of the Department of Confucianism (or "Confucian Religion") at the Chinese Academy of Social Sciences (CASS), and the current head of the Institute of World Religions, of which the Department of Confucianism is a part. The choice of interviewing the members of CASS was not an arbitrary one. Although it is called the Academy of Social Sciences, CASS is the national academy for the studies of both the humanities and the social sciences, with thirty-one institutes devoted to disciplines ranging from literature, history, religion, and philosophy to economics, sociology, and American studies. Established in 1977, CASS occupies the most prestigious position on the Chinese intellectual landscape as the highest ranking national research institution.[3] However, despite its close ties to the state (the head of CASS shares the same official rank as a vice-premier, and the current head is in fact a former vice-premier), CASS has had a long history of harboring intellectual dissenters. During the 1989 Tiananmen Square student movement, for instance, many members of CASS helped the students with political ideas and strategies, which led to the commonly shared view of CASS being a think tank of student leaders.

In the case of the controversy over Confucianism as a religion, CASS again has played an important role for both historical and political reasons. The Institute of World Religions was founded in 1964; it is the only institute at CASS that was established as a result of Mao's direct request.[4] Mao wrote in a memorandum dated December 30, 1963, that "there hasn't been a research institution led by Marxist scholars" to study the "three great world religions (Christianity, Islam and Buddhism)," yet "one cannot understand world philosophy, literature and history without critically examining and refuting theology."[5] The Institute of World Religions was set up only four months after Mao's written instructions;

from the very beginning it was laden with unambiguous political agendas, which have become a highly problematic legacy for its researchers.[6]

Rujiao shi, the only research facility in China bearing the name "Department of Confucianism (or Confucian Religion)," was created in 1979 under the Institute of World Religions at CASS. As we will see, the contemporary controversy centers around both its past and current members, and I demonstrate that, in this case, CASS is again the crucial cultural location where the state and the intellectuals encounter each other, and the consequences of such interactions reflect both the internal dynamics of this complex institution and the changing political climate of the country.

THE BIRTH OF THE FIVE MAJOR RELIGIONS CATEGORY IN SOCIALIST CHINA: 1949–1957

The conception of the Five Major Religions was formed in the 1950s behind the closed doors of the Chinese Communist leadership. To my knowledge there has been no scholarly account of what happened during those important deliberations of religious policy. The exclusion of Confucianism in particular has been very much a mystery: Why was it excluded? What were the reasons of the decision makers?

From various sources, including published materials and interviews with scholars from the CASS and an official from the National Bureau of Religious Affairs, which is part of the State Department, I learned that the notion of Five Major Religions was devised in the 1950s, when concerns for national security and social stability forced the newly formed government to find a way to deal with China's religious population. The religious organizations, especially the Catholic Church and the Protestant churches, were large enough to pose potential threats to the socialist state. In order to gain control of these organizations, the National Bureau of Religious Affairs was established solely for the management of such groups.[7]

In 1953 four religious associations were founded under the titles of "Patriotic Associations" of Chinese Catholics, Protestants, Muslims, and Buddhists. The Patriotic Association of Daoists didn't come into existence until 1957, when a Communist general intervened to make it an official religion.[8]

Apparently no one spoke out for the Confucians. But who were the Confucians? It seems plausible that Confucianism was left out of the official classification because there was no Confucian population perceived to be posing a political threat. And there also was no self-identified Confucian population to speak of in the first place. This was confirmed by Ren Jiyu, who was knowledgeable of the original discussion over the new China's religious policy: "The Five Religions policy was conceived because of political concerns; the more believers a religion had, the more seats for representatives they would get in the People's Political Consultative Congress. In Buddhism we had [representatives such as] Zhao Puchu; in the Christian Church we had Ding Guangxun. We knew there were relatively fewer believers of Taoism, but we couldn't find any Confucians at all."[9]

Many Chinese intellectuals might consider themselves living a life based on the Confucian virtues of learnedness and self-cultivation, yet none of them, at least in the mid-twentieth century, would call themselves "believers of the Confucian religion." Although the general atmosphere of scientism and atheism, which was part of the ideology promoted by the Enlightenment-minded Chinese Communists, must have played a role in people's silence about their religious beliefs, it is important to note that most people would have found the sentence "I am a believer of the Confucian religion" (*woshi yige rujiaotu*) deeply problematic, even though it is structurally similar to the sentence "I am a believer of the Christian religion" (*woshi yige jidutu*).

Although they share the exact same grammatical structure, the latter has been uttered countless times by Chinese Christians, whereas the former is rarely uttered since it is nonsensical to most Chinese people. Being a Confucian in traditional China means living a certain way of life; it's deeply embedded in everyday practice, and there is nothing in Confucianism that is akin to the Catholic or Jewish rites of confirmation, during which one declares one's belief or faith. Without a recognizable or identifiable base of believers, Confucianism as a religion has primarily been a matter of academic and political concern.

The Beginning of the Contemporary Confucianism as a Religion Controversy: Ren Jiyu and His Legacy

In 1978, two years after the end of the Cultural Revolution, at the founding meeting of the Chinese Association of the Study of Atheism, a state-run organization that counted many intellectuals, voluntarily or involuntarily, as its members, Ren Jiyu, a renowned scholar of the history of Chinese religion and philosophy who had since become the chairman of the association, made the proclamation that "Confucianism is a religion." His presentation later became the much-debated article "On the Formation of Confucian Religion," which was published in the leading state-supported academic journal *Chinese Social Sciences* in 1980.[10] But it was not an endorsement of Confucianism as a religion; far from it, it was the beginning of a prolonged effort to hold what Ren perceived to be the religious component of Confucianism responsible for many of the grave ills in the long history of China.

The article was controversial due to its bold statement that Confucianism should be considered a religion, like Buddhism and Daoism. As a historian, Ren offered concrete evidence to support his reading of Confucianism as a religion in the long course of Chinese history. But a close reading of the piece reveals familiar ideas about religion that were part of the Communist ideology at the time. Ren believed that Confucianism was a religion just like any other, and its influence in China had been largely negative, in the way that Christianity had been the tool of "coercion and oppression" in the Western world. He wrote that, because of its emphasis on "feudal rituals and restrictions," Confucianism as a religion "tortured the Chinese people" in the same way the Inquisition made people suffer in the Middle Ages.[11] He further argued that "Confucian religion limited the development of modern ideas, restricted the growth of technology and science in China."[12]

It would take a very detailed analysis to unpack the complex meanings of these passages. There is the Marxist denouncement of religion as the "opium of the people"; there is also the reiteration of Weber's verdict that Confucianism is responsible for China's failure to develop modernity, although this is more likely a coincidence since Ren probably had not read Weber's treatise on Chinese religions at the time (the Chinese translation of Weber's *Religions of China* didn't appear until 1991). For Ren, Confucian values such as filial piety and reverence toward the ruler are not cultural traditions worth preserving but signs of the harms done by religion. He concluded in his essay, "Hence, as history has shown us, the Confucian religion has brought us only disasters, shackles, and poisonous cancers, rather than valuable traditions."[13]

It became very clear in my interview with Ren, who was the director of the Chinese National Library until his death in 2009, that he still firmly believed that Confucianism as a religion is a negative force that prevented modernization in China. A lifelong Marxist, he also seemed to think that Confucianism was partly responsible for the fanaticism during the Cultural Revolution—too much reverence toward the ruler, for instance. This view was shared by many in the late seventies and early eighties, when they tried to place the blame for the Cultural Revolution on the "feudalistic traditions" in Chinese society, such as Confucianism.

However, it is important to note that although Ren believed that the Confucian religion had done much harm to modern China, he did not consider Confucianism to be a real, living religion in contemporary Chinese society. This explains his remark about the nonexistence of Confucians when the Five Major Religions policy was being formed in the 1950s. When I asked him whether Confucianism should be regarded as a religion today, Ren said that it was "a thing of the past," and a revival was impossible because of the "internal limitation of Confucianism due to its emphasis on tradition and filial piety, which is incompatible with modernity." He believed that Confucianism ceased to be a full-blown religion when the last Chinese imperial dynasty was overthrown in 1911 by the Republican Revolution: "Because there was no separation between the state and religion in Confucianism, the emperors had been serving as the heads of the religion, like the Pope. When the revolution put an end to the throne, it also marked the end of the Confucian religion. Today Confucianism as a religion no longer exists." For him, the continuation of certain Confucian ritual practices was simply a part of the "folk superstition" tradition, which is relatively insignificant; the important task is to uncover the true history of Confucianism as a religion in China before 1911, which is primarily an intellectual project.

Because of his high standing in the Communist Party and his reputation as a leading historian of Chinese religions, Ren was handpicked by Mao to found the Institute of World Religion in 1964. He became its first director, a position he held until 1985, when he took over the directorship of the National Library, although he remained the honorary director of the institute until his death. The establishment of the Department of Confucianism in 1979 was largely due to the influence of Ren and his strong interest in Confucianism as a religion. The department is still the only one of its kind in the entire country, and until 2003 the chair of the department had been held consecutively by three of Ren's former students. It's certainly an institution endorsed by the state, given Ren's political identity and his antireligion stance toward the religious nature of Confucianism.

THE CONTEMPORARY CONFUCIANISM AS RELIGION DEBATE: 2000–2004

The current Confucianism as a Religion Controversy refers to the controversy over the religious nature of Confucianism that in effect started in 2000. Although there were already discussions about Confucianism as a religion before that, most of them responses to Ren's work, it wasn't until 2000 that the debate became intense and widespread enough to be labeled "the red-hot topic in Chinese academia."[14] Even though Ren and his followers remain central figures in the current debate, the controversy is not simply a reevaluation of Ren's legacy; in many ways it also reflects the growing intellectual interest in the study of Confucianism in recent years.

During the so-called Culture Fever in the 1980s, when socialist China finally started to open its doors to the West, there was a general enthusiasm toward Western culture and ideas, and more and more foreign intellectuals were allowed to lecture and attend conferences in China. One of the visitors was Tu Weiming, the most influential scholar of Confucianism in the States and the longtime director of the Harvard-Yenching Institute, whose lecture on Confucianism at Beijing University in 1985 was a legendary event. Being a "New Confucian," Tu has long been interested in the religious dimensions of Confucianism, and his positive appraisal of the Confucian tradition (including its religiosity) as the core of Chinese culture was very inspiring to his audience.

At this time scholarly works on Confucianism from East Asian places such as Singapore, Taiwan, and South Korea were also being introduced. These works often treated the Confucian ethic as the driving force behind the industrial success of the "Four Little Dragons" of East Asia, the way the Protestant ethic was perceived as instrumental in the development of modern capitalism in Europe.[15] To the Chinese intellectuals who considered the question of modernization to be the most urgent one, such a Weberian take on Confucianism offered both a new solution and a new perspective on the Confucian tradition. There were also international conferences on Confucianism; one of the first was held in 1987 in Qufu, Confucius's birthplace, jointly hosted by the newly founded Confucius Foundation of China (a state-funded cultural organization to promote Confucian studies and Chinese culture) and the Institute for East Asian Philosophies in Singapore.[16] Such encounters with new interpretations of Confucianism from both East Asian regions and North America, along with the budding institutional encouragement from the state, indeed facilitated the changing attitude of the younger generation of Chinese scholars.

When Tu visited the Academy of Chinese Culture during his 1985 trip, the academy was one of the few institutions devoted to the studies of Chinese classics, or the "national learning" (*guoxue*), at the time. But the number of students who wanted to study Chinese classics was steadily on the rise, and the fervor for national learning became more prevalent in the 1990s, with many younger intellectuals joining the field, most of whom undertook their academic training after the Cultural Revolution. It should not come as a surprise that they began to question the legitimacy of the politically charged negative assessment of Confucianism as a religion.

But the debate didn't become sensational until October 2001, when the website Confucius2000.com was founded. The site was devoted to the scholarly study of all aspects of Confucianism, and soon the Confucianism as a Religion Debate dominated the site and brought the controversy to the attention of intellectuals nationwide.

The storm—for it was indeed a fierce storm—reached a feverish pitch in 2002–3, with hundreds of articles and responses posted on the Confucius2000 forum. In the postings the core participating scholars attacked one another with unprecedented candor, and their escalating quarrels were fueled by the speediness of internet publishing. The heated debate captured the attention of many intellectuals, especially the ones working in the fields of religion, philosophy, and history. In the words of one of the key participants in the controversy, in those two years the debate "reached a height and intensity that stunned the Chinese academic community."[17]

But before we turn to a detailed analysis of the debate, we need to first take a look at the cultural venues where the debate takes place. In today's China, there are two main channels of intellectual exchange for scholars who study religion, as is the case for most Chinese academics. One is the official channel, which includes numerous state-sponsored academic journals such as *Chinese Social Sciences* and state-sanctioned conferences. The other is the unofficial channel, which nowadays means mostly online publishing, since independent scholarly print journals normally don't last very long due to a lack of funding. The internet venue includes independent journals such a *Tracing the Dao*, a scholarly publication with its own website, as well as internet sites such as Confucius2000 that are dedicated to specific areas of scholarly interests.

Since the 1990s, the internet has been creating a virtual community of ideas for Chinese intellectuals, and this space has been expanding, particularly in the category of scholarly websites, which normally refrain from publishing direct criticisms of contemporary Chinese politics, and hence are relatively free from state censorship. Many such sites are expertly organized and maintained, and the involvement of leading intellectuals in the fields often provides these online ventures with a sense of academic legitimacy. The Confucius2000 site, for instance, counts many important scholars of Confucianism as its active contributors. About thirty or so similar sites on Chinese philosophy and religion are listed on Confucius2000 as members of a larger network of websites sharing common intellectual goals, which shows how such forums are thriving for people who wish to carry out serious exchange of ideas in cyberspace. Although none of these sites are state sponsored, there are often interactions between the official and unofficial channels; for example, relevant chapters published in state-run journals often end up on the Confucius2000 website.

There were various articles debating Ren's view on Confucianism in the official scholarly journals in the 1980s, but it was in 2001 that the debate reached a new phase, with many articles published in official as well as unofficial venues. The current controversy started when the two-volume *History of Confucianism as a Religion in China* was published in 2000. The author of the book is Li Shen, a former student of Ren's who at the time was the head of the Department of Confucianism (Confucian Religion), and his analysis of Confucianism as a religion closely resembles the substance of Ren's arguments. In other words, Li Shen carried out a systematic historical study of Confucianism as a religion with a similar negative value judgment, depicting the religious aspect of Confucianism as a fundamentally harmful element in Chinese culture and society.

A few months after the publication of the book, a review was posted on the Confucius2000 website with the title "The Federal Project Made of Tofu Dregs: Reflections on the First Volume of *History of Confucianism as a Religion in China*." The author was Chen Yongming, a colleague of Li's at the Department of Confucianism (Confucian Religion). It also carried the following postscript: "For various reasons this article has been rejected by many journals. The author hopes that a journal with the agenda of resisting academic mediocrity would be willing to publish this review."

But it turned out that the review did not need to be published anywhere else. Within a week Li posted a furious response on the same site, defending his interpretations of classical Confucian texts, which have been appraised by Chen as "full of nonsense" and essentially a "vulgarization and demonization" of Chinese cultural traditions.[18] In the months that followed, Li responded to dozens of similar attacks, which were often severe criticisms made by scholars who have an entirely different take on the impact and meaning of Confucianism as a religion. One strategy Li adopted was to ally himself with other intellectual authorities by listing well-known scholars as supporters of his work; he wrote that when he first started the project in 1996, "there were only five people in China who supported [Ren's] 'Confucianism is a religion' view." But now, he said, "there are more than thirty scholars who have endorsed my ideas."[19]

Unfortunately his tactic backfired when several of the people he mentioned posted pieces on Confucius2000 denouncing such alliance. At least two of them were Li's colleagues at CASS, although the entire debate involved participants from many different institutions. One further twist came when Li allegedly prevented the publication of his adversary Chen's review while publishing his own article attacking his opponent in the state-run *Confucius Studies*, which caused outrage among Chen's supporters.

Today, under the heading of "The Debate about Confucianism and Religion" on Confucius2000, there are at least two hundred related postings, although the later ones focus more on articulating the different understandings of Confucianism as a religion than on the actual disagreement between Li and his critics. It seems clear that Confucius2000 mainly represents scholars who want to restore a positive evaluation of Confucianism as a religion, even though it has also been publishing articles by Li and some of his associates. The overwhelming consensus on the site is that people might not agree with one another about whether or how Confucianism constitutes a religion, but unlike Ren and Li, most of them do agree that there is nothing inherently negative about the category of religion.[20]

What Is at Stake? Reclaiming the Category of Religion

In fact, many scholars have found positive reasons to support the notion of a Confucian religion. The newer generation of scholars of Confucianism is for the most part well-versed in both Chinese classics and Western theories, and they are more interested in a historically and philosophically nuanced understandings of Confucianism, with the religious element as an intriguing part of the Confucian tradition. The younger scholars I interviewed often expressed their desire to go beyond the Confucianism as a Religion debate, which they thought to be ideological, instead focusing on more productive discussions.

Some of them, however, also voiced their interest in locating a source for a stronger culture identity for China in the time of market economy, commercialism, and globalization. Lu Guolong, a renowned scholar of Daoism and Confucianism who replaced Li Shen in 2003 to became the head of the Department of Confucianism (Confucian Religion), said in our interview that Confucianism "is the host of our culture—all the other religions and traditions are secondary, like guests in our house." Like many other scholars, he also hopes for a revival of Confucian ethics, regardless of whether Confucianism can be revitalized as a religion.

In some ways, the controversy over the meaning of Confucianism as a religion between the older generation of Marxist scholars and the younger, more national-culture-minded intellectuals is a battle over the control of an important cultural and political asset. The newer generation has now accepted the notion that religion is an affirmative part of human experience, and now they are rehabilitating *rujiao*, the Confucian religion, from the weight of communist vilification.

What's really at stake is that the category of religion hasn't been value-free in socialist China, which is what many people sought to challenge through the Confucianism debate. Indeed, their disagreement with Ren and Li is not primarily about whether Confucianism is a religion, but about the value judgment that comes with such a conclusion. They might also speak of Confucianism as a religion, but their pronouncement comes with different intellectual justifications and completely opposite values. In this context the meaning of religion is at the center of the debate; the value of the category is something to fight for, and at the moment the Young Turks—those who no longer follow the socialist value judgment about religion—seem to have won the first round.

It is clear from the postings on Confucius2000 that the overwhelming majority of the participants disagree with Li Shen and his disparaging value judgment toward religion. Even though people are divided about whether Confucianism is a religion, there is no negative connotation when the religious aspects of Confucianism are discussed. But the most telling evidence comes from CASS. The Department of Confucianism, the symbolic center of the debate, had a changing of the guard in 2003, with Lu Guolong replacing Li Shen as the director.[21] To my knowledge the other six members of the department have either publicly opposed Li's view or stayed neutral throughout the controversy. The fact that Chen Yongming, the author of the article "The Federal Project Made of Tofu Dregs," which triggered the most intense episode in the debate, and Chen Ming, one of the leading opponents of Li's on Confucius2000, have stayed on as members of the department shows CASS's commitment to supporting the newer generation of scholars. Although internal politics must have played a role in this case, it is unlikely that broader intellectual and political considerations were not taken into account, such as the issue of the official position concerning the religions nature of Confucianism.

CONFUCIANISM AS A RELIGION: A NEW CLASSIFICATION IN THE MAKING?

What is the official position regarding Confucianism as a religion? There is no easy answer to the question, although there might be clues to be found. Besides the heated debates among Chinese scholars, it is also important to note what has been published in the official venues, for this could reflect the impact the intellectual debate might have had on the official religious classification. One of the best places to examine these shifting boundaries is the *Annual of Religious Studies in China*, the series of annual volumes reviewing the state of religious studies that first appeared in 1998 (*The Annual of 1996*). Since 2000, it has been published by Religion and Culture Press, a publishing house owned by the National Bureau of Religious Affairs, whose support is acknowledged in the preface to the latest *Annual*.[22] The series was edited by Cao Zhongjian, the deputy director of the Institute of World Religions at CASS when the first *Annual* was published; he is now the party secretary of the Institute of World Religions, the de facto head of the institute.

From the beginning of its publication, the structure of the *Annual* has closely followed the Five Major Religions category given by the Bureau of Religious Affairs. However, Confucianism has found its way into the official text. In the very first volume, the *Annual* of 1996, after three hundred pages of reviews about the scholarly work done on Buddhism, Daoism, Islam, and Christianity (both Catholic and Protestant), there was the category of "Others." Under "Others" we find the following classifications:

Others

The Studies of Confucianism
The Studies of Chinese Folk Religions

The Studies of Baojuan (popular texts based on oral telling of religious stories)
A Summary of the studies of New Religions

The article on "The Studies of Confucianism" was written by Li Shen.
In his short review, he recounted the debate initiated by his teacher Ren
in 1978, and concluded triumphantly that Ren's view had now been accepted by many scholars. He described a few events that he thought were
markers of the turning point, one being the inclusion of Confucianism as
one of the 350 items in the *Dictionary of Religion* in 1994, edited by Ren,
and another being a lecture given by Li himself at the inauguration of the
Department of Religion at Beijing University in 1996, titled "There Exists
a Confucian Religion in China."

The category of "Others" was suspiciously missing in the 1997–98
volume, and when it did return in the 1999–2000 volume, Confucianism was absent in the category. But in the bibliography accompanying
the articles, about a dozen books and articles on the religious nature of
Confucianism were mentioned. Then, in the 2001–2 volume, which was
published in 2003 during the heyday of the online Confucianism as a
Religion debate, we find Confucianism listed in the following way on the
content page:

The Studies of Buddhism
The Studies of Daoism
The Studies of Islam
The Studies of Judaism and Christianity
The Studies of Confucianism

Although "The Studies of Confucianism" is only a subheading, it seems
significant that Confucianism is listed for the first time as one of the major
religions in an official document. Given the official status of the *Annual* as
the authorized record of the state of religious studies in China, it is hard
not to speculate on a possible connection between the intensity of the ongoing Confucianism controversy and the government's potential interest
in revisiting the existing classification system of religions. But will such a
reclassification of the religious status of Confucianism ever happen?

Latest Developments in the Confucianism as a Religion Controversy

The heyday of the Confucianism as a Religion Debate was from 2000
to 2004; 2004 and 2005 marked the beginning of a new phase in the
controversy. Before 2004, the debate was a purely intellectual affair; to

participate meant posting one's views on Confucius2000.com or publishing them as in journal articles or books. Starting in 2004, some intellectuals ceased to take part in this academic debate by stopping arguing whether Confucianism had been a religion historically; instead, they started engaging in a variety of activities with the goal of making Confucianism into a state religion in contemporary China.

In July 2004, three leading figures in the promotion of Confucianism as a national religion hosted a symposium at the Yangming Spiritual House in the southern province of Guizhou. Jiang Qing, a former legal scholar who has been a leader in the revival of the Confucian religion movement, Chen Ming, a young philosopher who has been a key figure in the online debate, and Kang Xiaoguang, an environmental studies scholar, represented the leading voices in the so-called Mainland China New Confucianism, to be distinguished from the New Confucianism that refers to the group of Confucian philosophers active in Taiwan, Hong Kong, and North America.[23]

The year 2005 was also a turning point in the Confucianism as a Religion Controversy. For those endorsing Confucianism as a religion, suddenly they received mounting institutional support, from both official channels and private sectors. On June 14, 2005, the Center of the Study of Confucianism (or the Confucian Religion) was established; it was affiliated with the Department of Confucianism at the Institution of World Religions at CASS, and the director of the State Administration for Religious Affairs at the time, Ye Xiaowen, attended the opening ceremony. The establishment of the center was a serious blow to people who discredited the religious nature of Confucianism as well as those who had a negative assessment of Confucianism as a religion, such as Li Shen.

In December 2005, the center published its first newsletter, titled "Newsletter for the Study of Confucianism in China." The newsletter was published under the editorship of Lu Guolong, the head of the Department of Confucianism, with the assistance of Chen Ming, a leading activist in the Confucianism as a religion movement. And start-up funding for the newsletter came from Tang Enjia, the head of the Hong Kong Confucianity Academy and a wealthy merchant who has been donating "holy statues" of Confucius to universities throughout China.[24]

In March 2006, Wang Dasan, an independent scholar with a PhD in philosophy, established "China Confucianism as a Religion Online," which explicitly endorsed the position of Confucianism as religion.[25] The website has been publishing articles by "pro-Confucian religion" scholars, such as Jiang Qing, Chen Ming, and Lu Guolong.

Another important aspect of the development is the Reading of the Classics Movement (*dujing yundong*). It first started in the 1990s, and it has been growing steadily since then. It began as a grassroots movement of teaching children Chinese classics (with an emphasis on the Confucian canon) through reading and memorization, since such texts were not typically taught in schools. The scholars sanctioning the view that Confucianism is a religion in the academic debate are often supportive of the movement. In 2004, Jiang Qing edited with much fanfare a twelve-volume textbook titled *The Fundamental Texts of Chinese Culture Classics for Reciting.*[26] Jiang's edited volumes have received as much praise as criticism; it seems clear that the Reading of the Classics Movement has now been mobilized by the scholars endorsing Confucianism as a state religion, and the movement itself is often used as a target by people with opposing views.[27]

The involvement of private donors in the past few years is worth noticing, for they are supporting not only publications and conferences but also events such as retreats at Jiang Qing's Yangming Spiritual House.[28] In fact, the financial support of private donors, most of whom are successful businesspeople interested in traditional Chinese culture and values, has been instrumental to the success of the nascent Confucianism as national religion movement. Many of them are calling themselves Confucian Merchants (*rushang*), and there are now several associations of Confucian businesspeople throughout China, such as the Chinese Confucian Merchants International Business Club.

The question of the religious nature of Confucianism is an empirical one, although the right theoretical framework is crucial to a meaningful investigation, such as what constitutes a Confucian ritual. Nevertheless, it is obvious that there is a potential tension between the current revival of Confucian ritual practice (see chaps. 7 and 8) and the existing official classification of religion. The tension is only "potential" at the moment because although Confucian temples are clearly used for ritual purposes in recent years, organizationally they are not controlled by the State Administration of Religious Affairs, hence they are still technically below the radar that polices religious practice. Since most of these temples are historical buildings, they are managed by the State Administration of Cultural Heritage, and they have little contact with the officials working on religious affairs. This seems to be another indication of the conflicting status of Confucianism as a religion in contemporary Chinese society.

During one of my interviews with the official from the State Administration of Religious Affairs, I was told that the administration had been worrying about the current scholarly controversy, for "it might create a new religion." But how worried is the state? Has it started to participate actively in the reshaping and the redefining of the Confucian religion? The most telling sign—a rather surprising one—came in September 2004, during the celebration of the 2,555th birthday of Confucius.

Historically, such as during the Ming and Qing dynasties, there were official rites offered by the court at the Confucian temples in the city of

Beijing, and government officials were in charge of annual ceremonies at the Confucian temple in Qufu, Confucius's birthplace.[29] The rites were discontinued after the end of Qing dynasty in 1911, except for the few brief years when the political reformers attempted to make Confucianism into a state religion. It was indeed a gesture of open-mindedness of the socialist government when the annual ceremony on Confucius's birthday in Qufu was reinstated in 1993. Kong Deban, Confucius's seventy-seventh descendant, had been the chief official of ceremony until this year.

On September 28, 2004, for the first time since the founding of the People's Republic, the state officially took over, with government representatives presiding over the rites. In fact, the representatives choreographed the entire ceremony of the Veneration of Confucius, with several stage directors orchestrating the events, dozens of actors playing the roles of the disciples of Confucius, and thirty-six dancers re-creating a Confucian ritual dance. Although this ceremony was clearly a performance, the organizers wanted to make sure that it was an authentic Confucian ceremony, which they tried to achieve by copying most of the rituals after the ones depicted in Qing dynasty records. The emphasis on "authenticity" was the prevailing principle, and the seventy-seventh descendent of Confucius remarked that he felt more pious than ever during this first official ceremony for Confucius.[30]

Several weeks later, on November 16, 2004, the deputy secretary of the Department of Education announced to reporters that the Chinese government was planning to found one hundred Confucius Institutes globally in the next few years to promote the study of the Chinese language and Chinese culture. He explained that they are named "Confucius Institutes" because Confucius is an internationally recognizable symbol of Chinese culture, and the institutes will be teaching primarily language courses rather than classes on Confucian thought.[31]

This speech came during a ceremony unveiling a "holy statue" of Confucius on a university campus in Beijing. It is hard to ignore the quasi-religious undertones of the occasion, even though there was no suggestion of a religious dimension in the ambitious new plan for global Chinese language training. Interestingly, the "holy statue" was donated by Tang Enjia, the director of the Hong Kong Confucianity Academy, who has been promoting Confucianism as a religion for many years. The Chinese name of the academy, Hong Kong Kongjiao Xueyuan, literarily means the academy of "Confucian religion" (Confucianity). Tang has donated sixty such statues to leading universities in China so far, and it is clear from the warm welcome he received that his donation has been granted approval by high-placed political authorities.

The year 2005 also saw the increasingly elaborate public venerations of Confucius, organized by state agencies. In September, the Qufu city government continued to host the annual veneration ceremony celebrating Confucius's birthday in the Qufu Confucius Temple; in October, an official ceremonial event took place in Zhuzhou to venerate the legendary sage king Yan Di.[32]

It seems reasonable to suggest that there are indeed conflicting messages about the religious status of Confucianism being offered by the state. On the one hand, the state is not interested in supporting any new religion; it has enough trouble with the existing ones. On the other, the state is beginning to recognize the importance of identifying Confucianism, or Confucius, as a unifying element in Chinese society. It is needed for the representation of a Chinese national culture in the global context, and it is also needed for the centering of the increasingly shaky collective sense of morality in the country's fast transition into market economy and capitalism.

A recent news report is a good illustration of the latter endeavor. At a "renewal of marital vows" ceremony taking place in Beijing during the moon festival in 2004, which is a traditional holiday celebrating familial harmony, 180 couples renewed their vows in a hotel ballroom among friends and family, with government officials as special guests. What was highly unusually about this ceremony was that the couples declared in front of a "holy portrait of Confucius" that they "will never divorce."[33] This is certainly not a traditional Confucian practice, for the notion of legal divorce did not exist in China until the early twentieth century. Today the divorce rate is about 21 percent (a tremendous increase from 7 percent in 1980), according to the Ministry of Civil Affairs, and the ceremony reflected a societal need to promote marital stability.

The growing number of worshippers at Confucian temples also suggests an increasing need among ordinary people for a religious system that is deeply rooted in Chinese tradition, with long-established customs and rites, such as the blessing of exam-taking students. Fenggang Yang has pointed out that the religious economy of China is one of economics of shortage. In his valuable triple-market theory of religion, a red market "consists of all legal (officially permitted) religious organizations, believers, and religious activities," whereas a black market "consists of illegal (officially banned) religious organizations, believers, and religious activities" and a gray market "consists of all religious and spiritual organizations, practitioners, and activities with ambiguous legal status."[34] In this framework, it seems that Confucianism has the potential of offering an alternative that could satisfy the religious needs of many people on the gray market, and it might have the advantage over the other religious options because of its time-honored ethical system (as a moral foundation for the entire society) and its symbolic significance (as an indigenous tradition).

To conclude, the Confucianism as a Religion Controversy in China has already moved from an intellectual debate to a more diverse social phenomenon, with key actors deliberately promoting the social and potentially political agenda of legitimizing Confucianism as China's national religion. The state has been tolerant—and even supportive in certain instances—of this emerging movement since their endorsement of Confucianism and Confucian traditions is in line with their current political goal of maintaining "a harmonious society" (*hexie shehui*) through promoting traditional culture and values. But it remains to be seen whether they would go as far as accepting Confucianism as the state religion of a socialist country. In addition, there is still the remaining issue of who the Confucians are in China, other than the handful of fundamentalist Confucian scholars discussing Confucian classics in flowing traditional robes in the picturesque mountains of Guizhou.

There have been rumors that, during one of the more dramatic moments of internal conflict within the Department of Confucianism at CASS, higher political authorities were appealed to, and their endorsement was crucial to the settlement of the disagreement. The current regime has been very pragmatic in its dealings with the possibility of the revival of Confucianism as a religion, and it remains to be seen how the political climate will affect the academic discourse about Confucianism as a religion. It also remains to be seen how the academic categorization might play a role in the possible reinvention of Confucianism: as a national cultural identity, as a revival of ritual practices, or as a full-fledged religious movement with intellectuals acting as its spokespeople.

PART II

THE PROBLEM OF METHODOLOGY

Who Are the Confucians in China?

CHAPTER 4

Confucianism as a World Religion

The Legitimation of a New Paradigm

SINCE THE TURN OF THE TWENTIETH CENTURY, the classification of Confucianism as a world religion, which originated in Max Müller's *Sacred Books of the East* series, has been accepted by generations of comparative religion scholars as well as scholars in related fields in the humanities and social sciences. Among social scientists, the most significant early adherent of this framework was Max Weber, who adopted the classification of world religions for what he called his "sociology of world religions" project. In his essay "The Social Psychology of World Religions" (1913–15), he explained his approach:

> By "world religions," we understand the five religions or religiously determined systems of life-regulation which have known how to gather multitudes of confessors around them. The term is used here in a completely value-neutral sense. The Confucian, Hinduist, Buddhist, Christian, and Islamist religious ethics all belong to the category of world religion. A sixth religion, Judaism, will also be dealt with. It is included because it contains historical preconditions decisive for understanding Christianity and Islamism, and because of its historic and autonomous significance for the development of the modern economic ethic of the Occident—a significance, partly real and partly alleged, which has been discussed several times recently. References to other religions will be made only when they are indispensable for historical connections.[1]

Weber's utilization of the world religions framework formed the foundation of his work in the sociological study of religion, starting with his seminal analysis of one of the world religions, Christianity, in *The Protestant Ethic and the Spirit of Capitalism* (1904–5),[2] followed by *The Religion of China: Confucianism and Taoism* (1915),[3] *The Religion of India: The Sociology of Hinduism and Buddhism* (1916–17),[4] and

Ancient Judaism (1917–19).[5] Hans H. Gerth and Don Martindale note that "Max Weber's untimely death in 1920 prevented him from rounding out his studies with an analysis of the Psalms, the Book of Job, Talmudic Jewry, Early Christianity, and Islamism."[6] Sociologists today are still dealing with the rich legacy of Weber's sociology of world religions.[7]

How do we assess the successful spread and legitimation of the world religions paradigm in general, and the classification of Confucianism in particular? In his groundbreaking study of history of science, *The Structure of Scientific Revolutions*, Thomas Kuhn uses the concept of "paradigm" in his investigation of the historical and social nature of scientific knowledge. By "paradigm" he refers to the "universally recognized scientific achievements that for a time provide model problems and solutions to a community of practitioners."[8] Although Kuhn's discussion of what he calls "normal science" is limited to natural scientific disciplines such as physics and biology, his notion of "normal science" can indeed be applied to other knowledge-producing disciplines, such as religious studies: "'[N]ormal' science means research firmly based upon one or more past scientific achievements, achievements that some particular scientific community acknowledges for a time as supplying the foundation for its further practice."[9]

If we view a humanistic or social scientific discipline such as religious studies or sociology in the same light, then what Kuhn says in the following passage about the signs of the implementation of "a single paradigm" in a given field can also be applied to non-natural-science disciplines:

> In the sciences (though not in fields like medicine, technology, and law, of which the principal *raison d'être* is an external social need), the formation of specialized journals, the foundation of specialists' societies, and the claim for a special place in the curriculum have usually been associated with a group's first reception of a single paradigm.[10]

In other words, we can examine the reception or legitimation of a paradigm through many observable social facts. In the rest of this chapter, I argue that the notion of world religions, in particular the notion of Confucianism as one of the major world religions, has indeed become the universally recognized "achievement" that provides "model problems and solutions to a community of practitioners," in this case scholars in religious studies, as well as scholars who study Chinese religions in other fields, such as sociology, history, philosophy, and Asian studies.

My focus is on the following aspects that constitute a classical establishment of a paradigm: popular publications and textbooks, scholarly publications in various related disciplines from the nineteenth century to today, the establishment of scholarly associations, new academic departments, and new academic curricula. In order to simplify my argument, I chose to center on the acceptance and implementation of this paradigm in American academia, rather than comparing it to academia in another country, such as Great Britain.[11] However, the publications examined are not simply publications in the States but include English-language scholarship from international libraries and databases, which also reflect the increasingly global nature of knowledge production today.

CONFUCIANISM AS A WORLD RELIGION IN TODAY'S POPULAR BOOKS AND TEXTBOOKS

Searching the keywords "world religions" in the "books" category on Amazon.com produces 110,997 titles (as of May 20, 2012). There are 422 titles if we narrow the search by using the keywords "world religions Confucianism." If we search "world religions textbook" under "Religion and Spirituality," 1,011 results appear. When we select the books through the Amazon.com search function "popularity," we can see easily which textbooks on world religions belong to the top ten. Do they all discuss Confucianism as a world religion?

Among these best-selling titles is Huston Smith's *The World's Religions: Our Great Wisdom Traditions*, a top-seller since its first publication in 1958.[12] Smith's *The Illustrated World's Religions: Guide to Our Wisdom Traditions* is another popular choice.[13] Prentice Hall's *Religions of the World* is now in its tenth edition, and McGraw-Hill's *Experiencing the World's Religions* is also a popular title.[14] All these books on world religions include Confucianism as a world religion.

The Complete Idiot's Guide to World Religions is another well-liked choice, with a chapter titled "Confucianism: Human Relations 101."[15] Descriptions such as "spiritual beliefs" and "ancient system of Chinese ethical thought" are used interchangeably when it comes to Confucianism. Another book, *The World's Wisdom: Sacred Texts of the World's Religions*, offers a selection of "sacred texts" of world religions.[16] A review from a librarian is worth citing:

> This is a compendium of sacred texts of the religions of the world, written as a companion for Huston Smith's classic *The Religions of Man*. Chapters cover Hinduism, Buddhism, Confucianism, Taoism, Judaism, Christianity, Islam, and Primal religions (e.g., Native American, African, etc.). The intent of the book is clearly to whet the appetite of the first-year college student by offering tidbits from the New Testament, Tao Te Ching, Qur'an, Hebrew Bible, etc., in small, tasty portions, easily consumed without any need for deep reading or reflection.[17]

The "tidbits" from Confucianism include passages from the *Analects*, *Mencius*, *Daxue* (the *Great Learning*), as well as a few Chinese proverbs.

The book is recommended by the reviewer "as a good text and supplementary reader for any college introductory class in religious studies."

In *World Religions in America: An Introduction*, it is stated that "the major religious traditions of East Asia are Buddhism and Confucianism, both of which have profoundly influenced all East Asian societies."[18] In *Oneness: Great Principles Shared by All Religions*, with a glowing blurb from the Dalai Lama on the cover ("As this book shows . . . every major religion of the world has similar ideas of love [and] the same goal of benefiting humanity through spiritual practice"), there are quite a few principles attributed to Confucianism.[19] In Pope Benedict XVI's *Truth and Tolerance: Christian Belief and World Religions*, he speaks of Confucius as one of "the great founders of East Asian Religions."[20]

This narrative of major world religions is often connected to the narrative of world history. For example, Confucianism as a world religion appears in popular textbooks such as Oxford University Press's *Atlas of World History*, edited by Patrick K. O'Brien,[21] as well as in the bestselling book *How to Prepare for the AP World History*, in which categories such as "world civilizations," "world cultures," and "world religions" are used abundantly, and Confucianism is discussed as one of the world religions.[22]

This general discourse of world religions, of which Confucianism is a vital part, has permeated not only secondary and postsecondary education but also the education of children. One of the top twenty best-selling books on world religion on Amazon.com is titled *One World, Many Religions: The Ways We Worship*. In this book for kids aged nine to twelve, Mary Pope Osborne promises to "survey the origins, traditions, sacred writings, forms of worship, and major holidays of Judaism, Christianity, Islam, Hinduism, Buddhism, Confucianism, and Taoism."[23] In *The Kids Book of World Religions*, another book aimed at the same age group, Confucianism is depicted as a major world religion, along with a colorful illustration of Confucius.[24]

It is important to note that some authors of these introductory texts seem to be uneasy about including Confucianism in the pantheon of world religions, and yet they are compelled to do so due to existing categories and conventions. For instance, although John Bowker includes Confucianism in his chapter on "Chinese Religions" in his widely read *World Religions*, he does not speak of it as one of the major faiths of the world.[25]

Some of the authors are also concerned about the term "Confucianism," conscious of its Western origin; we find the following explanation in *World Religions Today*: "We use Confucianism, a Western term originated in eighteenth-century Europe [in fact the word "Confucianism" did not come into existence until the nineteenth century], instead of the corresponding Chinese term *rujia*, meaning 'literati tradition.'"[26]

Confucianism as a World Religion in Book Publications

If we conduct a brief overview of the publication of books in English related to Confucianism as well as world religions through the WorldCat catalogue, the world's largest network of library content and services, we can see that there were essentially three stages in the development of such publications:[27]

1. The first stage of publications (pre-1870): the beginning of the development of a historical and comparative understanding of religion through a small number of publications.
2. The second stage of publications (1870–1960): the gradual establishment of the world religions discourse and the corresponding establishment of Confucianism as a world religion through larger numbers of scholarly as well as popular publications on these topics.
3. The third stage of publications (1960–today): the full acceptance and recognition of the world religions discourse as the central framework in the comparative study of religions are demonstrated through the abundant publications that support and rely on this paradigm.

First, let us look at the publications connected to world religions.[28] Although there were some books with the keywords "world religions" published between 1800 and 1870 (e.g., 141 such books were published between 1860 and 1870), which is what I call the first stage, we can see clearly that there was a period of growth of such books between 1870 and 1960. In the second stage, there were 645 such books being published between 1890 and 1900 and 612 between 1950 and 1960—not much change from the end of the nineteenth century to the middle of the twentieth century, given the explosion of the publishing industry in the twentieth century. In the third stage, between 1960 and 2007, there was an enormous growth of such publications, indeed a boom: between 1960 and 1970, 1,085 titles; between 1970 and 1980, 1,467 titles; between 1980 and 1990, 2,205 titles; between 1990 and 2000, 4,009 titles.

If we search for books with the keyword "Confucianism," published between 1800 and 2007, a similar pattern emerges. Again, this can be easily divided into a three-stage development, although the beginning of the publication of books relating to Confucianism was a lot later than the books relating to world religions. A search shows that there was nothing published on Confucianism between 1800 and 1830.[29] Between 1830 and 1870, which is within the first stage, there were ten titles, three of which were written by Legge,[30] and the rest were missionary texts such as the 1859 book by Joseph Edkins (1823–1905) titled *The Religious*

Conditions of the Chinese: With Observations on the Prospectors of Christian Conversion amongst that People.[31] However, from 1870 to 1960, the second stage of growth, we see a steady rise in the numbers of books relating to Confucianism. Further searches on WorldCat show that in the twenty years before the publication of the first *SBE* volume on Confucianism, namely between 1858 and 1878, there were thirty published books on Confucianism, most of which were written by missionaries, most notably Legge and Elkins. In the twenty years after the publication of the last *SBE* volume on Confucianism, between 1887 and 1907, there were 118 published books on Confucianism, most of which were written not by missionaries who had spent time in China but by people who were interested in the comparative study of world religions, with titles such as *Comparative Religion: Its Genesis and Growth* (1905).[32]

However, starting in the 1960s, a significant rise took place: between 1960 and 1970, 171 titles concerning Confucianism were published; between 1980 and 1990, 373 titles; between 1990 and 2000, 605 titles; and between 2000 and 2007, not yet a full decade, 445 titles. A parallel can be found when we search under the keywords "world religions," and "Confucianism" or "Confucius."

What this shows is that there is a similar pattern between the rise of numbers of books on Confucianism as a world religion and the rise of numbers of books on world religions, and this connection can still be seen through the many publications on both world religions and Confucianism on the Amazon.com top-selling list today. In order to understand how and why they are connected, we need to turn to explanations that are intellectual, political, as well as social. Here let us continue our assessment of the acceptance of the world religions paradigm in American academia through an examination of academic curricula and scholarly associations.

The Teaching of Confucianism in American Academic Curricula Today

In order to get a concrete sense of whether the world religions paradigm has indeed become the foundation for the practice of teaching among religion scholars, and whether Confucianism is taught as a world religion within this framework, I sampled the curricula in two types of American higher education institutions that are devoted to the study of religious knowledge: religious studies departments as well as divinity schools. As we shall see, today Confucianism is considered by many religious studies departments and divinity schools in American universities to be one of the major world religions.

TABLE 4.1. Top-Selling Books in English on World Religions

Ranking on Amazon.com	Title	Author	Confucianism as a World Religion?
1	*Experiencing the World's Religions*	Michael Molloy	Yes
2	*The World's Religions*	Huston Smith	Yes
3	*Buddhism Plain and Simple*	Steve Hagen	Not applicable
4	*Encountering the New Testament: A Historical and Theological Survey*	Walter Elwell and Robert Yarbrough	Not applicable
5	*Living Religions*	Mary Pat Fisher	Yes
6	*100 Top Picks for Homeschool Curriculum*	Cathy Duffy	No
7	*The Sacred and the Profane: The Nature of Religion*	Micrea Eliade	Yes
8	*Gospel in Life Study Guide: Grace Changes Everything*	Timothy Keller	Not applicable
9	*World Religions: The Great Faiths Explored & Explained*	John Bowker	Yes
10	*The Illustrated World's Religions: Guide to Our Wisdom Traditions*	Huston Smith	Yes

Source: Amazon.com; ranking as of May 20, 2012.
Note: "Not applicable" because these are texts specifically about a single religious tradition, such as Buddhism or Christianity.

TABLE 4.2. University Course Offerings on World Religions

Ranking/Curriculum	Courses on World Religions such as Buddhism, Hinduism, Judaism, Islam	Courses That Include Confucianism as a Religion or World Religion
1. Harvard	Yes	Yes
1. Princeton	Yes	No
3. Yale	Yes	Yes
4. Columbia	Yes	Yes
5. California Institute of Technology*	Not applicable	Not applicable
5. Massachusetts Institute of Technology*	Not applicable	Not applicable
5. Stanford	Yes	Yes
5. University of Chicago	Yes	Yes
5. University of Pennsylvania	Yes	No
10. Duke	Yes	Yes

Source: "National University Rankings," US News & World Report (2012).
* This university does not have a religious studies department.

Let us first examine religious studies departments (or departments of religion) at the top ten universities listed in the 2012 *US World News & World Report* rankings. Table 4.2 shows an overview of the course offerings in these religious studies departments.

At Harvard University, where "Committee on the Study of Religion" is the official title of the program in religious studies, the introductory course on world religion, "Religion 11: World Religions: Diversity and Dialogue," is required of all undergraduate concentrators.[33] For PhD students, it is stated that students need to focus on "historical complexes" that include "the Greco-Roman or Hellenistic world, the modern West, East Asia, China, Japan, South Asia," and religious traditions that include "Buddhist, Christian, Confucian, Hindu, Islamic, and Jewish."[34]

At Yale University, the Department of Religious Studies at one point offered not one but three courses related to world religions.[35] They are "RLST 100b: Introduction to World Religions," "RLST 101a: World Religions in New Haven," and the following course:

RLST 103b World Religions and Ecology: Asian Religions

The emerging relationships of world religions to the global environmental crisis. Attention to both the problems and the promise of these relationships. Ways in which religious ideas and practices have contributed to cultural attitudes and human interactions with nature. Examples from Hinduism, Buddhism, Confucianism, and Taoism.[36]

At Stanford, although there is no course on world religions, the undergraduate program asks the students to study the "major questions, themes, developments, features, and figures in the world's religious traditions." The following course on Chinese religions was offered in the academic year 2006–7, which adopted a classification of Chinese religions legitimized by the world religions paradigm:

RELIGST 35 Introduction to Chinese Religions

Confucianism, Daoism, Buddhism, and the interchange among these belief systems and institutions. Set against the background of Chinese history, society, and culture, with attention to elite and popular religious forms.[37]

At the University of Pennsylvania, although the Department of Religious Studies offers no course on world religions, there is the following course on religions of Asia, in which Confucianism features prominently:

RELS001 Religions of Asia

This course is an introduction to the religious traditions of Southern and Eastern Asia. It surveys the beliefs, rituals, and thought of major traditions—Hinduism, Buddhism, Confucianism, Taoism—and less well known traditions—Jainism, Zoroastrianism, Sikhism, Shintoism. The focus of the course will be on the lived experience of each tradition, looking at the worldviews, motives and aspirations of religious figures.[38]

At Duke University, where "the Department of Religion is one of the largest Humanities departments at Duke and one of the most prestigious departments of religion in the country," the department offers courses in different religious traditions.[39] Although Confucianism is not explicitly mentioned among the traditions, the following course was offered as recently as spring 2012:

AMES 118S/REL 161YS Religion and Culture in Korea

This course introduces you to the dynamics of contemporary Korean religions: Shamanism, Buddhism, Confucianism, Christianity, Islam, and new religions including Kimilsungism. From a global perspective, we look critically at the diverse expressions of Korean religions in popular culture, politics, economy, literature, sports, and media.[40]

However, it is worth noticing that the department's "New Graduate Track in Asian Religions" does not mention Confucianism at all.

At Princeton University, although there isn't a course focusing on Confucianism in the Department of Religion, Confucian tradition is still discussed in the East Asian context as a religious tradition:

REL 228 Religion in Japanese Culture (also EAS 228)

An introduction to Japanese religion from ancient to modern times, focusing on its role in culture and history. Representative aspects of Shinto, Buddhist, Confucian, and other traditions will be studied, as well as such topics as myth, ritual, shamanism, and ancestor worship.[41]

At Columbia University, although we cannot find a course devoted to world religions, Confucianism is once again covered, here in a course on Chinese religious traditions:

RELI V 2405x Chinese Religious Traditions

Development of the Three Teachings of Confucianism, Taoism, and Buddhism: folk eclecticism; the contemporary situation in Chinese cultural areas. Readings drawn from primary texts, poetry, and popular prose.[42]

For the divinity schools, let us look at five leading divinity schools in the country, a list partially based on the National Research Council rankings of PhD programs in religious studies and theology.[43] Here we see that Confucianism is indeed viewed as one of the major religious traditions or a world religion. For instance, Confucianism is one of the world religions being studied at the Center for the Study of World Religions at Harvard; at Harvard Divinity School, Tu Weiming offered courses as the Harvard-Yenching Professor of Chinese History and Philosophy and of Confucian Studies until his retirement in 2010.

At Yale Divinity School, courses such as "REL 817b World Religions and Ecology: Asian Religions" are offered; this course "explores the various ways in which religious ideas and practices have contributed to cultural attitudes and human interactions with nature. Examples are selected from Hinduism, Buddhism, Confucianism, and Daoism."[44] At Princeton Theological Seminary, one component of the comprehensive PhD examinations is the following: "Religious and Social Ethics of a Non-Christian Tradition (Confucian, Buddhist, Hindu, Islamic, Indigenous, Judaic), with special reference to its encounter with Christianity in at least one context."[45]

At the Divinity School at the University of Chicago, Anthony Yu, professor emeritus of religion and literature, taught courses that "reinterpret classical Chinese narratives and poetry in light of Buddhism, Taoism, and Confucianism."[46] And at the Boston University School of Theology, John H. Berthrong, the associate professor of comparative theology and deputy director of the Division of Religious and Theological Studies, has written extensively on Confucianism.[47] Another well-known scholar of Confucianism, Robert Neville, professor of philosophy, religion, and theology, is the author of *Boston Confucianism: Portable Tradition in the Late-Modern World*.[48]

SCHOLARS OF CONFUCIANISM IN AMERICAN ACADEMIC ASSOCIATIONS

In *The University Gets Religion: Religious Studies in American Higher Education*, D. G. Hart writes about the "formal emergence of the field in the period from 1925 to 1965" in American higher education:

> These four decades witnessed the formation of a body of scholars with a common interest in teaching religion in an academically respectable manner. This was also the time when religion emerged institutionally as an academic department at most of the colleges and universities where it is now taught and studied.[49]

Hart divides his study into three parts:

> Part I: The Age of the University, 1870–1925
> Part II: The Age of the Protestant Establishment, 1925–1965
> Part III: The Age of the American Academy of Religion, 1965–Present

This indeed corresponds well with the pattern we saw in the world religions publications. What we view as the second stage of such publications, from 1870 to 1960, can be split into two phases in the context of the institutionalization of religious studies in American higher education: from 1870 to 1925, the formative years of the paradigm of historical and comparative study of world religions; from 1925 to 1965, as Hart argued, "the time when religion emerged institutionally as an academic department at most of the colleges and universities where it is now taught and studied."[50]

According to Hart, the first professional society for religion scholars in America was the Society of Biblical Literature, founded in 1880, which published the quarterly *Journal of Biblical Literature*.[51] Shortly afterward, in 1909, Professor Ismar J. Peritz of Syracuse University founded the Association of Biblical Instructors in American Colleges and Secondary Schools, with the purpose of stimulating "scholarship and teaching in religion":

> The group continued to meet under the original name until December of 1922 when members voted to change the name to the National Association of Biblical Instructors, and thereby acquired the acronym NABI ("prophet" in Hebrew). In 1933, the Journal of the NABI was launched and published twice a year until 1937 when the name was changed to the *Journal of Bible and Religion*, a quarterly periodical. By 1963, the association, sparked by dramatic changes in the study of religion, was ready for another transformation. Upon the recommendation of a Self-Study Committee, NABI became the American Academy of Religion (AAR) and was incorporated under this name in 1964. Two years later, the name of the journal was changed to the *Journal of the American Academy of Religion (JAAR)*.[52]

In other words, the AAR as we know it today was founded in 1964, and the "dramatic changes in the study of religion" were as much about the tension between the older Protestant curriculum and more critical inquiries in religious studies as about the radical changes in cultural and political values in the 1960s.[53] The AAR's rapid growth testifies to the institutional strength that contributes to the continuing expansion of what was coming to be called "religious studies":

> From a base of four founding members in 1909, the AAR has grown to 9,000 members today. Members are largely faculty at colleges, universities, and divinity schools in North America, with a growing percentage located at institutions of higher education in Asia, Africa, and Europe.[54]

From the AAR "Annual Report 2006," we learn that in 2005 the AAR experienced a watershed event, passing the 10,000-member mark for the first time in its history.[55] Among these members, most of them "teach in more than 1,500 colleges, universities, seminaries, and schools in North America and abroad."[56]

Not surprisingly, one of the key academic associations that scholars of Confucianism today gravitate toward the most is AAR. With its many sections and groups dedicated to comparative and/or Asian topics, such as Comparative Studies in Religion, Religion in South Asia, Japanese Religions, Korean Religions, Sacred Space in Asia, Daoist Studies, and Religions in Chinese and Indian Cultures, many scholars of Chinese religions have found their academic community at the annual AAR meetings. For people who study Confucianism, there are two groups that are particularly hospitable to them: the Chinese Religions Group and the Confucian Traditions Group. The Confucian Tradition Group is arguably the most welcoming intellectual home for scholars of Confucianism at AAR, with its statement that it is "committed to the study of the diversity of religious traditions associated with Confucius. It embraces historical, philosophical, and dialogical approaches, and is not located in any single country or discipline."[57] At the 2007 AAR annual conference, there were three sessions organized by the Confucian Traditions Group, with topics ranging from "The Religious Status of Confucianism" to "Values in Conflict: Confucian Attempts to Resolve Moral Dilemmas."[58] In 2007, the Chinese Religions Group had 101 members on its email list, the Confucian Tradition Group 120.[59]

If AAR is the most established association of scholars of religious studies in America, then the American Philosophical Association is undoubtedly the most established association of academic philosophers. Although there are often papers on Confucianism presented at meetings of this association, the approach is primarily philosophical, with little or no discussion on Confucianism as a religion, unlike the situation at AAR meetings.

There are very few scholars working on Confucianism in social science disciplines; besides attending large disciplinary conferences such as the American Sociological Association meetings, they can attend two other types of association meetings: those of associations focusing on the sociological study of religion, such as the Society for the Study of Religion (SSSR) and the Association for the Sociology of Religion (ASR), and conferences dealing with religion and regional studies, such as the AAR and the Association for Asian Studies (AAS).[60]

To conclude, although scholars who study Confucianism as a religion or world religion do not have their own academic association, they have indeed established themselves as part of the larger intellectual community of religious studies scholars, and their membership in associations such as the AAR is not only uncontested, but warmly welcomed. The growth and strength of the discipline of religious studies have created a solid institutional structure for people who study Confucianism as a religion, and the fact that there have been major disagreements regarding the religious nature of Confucianism among these scholars for several decades shows only the overall stability of the world religions paradigm in the field of religious studies.

CHAPTER 5

Counting Confucians through Social Scientific Research

In this chapter I examine different types of empirical data—national censuses as well as various surveys—from Mainland China, as well as from Taiwan, Japan, and South Korea, in order to answer the following two questions: (1) whether "Confucianism" is a category in religious classifications in these East Asian countries and regions and (2) whether we know how many people are counted as "Confucians" in China. I hope this investigation will establish a dialogue about the empirical classification of Confucianism and its implications, as well as the complex social meanings of being a Confucian in contemporary life.[1]

Counting Confucians in East Asia: An Overview

Social scientists have long been interested in the role of Confucianism in the development of modern Asia. Following the publication of Weber's *Religion of China: Confucianism and Taoism*, especially its English translation in 1951, many scholars have connected Confucian values with the so-called "modernization process" in Asian countries such as China, Taiwan, Japan, South Korea, Vietnam, and Singapore. The most noticeable examples include Tu Weiming's edited volume *Confucian Traditions in East Asian Modernity: Moral Education and Economic Culture in Japan and the Four Mini-Dragons*, as well as *Modernization, Globalization, and Confucianism in Chinese Societies*, the examination of the impact of modernization and globalization on Confucianism in Mainland China, Taiwan, and Singapore by sociologists Joseph B. Tamney and Linda Hsueh-Ling Chiang.[2]

It is a fact that Confucianism has been flourishing for hundreds of years outside of Mainland China, especially in Korean, Japan, Taiwan, and Vietnam. In their book *Rethinking Confucianism: Past and Present in China, Japan, Korea, and Vietnam*, Benjamin Elman, John Duncan, and Herman Ooms speak of Confucianism as a repertoire of common techniques (*rushu*)—civil service bureaucracy, Confucian academies, and rituals as a balance to legal system—that link different social groups together: the literati elites in China, the warriors and merchants in Japan, the *yangban* aristocrats in Korea, and the rural literati in Vietnam.[3]

It is often acknowledged that ritual practices associated with Confucianism are better preserved in Korea than in Mainland China. The National Confucian Shrine in Seoul was founded in 1397, and ritual worship of Confucius has since been conducted there twice each year. Hongkyung Kim speaks of Korean Confucian ritual practice as having three components: formal institutionalized practices (including rituals for Confucius), practices within the household (including rites for worshiping the ancestors), and practices to inform one's personal conduct.[4]

Confucianism has long been seen as one of the key elements in Japanese religious, cultural, and political life, and scholars from Robert Bellah to Edwin O. Reischauer have emphasized its significance.[5] According to Kazou Kasahara in *A History of Japanese Religion*, "For two thousand years Shinto, Buddhism, and Confucianism had dominated the Japanese religious consciousness. . . . Confucianism, the official philosophy of the Tokugawa shogunate, was also absorbed by Japanese of all social classes."[6] In *Religion in Contemporary Japan*, Ian Reader shares a similar view: "If the influences of Taoism may be seen mostly at the folk and populist levels, Confucianism's can be perceived running through much of Japanese society in general, instilling ideals of order and structuralising respect for one's elders and seniors both in family and social terms and asserting the importance of harmony as a social ideal."[7]

But how have the social scientists been dealing with the empirical question of who the Confucians are in Asia? In fact, as early as 1892 there were already social scientists trying to come up with an account of the number of Confucians in China. In an article titled "Development of Statistics of Religion," in *Publications of the American Statistical Association*, M. Fournier De Flaix wrote,

> *The worship of Ancestors and Confucianism.* As has been already indicated, the Worship of Ancestors is the true religion of China. It is also the official religion, while the Chinese enter indiscriminately into all the temples of the Buddhists and Taoists to burn their incense or bring their flowers. . . . It is important not to depreciate the influence of the Worship of Ancestors and Confucianism in order to magnify that of the true Buddhists and Taoists. Consequently, with at least 256,000,000 followers, Confucianism and the Worship of Ancestors becomes the second religion of mankind [after Christianity].[8]

This is by no means an isolated endeavor. Right next to the title page in his 1905 book *Comparative Religion: Its Genesis and Growth*, Louis

Henry Jordan, the special lecturer in comparative religion at the University of Chicago, presents a colored chart showing the numbers of "adherents" of all the major world religions; on the chart, Confucianism is listed as the second largest religion on earth, with 240 million believers, almost half the size of all Christians in the world, 520 million.[9]

A closer look at the numbers reveals the nature of the empirical predicament. There are in fact two related problems, both deeply rooted in the intellectual and social history of comparative studies of religions as well as Confucian studies:

1. Should we consider Confucianism as a religion? In other words, would its religiosity and/or ritual practices qualify it as a religion?
2. If Confucianism can be counted as a religion, who are the Confucians in East Asia?

The first question is a matter of definition of religion, which requires a critical and reflective view of the history of religious taxonomies, an issue that has been eloquently discussed by scholars such as Talal Asad, Jonathan Z. Smith, and Tomoko Masuzawa. If we assume that the answer to the first question is yes, based on historical, sociological, and anthropological evidence, then we have to deal with the equally difficult second question.

The second question is a matter that extends to the classification of all Asian religions, not just Confucianism. The astonishing number proposed by Louis Henry Jordan (240 million Confucians in China in 1905) is very likely his estimate of the Chinese population at the time. The reasoning seems to be that, since China is a Confucian country, and Confucianism is the orthodoxy in Chinese society, all Chinese people must be Confucians, unless they are Buddhists or Daoists. This is very much a view that Weber took for granted; in fact, part 2 of *The Religion of China*, which focuses on Confucianism, is simply called "Orthodoxy."

In what follows, I first look at whether Confucians are counted in contemporary survey data, which leads to an examination of the problematic ways in which Asian religious life is studied in social science survey research. I then focus on ancestral worship as a possible Confucian practice, which might be one possible way of identifying Confucians in East Asia.

LOOKING FOR CONFUCIANS IN CHINA, TAIWAN, JAPAN, AND SOUTH KOREA THROUGH THE WORLD VALUES SURVEY

A little over one hundred years after M. Fournier De Flaix gave us his estimated numbers of religious believers in China in 1892, the 2001 World Values Survey attempted to calculate a more accurate account of religious life in China. However, the questions regarding religion started very much on the wrong foot:

Question: Do you belong to a religious denomination?[10]

> Yes 6.1%
> **No 93.9%**[11]

The next two questions are not much better:

Question: Independently of whether you go to church or not, would you say you are:

> A religious person 13.7%
> **Not a religious person 55.3%**
> A convinced atheist 24%
> Don't know 6.8%
> No answer 0.2%

Question: How often do you attend religious services?

> More than once a week 0.7%
> Once a week 1.5%
> Once a month 0.9%
> Only on special holy days (Christmas, Easter days) 5.4%
> Once a year 0.8%
> Less often 1%
> **Never, practically never 89.7%**

The next question is the trickiest, since it deals with religious classification. The question would not have been difficult for a survey carried out in the States, yet it poses a real challenge to social scientists studying Chinese religions:

Question: Do you belong to a religious denomination? In case you do, answer which one:

> Buddhist 2.1%
> Muslim 0.4%
> Other 0.2%
> Protestant 2.5%
> Roman Catholic 0.8%
> Don't know 0.4%
> No answer 0.6%
> **Not applicable 93%**

Based on these data, it is easy to conclude that the Chinese people must be the most unreligious in the world.

But if we contrast these World Values Survey questions with one question from the 2004 Taiwan Social Change Survey, which presented much more nuanced questions regarding religious practices, we can see how the real story has been missed:

Question: Have you ever worshipped gods (*baishen*) or worshipped ancestors (*baizuxian*)?[12]

> Yes 84.8%
> No 15.2%

In other words, most people surveyed have practiced the most prevailing rites in Taiwan society: the worship of gods and ancestors.

Once the right questions are asked, a new picture of religious life emerges, and as a result more questions are opened up for investigation. For instance, what does it mean when someone answers yes to the last question? Does it mean that this person is a Confucian? But the question is about worshipping "gods" as well as "ancestors." Indeed, the empirical problem with classifying Confucianism isn't caused just by its contested religious status, but also by the fact that many Chinese people carry on ritual practices from many different religious traditions simultaneously. Such empirical difficulties demand more nuanced survey questions, as well as more sophisticated ways of classifying Asian religions.

Table 5.1 is a summary of the answers to the question of religious affiliation in China, Taiwan, Japan, and South Korea, based on the 1981–2002 four-wave integrated data set of the World Values Survey (WVS). As we can see, among the 13,581 people surveyed, only 21 individuals considered themselves Confucians.

The percentage of Confucians in Korea in the WVS data is in fact quite close to the percentage of Confucians in South Korean census data (see table 5.2). In the latest survey on religion in China, titled Spiritual Life Study of Chinese Residents (SLSOCR), conducted in 2007, similar questions about religious affiliation were asked, with results similar to those of the WVS (see table 5.3).[13] Here, among the 6,984 people surveyed, only 12 individuals considered themselves Confucians.

As we will see, a more accurate picture of who the Confucians are in East Asia will come into view only once we start asking questions that are relevant to ritual practices in the Confucian tradition, instead of simply following the routine questions about denominational affiliation that are rooted in the monotheistic, Judeo-Christian framework of religion. Indeed, once we bring questions of ancestral rites to our surveys, which the Horizon 2007 survey did in questions regarding everyday ritual practice, we will be much closer to capturing the reality of Confucianism as a living tradition in our contemporary world.

TABLE 5.1. The World Values Survey: Religious Affiliations in China, Taiwan, Japan, and South Korea

Religious Denomination (N =13,581)	Total (%)	Country/Region			
		China (%)	Taiwan (%)	Japan (%)	Republic of Korea (%)
Buddhist	22.7	0.9	30.8	35.6	24.9
Confucian	**0.2**	—	—	—	**0.4**
Hindu	*	—	—	0.1	*
Jew	*	—	—	*	*
Muslim	0.2	0.5	—	—	0.1
Orthodox	0.9	—	—	2.3	0.5
Other	2.1	0.1	—	2.7	3.2
Other: Taiwan (Daoism, Protestant fundamentalism, ancient cults)	2.5	—	44.0	—	—
Protestant	7.4	0.7	2.4	0.9	19.6
Roman Catholic	4.9	0.3	1.9	0.6	13.0
Don't know	0.3	0.1	—	0.7	0.1
No answer	1.0	0.2	—	2.4	0.5
Not applicable	**43.2**	**54.2**	**20.9**	**44.8**	**37.0**
Not asked in survey	11.0	42.9	—	—	—
Missing	3.5	—	—	9.7	0.6
Total	13,581 (100%)	3,500 (100%)	780 (100%)	4,631 (100%)	4,670 (100%)

Note: Selected countries/samples: China (1990, 1995, 2001), Japan (1981, 1990, 1995, 2000), South Korea (1982, 1990, 1996, 2001), Taiwan (1994), the World Values Survey.

TABLE 5.2. Confucians in South Korea

	1985 (%)	1995 (%)	2005 (%)
Total population	1.3	0.4	0.2
Aged 18 and over	1.7	0.6	0.3

Source: South Korea census microdata.

COUNTING CONFUCIAN PRACTICES: FROM INSTITUTIONAL MEMBERSHIP TO RITUAL PRACTICE

Is there a better way to count Confucians in East Asia besides asking whether they are a Christian, Buddhist, Daoist, or Confucian? The answer is a tentative yes. According to a recent Gallup survey on religions

TABLE 5.3. The Horizon Survey: Religious Beliefs in China

Question: Regardless of Whether You Have Been to Churches or Temples, Are You a Believer of Any of the Following Religions?

Religion	Frequency	Percentage
Buddhism	1,164	16.7
Daoism	23	0.3
Confucianism	**12**	**0.2**
Protestantism	163	2.3
Catholicism	15	0.2
Islam	30	0.4
Other	2	0.0
I don't believe in anything	**5,452**	**78.1**
Hard to say	118	1.7
Refuse to answer	5	0.1
Total	6,984	100.0

Source: Spiritual Life Study of Chinese Residents Survey, Horizon 2007.

in Korea, in answering the question "If your ancestor's tomb is in good location, the lives of your descendants will be good," about 55 percent said yes (Korean Gallup). According to the Religious Consciousness of the Japanese Survey, conducted by the NHK Broadcasting Corporation in 1981 and cited in Jan Swyngedouw's article in *Religion and Society in Modern Japan*, "paying a visit to the ancestral tombs at *o-bon* ('the feast of the dead' in July or August) and *higan* (the spring and autumn equinoxes) is a custom that 89% (69% regularly and 20% sometimes) observe."[14]

Indeed, ancestral worship might be a much better indicator of "Confucianness" than membership in a denomination or belief systems in a religion, yet it has been overlooked by most contemporary surveys, which emphasize membership in institutionalized denominations and belief systems, a paradigm based on Judeo-Christian understandings and practices of religion. We might want to view the assorted Chinese ritual practices as parts of a "Chinese religious tool kit," which refers to the sets of diverse religious habits, rituals, and beliefs from different religious traditions that are more or less commonly shared by the Chinese people.[15]

If we ask questions about practices instead of beliefs or religious memberships in China, for instance, we will get a much higher number of people who say that they practice religious rituals. When questions about ancestral rites were asked as part of the Horizon 2007 survey, for instance, about 70 percent of people interviewed said that they visited their ancestors' graves in the past year. But the follow-up question for us is whether we should count these people as Confucians. In other words, is ancestral worship *necessarily* a Confucian practice? Let us first look at the case of ancestral worship in China, and then briefly turn to ancestral worship in Japan and Korea.

ANCESTRAL WORSHIP: THE RITUAL PRACTICE OF CONFUCIANS?

Scholars have long argued that the worship of ancestral spirits can be traced back to the beginning of the traditional ritual system of China.[16] Although it existed in China long before the rise of Confucianism, it became appropriated by disciples of Confucius as an essential ritual in Confucianism. In the Chinese Rites and Term Controversy, the heart of the matter was Franciscan and Dominican missionaries' (and later the Vatican's) objection over Chinese converts' participation in what they believed to be Confucian ancestral rites, as well as the worship of Confucius.

As we have seen in examining the Horizon 2007 survey, there has been a great increase in the number of people making annual trips to their ancestral hometowns to perform rituals at the grave sites of their deceased family members. The rituals are sometimes called *saomu* (tomb sweeping) since the primary rituals involve the cleaning of graves and the displaying of sacrifices (such as food, drinks, or paper goods that are made to resemble luxury products). It is believed that the ancestors' blessing can guarantee good fortune in one's personal affairs. As Michael Nylan and Thomas Wilson argue, historically the cult of ancestors constitutes "the only rites practiced by Chinese of every social status and educational background," which I suggest remains the case today.[17]

It is important to point out that although these rituals are generally considered "Confucian" by scholars of Chinese religion, it is unclear whether the practitioners actually view them as Confucian rituals. Indeed, as sociologists and anthropologists such as Herbert Spencer, E. B. Tylor, and E. E. Evans-Pritchard have long pointed out, ancestral worship is very much a universal human practice. In their 2008 study *The Supernatural and Natural Selection: The Evolution of Religion*, Lyle B. Steadman and Craig T. Palmer call it "the most common supernatural claim found in traditional societies," and they argue that it encourages cooperation among living kinsmen, hence promotes the "transmission of traditions from ancestors to descendants."[18]

However, scholars of Asian religions would disagree with their claim that "the significance of ancestors and traditions has become obscured in modern societies."[19] Indeed, through meticulous fieldwork, Robert Smith has shown that ancestral worship is still a significant part of Japanese contemporary religious life.[20] He also offers an interestingly ambiguous account of the origin of ancestral worship in Japan:

> There must always remain some uncertainty about the origin of ancestor worship in Japan. To some it has seemed obviously a cult imported from China; but they have been unable to show how a phenomenon so thoroughly bound up with lineage principles could operate in a society lacking lineage organization altogether. To others it is equally apparent that ancestor worship lies at the heart of the indigenous belief system of Japan and thus predates the introduction of Buddhism and Confucianism. Still others argue that although the Japanese practices resemble ancestor worship they fall short of the full-fledged development to be seen in China or in some African societies. We cannot finally know which of these positions comes closest to the truth, but we can be certain that insofar as the practice of ancestor worship in Japan owes anything at all to continental sources, it has not unexpectedly taken on emphases without analogue in any other Buddhist country of Asia. In this respect ancestor worship is like all other features of Japanese culture that are wholly or partially of alien derivation—the transformations wrought by the Japanese have been profound.[21]

In other words, although there might be a connection between ancestral rituals and Chinese Confucianism, the rituals have been thoroughly appropriated and transformed by Japanese practitioners.

Turning to the case of Korea, here the connection between ancestral rituals and Confucianism seems to be much more pronounced. In *The Confucian Transformation of Korea: A Study of Society and Ideology*, Martina Deuchler argues that

> the undoubtedly most fundamental feature of the Confucianization of Korean society was the development of the patrilineal lineage system. . . . Ancestor worship clarified the lines of descent and marked kinship boundaries as well. . . . Ancestral rites thus introduced a kind of ideological corporateness that, detached from political and economic conditions, functioned as a prime mover in the formation of patrilineal descent groups in Choson Korea.[22]

Edward Y. J. Chung gives concrete accounts of how such rites still constitute a living tradition in South Korea in "Confucian *Li* and Family Spirituality: Reflections on the Contemporary Korean Tradition of Ancestral Rites":

> Various [seven] types of memorial rites were commonly held in traditional Korea. They are mentioned in the Korean Confucian handbooks such as *Sarye Pyŏllam* (Manual of the Four Rites), a famous mid-18th century edition of Chu Hsi's Chinese work, *Family Rites (Chiali)*. Four of the rites that are still commonly held in South Korea are as follows:

- *ch'arye*, special holiday rites;
- *kije(sa)*, death commemoration held at home—traditionally at midnight. on the anniversary of the ancestor's death;
- *sije*, held on an extended family basis in the tenth lunar month; and
- *myoje*, gravesite rite commemoration (now more commonly as *sŏngmyo*).[23]

These rites, especially the grave site commemoration, indeed seem to be deeply rooted in the Confucian tradition.

However, Hongkyung Kim argues that although the Choson dynasty adopted Confucianism as its state ideology in 1392, and texts such as *The Multifarious Rites for Worshipping the Ancestors*, written by Yi Onjok (1491–1553), became widely influential, it is still not easy to tell whether Confucianism is a religion for Korean people:

> Today, despite some seven hundred years of development, it is still not easy to determine how many people in Korea have accepted Confucianism as their religion. This is primarily because Confucianism, unlike Christianity and Buddhism, is not a typical religious organization supported by the two pillars of believers and clergymen. The Songgyun'gwan uses as its religious barometer the issue of whether a household performs rituals for ancestors. Based on this barometer, it has boldly declared that more than half of the entire population in Korea could be considered Confucian. This conclusion may of course be an exaggeration, since many people who observe ancestor worship rituals identify themselves with other religious, such as Catholicism or Buddhism. (Unlike Catholicism, Protestantism in Korea doesn't allow its believers to participate in ancestor worship in general.) However, their declaration reflects the fact that a significant number of Korean people participate in ancestor worship rituals, which are the core religious activity of Confucianism.[24]

One can easily imagine continuing debates among scholars over the Confucian nature of ancestral worship in Korea, as well as in Japan and China; this is indeed a fascinating subject for both historical analysis and contemporary social scientific research.

The larger debate over who the Confucians are in these East Asian countries—and in other parts of Asia, such as Singapore, Vietnam, and Indonesia—will not likely be resolved soon in the future. This could be seen as a failure for those of us who try to define, classify, and identify the social reality of a complex set of ideas and practices that is Confucianism, or this could be seen as a sign of the vitality and strength of Confucianism as an ever-changing, ever-evolving, and dynamic religious, social, and cultural tradition.

CHAPTER 6

To Become a Confucian

A New Conceptual Framework

VERY OFTEN THE IDEA OF CONVERSION brings to mind passionate experiences of religious awakenings and radical transformations of individual lives, as well as large-scale transformations of societies—both peaceful transitions and fervent clashes—throughout history. In her introduction to the edited volume *The Anthropology of Religious Conversion*, Diane Austin-Broos describes conversion as a fundamental change in one's worldview: "To be converted is to reidentify, to learn, reorder, and reorient."[1] And William James famously formulates the experience of conversion in the following way:

> To be converted, to be regenerated, to receive grace, to experience religion, to gain an assurance, are so many phrases which denote the process, gradual or sudden, by which a self hitherto divided, and consciously wrong and inferior, becomes unified and consciously superior and happy, in consequence of its firmer hold upon religious realities. This at least is what conversion signifies in general terms, whether or not we believe that a direct divine operation is needed to bring such a moral change about.[2]

However, in the case of Confucianism, the process of becoming a Confucian is in most cases not an impassioned engagement but a gradual process that involves ritual practices, academic education, and moral self-cultivation, as well as participation in certain Confucian social institutions. Historically, to become a Confucian in China has not been about the renunciation of other religious beliefs or the exclusion of other religious practices but rather a deepening of one's bonds in a given

This chapter was adapted from "To Become a Confucian" by Anna Sun in *Oxford Handbook of Religious Conversions* edited by Lewis Rambo (forthcoming) and published here by permission of Oxford University Press, Inc.

community and tradition and a consolidation of one's different social and cultural identities.

Moreover, to be a Confucian has meant very different things in different historical periods and in different cultural contexts in China. Indeed, to be a Confucian is to have one of the most fluid religious identities. The traditional concept of conversion cannot be applied in a straightforward way to Confucianism, for the process of *becoming* a Confucian has had radically different forms over the course of Chinese history.

Although here I speak of being a Confucian as a religious identity, I am not directly addressing the question of whether Confucianism *is* a religion. In this chapter I am assuming the following three premises without further argument: (1) Confucianism is seen as one of the major world religions today, both in the popular imagination and in academic work (notwithstanding the fact that its religious nature has been constantly contested by scholars); (2) the definition of religion, like the definition of many important concepts, is produced by consensus of communities of practitioners and scholars, and it is a historical product rather than an ahistorical, normative concept; and (3) because of the nonstatic nature of both the definition of religion and the ideas and practices associated with Confucianism, it is entirely plausible for Confucianism to be seen or understood as a religion by both practitioners and scholars in a given social and historical context, and not as a religion in a different context.

In his discussion of conversion to Buddhism in India, Torkel Brekke makes a distinction between two basic modes of understanding religious conversions: the "Pauline paradigm" (following J. T. Richardson), which uses the conversion of St. Paul as the paradigm case, emphasizing the power of an external force—e.g., the voice of Jesus—over the converted person, versus the "activist paradigm," which stresses the choices made by rational individuals in the conversion process.[3]

If we follow these two basic definitions of religious conversion, we may formulate a conversion process as follows:

One converts to X.

This formula can be easily understood when we discuss the case of someone converting to Catholicism or Islam:

One converts to Catholicism.

or

One converts to Islam.

We know what the act of "converting" refers to, regardless of whether we know what "Catholicism" or "Islam" entails. Such acts of conversion are common occurrences in our contemporary social life as well as throughout history, and although social scientists might disagree on how to best analyze them from sociological or psychological perspectives, they would all agree that such religious conversions are social facts that can be examined, for there are doctrinal rules and procedures regulating the conversion process, such as the *Catechism of the Catholic Church* and the Catholic *Rite of Christian Initiation of Adults*. In addition, there are tangible, historically rooted, and standardized ritual ceremonies that formalize the conversion process, sanctifying a person's new identity as a convert and marking his or her acceptance into a new religious community.[4]

Yet the situation is very different in the case of Confucianism. Let us consider the following formulation:

One converts to Confucianism.

What does the phrase "one converts to Confucianism" mean, exactly? The truth is that very few people have ever uttered these words to describe their experiences in relation to Confucianism. Historically, no Chinese person has described his or her affiliation with Confucianism in terms that can be translated as "conversion," even though terms that mean "conversion" are often used in relation to Buddhism, such as *guiyi* (converting to Buddhism). Furthermore, although there are voluminous studies of Chinese converts to Catholicism, Protestantism, or Islam, we do not know of cases of Catholics, Protestants, or Muslims who have been "converted to Confucianism."

There are two main difficulties in describing Confucianism in the traditional language of conversion. The first lies in the fact that there are no definitive conversion rites in Confucianism, such as baptism in Catholicism and Protestantism. In traditional China, one becomes a Confucian through a process that involves undergoing a Confucian education and living a certain form of life. Although one also participates in Confucian rituals, there is no official conversion rite to signify one's acceptance into this particular religious tradition. In other words, there is no formal religious ceremony marking one's transformation from being a non-Confucian into being a Confucian; the process is a much more gradual one, and most people who are considered Confucians might not be able to identify the precise moment at which they became Confucian. Indeed, there is no membership record for Confucianism, as opposed to the case for Christianity.

The second difficulty comes from the fact that there are no official religious organizations in Confucianism, such as churches or mosques, nor is there an official priesthood or clergy. As a result, there is no religious authority in charge of the acceptance of new members, nor a religious authority to administer official certificates of conversions, as in many other traditions. In fact, it is difficult to speak of membership in Confucianism in general, since the foundation of Confucianism is not religious institutions but diverse and interconnected social and education systems.

In his influential book *Religion in Chinese Society*, C. K. Yang makes the distinction between what he calls "institutional religion" and "diffused religion."[5] For instance, in the case of institutional religions, we find temples or churches with their own clergy and clear institutional structure; in the case of diffused religion, the religious activities are conducted in more secular settings, such as the family. Joseph Adler argues that Confucianism is a diffused religion according to Yang's definition: "This is one of the reasons why it is so difficult to speak of Confucianism as 'a religion': this terminology implicitly reifies the phenomenon as a distinct 'thing,' yet as diffused religion Confucianism does not exist separately and apart from the secular social settings in which it is practiced."[6] This is particularly true of Confucian rituals; they can be performed on the grounds of Confucius temples, in front of the ancestral tablets in one's household, or at the graveside of one's deceased family members.

Due to the unique nature of Confucianism, instead of using the formulation of "One converts to X," I propose the following modified formula:

One becomes a Confucian.

Here the emphases are on both *become* and *Confucian*, for there are many different ways of *becoming* a Confucian and many different ways of *being* a Confucian. Indeed, the term "Confucian" has meant a wide range of things throughout the course of Chinese history.

HISTORICAL CONSIDERATIONS

Even though Confucius famously said that he prefers not to address matters related to gods and spirits (*Analects*, 7.21), discussions about the appropriate performance of rituals can be found in many passages in the *Analects*. It is clear that living a life of proper ritual practice is central to Confucius's teaching.

Although Confucius was highly regarded as a teacher and sage prior to the Han dynasty, the so-called "cult of Confucius" did not start until the Han dynasty (206 BCE–220 CE). The worship of Confucius through rituals performed by the emperor or his surrogates can be dated to the late sixth or seventh century. The historian Thomas A. Wilson notes that, starting in the Tang dynasty (618–907), a liturgy for the worship of Confucius was constructed based on ancient canonical texts on rituals, and these codes for sacrifices were used throughout imperial China, with modifications along the way. For instance, the Tang codes required the first offering to be presented by the crown prince and the second and the third by the two top officials of the Directorate of Education; in the Ming dynasty (1368–1644), the ritual sacrifices were supervised by senior officials from the Court of Imperial Sacrifices, the Directorate of Education, and the Ministry of Rites.[7] Such formal and official ritual performances are often referred to by scholars as the "state cult of Confucius." These ritual practices were carried out by the royal court of different dynasties, and temples devoted to the veneration of Confucius flourished in major cities until the Republican Revolution in 1911 put an end to the last imperial dynasty, the Qing (1644–1911), as well as to the court worship of Confucius.

Michael Nylan and Thomas Wilson persuasively divide the history of the cult of Confucius into three periods or stages:

1. From some time after Confucius's death in 479 BCE until after the fall of the Han dynasty, generations of his followers and descendants venerated Confucius in a local cult celebrated in Qufu, with only occasional official patronage.

2. With the first sacrifice to Confucius by court officials in the capital in the mid-third century CE, the cult emerged from the local circumstances of its beginnings, to become gradually integrated into imperial institutions. During the next five hundred years, imperial officials performed sacrifices to Confucius at educational sites with increasing frequency, but several key elements of a cult, such as the identity of its principle sage—Confucius or the Duke of Zhou—and the classical precedent that sanctioned it, remained unsolved.

3. A cult devoted to Confucius as its sage, with a regular liturgy based on a widely accepted classical precedent, was fully intergraded into the imperial cults celebrated in and around the capital from the mid-eighth century. The cult of Confucius, patronized by classically educated civil officials and Confucian literati, grew in prominence during the late imperial period and thrived until the end of nineteenth century. During this third period the cult continued to evolve along with fundamental changes in society as well as within Confucian learning itself.[8]

Besides ritual performed in Confucius temples, another important component of Confucian ritual practices is the personal worship of ancestral spirits. Although this practice existed in China long before the rise of Confucianism,[9] ancestral rites have been appropriated by the disciples of Confucius as an essential ritual.

Another unique feature of Confucianism is how closely related the rise of the civil examination system in imperial China is to the development and continuity of Confucian rituals. The civil service examination system started in 605 and ended in 1904, shortly before the fall of the imperial dynasty in 1911 and the birth of the Republic of China. In some ways the exam system served as the bridge between Confucius worship and Confucian elites. In *Sages and Saints*, Chin-shing Huang makes the important point that, unlike Christian churches where everyone is welcome to enter, Confucius temples in imperial China were sacred spaces reserved for imperial courtiers, scholar-officials, and Confucian students (*rusheng*), people who either had passed through the civil examination system or were about to enter it. Newly appointed local officials were often required to pay respect to Confucius in the local Confucius temple before they could begin their official duty, and the Confucius temples were also the sites where Confucian students celebrated their success on the civil examination exams by offering their thanksgiving to Confucius. Such rituals marked their transformation into officialdom—and, indeed, their new identity as full-fledged Confucians.[10] This is indeed a unique feature of membership in Confucianism; it existed only in imperial China, and it had little to do with a formal process of conversion but had everything to do with one's acceptance into the learned world of Confucian social and political elites.

The Jesuit missionaries in China were forced to deal with the issue of such rituals in the seventeenth century during the "Chinese Rites Controversy." The "Chinese Rites Controversy" highlighted the diffused nature of Confucian ritual practice. As Liam Matthew Brockey puts it, the Jesuits considered Confucianism, especially the worship of Confucius, "the sect of the literati," and they saw "the yearly participation of Christian literati in rituals at Confucian temples as a solemn expression of remembrance for a revered master."[11] Their accommodation policy came from their realization that they needed the support and protection of the dominant social and political elites, who were "by profession, committed Confucians."[12]

However, the Franciscan and Dominican missionaries objected to Chinese converts' participation in certain Confucian rites. Brockey notes, "These missionaries especially objected to seeing Christian literati participate in Confucian ceremonies and ordinary Christians keep tablets inscribed with their ancestors' names in their homes. In the friars' opinion, both were intolerable manifestations of idolatry and not, as the Jesuits claimed, merely political and social customs."[13] Their response to the Jesuits' accommodation policy was "roaming the streets of Peking, preaching that 'the king was wrong and Confucius was in hell.'"[14]

THEORETICAL CONSIDERATIONS

Given the complex history and reality of Confucianism, how do we find a theoretical model that can encompass the many different ways through which one becomes a Confucian? Lewis Rambo has offered a very useful typology of conversion in his study, *Understanding Religious Conversion* (1993):

> *Apostasy, or defection*: the repudiation of a religious tradition or its beliefs by previous members.
>
> *Intensification*: the revitalized commitment to a faith with which the convert has had previous affiliation, formal or informal.
>
> *Affiliation*: the movement of an individual or group from no or minimal religious commitment to full involvement with an institution or community of faith.
>
> *Institutional Transition*: the change of an individual or group from one community to another within a major tradition (such as denominational switching).
>
> *Tradition Transition*: the movement of an individual or a group from one major religious tradition to another.[15]

The case of Confucianism seems to lie between the modes of *Intensification* and *Affiliation*, for the process of becoming a Confucian can be seen as an intensification of one's previous bonds with the Confucian tradition through ritual practices (especially ancestral rites) as well as self-cultivation through education and spiritual exercises. And it is also an official affiliation in the case of the Confucian elites in imperial China, who were entitled to participate in the formal rites venerating Confucius in Confucius temples, a privilege that was reserved for members of the imperial court and scholar-officials who were selected through national civil examinations.

In contemporary China, however, with the absence of the imperial "state cult of Confucius" and the officiating process of one's status as a Confucian through the imperial civil service examination, how do we identify who the Confucians are, and how do we differentiate the varied ways through which they become Confucians? Furthermore, how do we convey the rich inclusiveness of religious ritual life in the Chinese context, where, unlike in monotheistic traditions such as Christianity and Islam, a person can carry out diverse ritual practices from different religious traditions in one's life—Confucian, Buddhist, Daoist, etc.—without seeing them as contradictory?

I propose the following three criteria to define whether someone is behaving as a Confucian in terms of his or her participation in Confucian practice. I am not using these criteria to define *whether* someone is a Confucian, which suggests an exclusive religious identity that is not suitable in the discussion of Confucianism. Rather, these criteria define *when* someone is a Confucian, meaning the occasions during which one behaves as a Confucian.

The Minimal Criterion: Confucius Worship

The Minimal Criterion: Confucius Worship declares that one is a Confucian when one practices any of the following rituals that take place in a Confucius temple:

a. Burning incense;
b. Praying to the statue or the tablet of Confucius;
c. Writing prayers on prayer cards that hang in trees or a placed on special shelves within the temple;
d. Any other rituals that take place in a Confucius temple.

This criterion refers to the people who participate in Confucius worship in Confucius temples. The Minimalist Criterion ensures the undeniable religious dimension of Confucianism; these are religious rituals performed in a sacred space.

The Inclusive Criterion: Ancestral Rituals

According to the Inclusive Criterion: Ancestral Rituals, one is a Confucian when one practices any of the following rituals:

a. Any ritual practices in an ancestral temple;
b. Any ritual practices at the grave site of one's deceased ancestors/ family members.

These practices refer to people who participate in either Confucius worship or ancestral worship. As the name suggests, this is a more inclusive criterion than merely Confucius worship, for it includes all the religious rituals that are commonly seen as Confucian.

The Extended Criterion: Cultural Confucianism

The Extended Criterion: Cultural Confucianism states that one is a Confucian when one does any of the following:

a. Practicing filial piety and other Confucian virtues;
b. Practicing Confucian spiritual exercises in order to live a more Confucian life, such as reading the Confucian classics and meditating;
c. Practicing other Confucian social rituals, such as family rituals (*jiali*).[16]

This refers to people who may or may not participate in Confucian religious rituals such as ancestral worship or Confucius worship but who are "culturally Confucian" because of their practices of Confucian virtues and spiritual exercises that aim at cultivating their mind and body and/ or their practices of Confucian social rituals such as the proper way to interact with their family members and friends.

For instance, if someone takes the virtue of filial piety—one of the most fundamental Confucian virtues—seriously in one's life by behaving in a certain way toward one's parents, one can be seen as a "Cultural Confucian" according to this criterion. This also includes people who are involved in the study of classical texts in the Confucian canon, such as the *Analects* and the *Mencius*, as well as more popular Confucian texts such as *The Classic of Filial Piety* (*xiaojing*) or *The Book of Three-Character Verse* (*sanzi jing*), in order to use Confucian ideas as the guiding ethical principles in their life (and often also as the foundation of the education of their child or children).

The relationship among the three criteria can be seen in figure 6.1.

There is an additional aspect of Confucianism that might be called "Political Confucianism," a term promoted by the contemporary scholar and Confucian activist Jiang Qing. This refers to the idea that Confucianism should serve as the foundation of Chinese politics and culture and

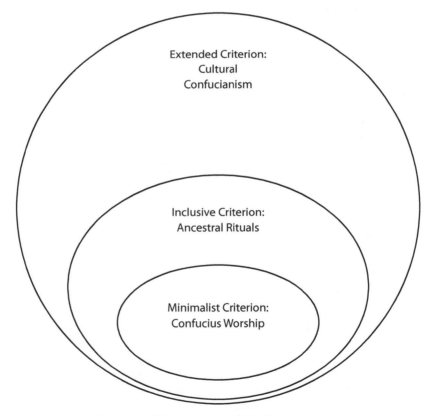

Figure 6.1. Three Criteria of Confucian Practice

that Confucian political philosophy should be the guiding force in China's transformation from a socialist state to a new political system. This has become an influential way of understanding Confucianism in China among intellectuals who are increasingly nationalistic in their cultural and political outlook; Jiang Qing and Kang Xiaoguang are two leading voices in this reformulation of Confucian politics.[17] Indeed, today Confucianism is being considered as a viable alternative to Western liberal democracy, although the official discourse of Confucianism is still full of ambiguities.[18]

As Prasenjit Duara has suggested, there is a long-standing "transmutation (or traffic) of religious ideas into political ideas," especially in the case of Confucianism, which has a long, entangled history with dynastic rulers, political reformers, and the creation of a modern "national citizenry" in China.[19] So it should not come as a surprise that "Political Confucianism" is experiencing a new wave of revival in China, and it remains to be seen whether it will make use of the religious aspects of Confucianism in the legitimation of its authority.

In his insightful book *Contemporary Confucian Political Philosophy: Toward Progressive Confucianism*, Stephen Angle divides contemporary Confucian political philosophers into the following seven types: the philosophical historians, the Confucian revivalists, the institutional Confucians, the Kantian New Confucians, the Critical New Confucians, the Neo-Classical Confucians, and the synthetic Confucians. He writes, "Confucian civil society organizations, both formal and more informal (like the community of like-minded people who contribute to a particular internet site), have also begun to serve more than merely academic functions. A mix of scholars and what can only be called Confucian activists have started to take and publicize positions on matters of public interest, sometimes in direct opposition to governmental entities."[20] There are both positive and negative effects of such intense Confucian political activism, which can be seen from emerging conflicts over different cultural, political, as well as religious values.

THE ROAD TO BECOMING A CONFUCIAN: SELF-CULTIVATION THROUGH EDUCATION, SPIRITUAL EXERCISES, AND SOCIAL RITUALS

Since one becomes a Confucian not through a radical transformation of one's fundamental beliefs or worldview but rather through steady practice of Confucian rituals and an ongoing commitment to the Confucian way of life, the idea of self-cultivation is central to the process. One becomes a true Confucian, a *junzi* (virtuous person), through intense self-cultivation, and the Confucians see the techniques of the cultivation of the self as involving all aspects of one's being: intellect, sensibility, imagination, temperament, and relation to others, as well as manners and all other physical manifestations of oneself.

In Pierre Hadot's articulation, the main aspects of spiritual exercise in Hellenistic philosophy are strikingly similar to the components of self-cultivation in the Confucian tradition:

1. Learning to Live: Learning the art of living though a transformation of one's inner self.
2. Learning to Dialogue: Learning to have genuine dialogues with others as well as with oneself.
3. Learning to Die: Training for death through contemplation of the nature of life and death.
4. Learning How to Read: Learning "how to pause, liberate ourselves from our worries, return into ourselves, and leave aside our search for subtlety and originality, in order to meditate calmly, ruminate, and let the texts speak to us."[21]

For Confucius, it is through observing *li* (social rules and rituals) that one cultivates virtuous desires, and one must be guided by teachers and helped by virtuous friends along the way. This is why the internalization and mastery of *li* is essentially a social process that includes both education and spiritual exercise.[22] Confucius calls this process "restraining oneself with social rules and rituals" (*Analects*, 6.27, 9.11), "establishing oneself through social rules and rituals" (*Analects*, 8.8, 20.3), and "self-disciplining by submitting oneself to social rules and rituals (*keji fuli*)" (*Analects*, 12.1). Confucius says that at age seventy he was able to "follow all the desires of his heart without breaking any rules," because all the rules have become constitutive of his self (*Analects*, 2.4).

Self-cultivation through education and spiritual exercise remains a central concern in Confucianism throughout Chinese history. Partly due to the influence of Daoism and Buddhism, the Neo-Confucian philosophers in the Song dynasty (960–1279) and the Ming dynasty (1368–1644) developed elaborated theories of Confucian self-cultivation as well as rich techniques, making use of ideas and methods from Zen Buddhism.[23]

It was Zhu Xi (1130–1200), a leading Neo-Confucian philosopher, who was one of the first to advance the idea of the Four Books, which included the *Analects*, the *Mencius*, the *Great Learning*, and the *Doctrine of the Mean*, texts Confucius considered to be the most significant parts of Confucian canon. Through the Four Books, Zhu Xi advocated the idea of self-cultivation through both philosophical and spiritual exercises such as contemplation and reading, pointing to an "inward" shift toward inner sources of personal morality.

However, this does not mean that social rituals such as family rituals are no longer important. Commenting on Zhu Xi's manual on family rituals, Patricia Ebrey remarks,

> Although the main focus of Zhu Xi's work was the theory and practice of self-cultivation, the defining and shaping of the self always took place in a social context, and the study of rites remained a major concern of his, as it has been earlier for the Confucius of the *Analects*, in which humanness and rites were twin themes. . . . As a practical matter for the local elite, Zhu gave family ritual priority over the royal and state rituals that occupied so much of the Zhou texts [ancient ritual texts]. . . . Subsequently, Zhu's prescriptions became models for the cultural and social elite, adapted widely in premodern East Asia.[24]

In other words, even for Neo-Confucians like Zhu Xi, who emphasized the kind of contemplative practices of meditation and reading that were not unlike the intense contemplative practices of prayers and sacred reading (*lectio divina*) found in Catholic monastic life, the religious and social rituals of everyday life were still indispensable.

These aspects of Confucian self-cultivation—education in the Confucian canon, various forms of spiritual exercises, emphasis on social rituals—can be felt clearly in the contemporary revival of Confucian practices. The Reading of the Classics Movement began in the 1990s as a grassroots movement designed to teach children Confucian classics through reading and memorization, and it has now spread widely throughout China, with classes offered in private schools and its impact felt in state-run educational institutions.

There are also efforts to bring back classical Confucian social rituals, to relearn the proper ways of behaving in the Confucian tradition. Such social rituals include the veneration of one's parents through proper etiquette at formal occasions, such as weddings, as well as at informal occasions, paying respect to one's teachers with deferential manners in the classroom, and the general Confucian way of conduct of treating people as well as oneself with dignity and reverence.

It might be useful to think of Confucianism as the foundation of contemporary Chinese moral economy. Here I use the definition of moral economy as formulated by Lorraine Daston: "What I mean by a moral economy is a web of affect-saturated values that stand and function in well-defined relationship to one another."[25] A good example of contemporary Chinese moral economy can be found in an article published in the *New York Times* on January 29, 2011. Titled "China Might Force Visits to Mom and Dad," the article reports, "On the eve of the Lunar New Year festival, when Chinese flood train stations, bus terminals and airports to reunite with loved ones, one Chinese ministry is proposing that the government mandate closer families. Under a proposal submitted last Monday by the Civil Affairs Ministry to China's State Council, adult children would be required by law to regularly visit their elderly parents. If they do not, parents can sue them."[26]

Although the *New York Times* article did not mention Confucianism as behind the value embedded in this proposed legal measure, it is clear that its justification is Confucian. Indeed, in Confucian ethics, one of the most important virtues is filial piety: one's unconditional reverence and devotion to one's parents. Many Confucian values have been incorporated into the very fabric of everyday life in China to such an extent that people are no longer conscious of their Confucian origins. These values have been internalized in individual lives, and they have become social norms of behavior. Such values include filial piety, reverence toward teachers, benevolence toward others, and respect for tradition and social rituals. Such values and ideals are taught through manuals of correct behavior for children, handbooks of self-cultivation, and many other institutional, ritual, and cultural means.

Becoming a Confucian in the Global World

What makes one a Confucian in today's world? Among the various criteria we have discussed, which are the most fundamental, the most essential to becoming Confucian today? Is someone who worships Confucius in a Confucius temple more Confucian than someone who practices filial piety toward his or her parents, or someone who reads the *Analects* as his or her spiritual manual for life? And does it matter whether one is Chinese if one wants to become a Confucian?

To answer these questions is to confront the internal tensions in Confucianism in the contemporary world; they are not necessarily causes of conflicts, but often sources of renewal and innovation. Confucianism is often seen as a conservative force, for historically it has placed great emphasis on preserving canonical texts, maintaining ritual traditions, defending existing social hierarchies, and protecting a uniquely *Chinese* social, cultural, and political identity.

Yet we also know that the Confucian canon has been remade over and over by countless generations of scholars who have transformed it through extensive commentaries over two thousand years of intense hermeneutic practices. And numerous Confucian scholars and politicians have acted as agents of change, such as becoming some of the earliest Catholic converts in China or serving as leading political reformers in the twentieth century. And rituals such as Confucius worship ceremonies have gone through a striking alteration, changing from ceremonies conducted by imperial courts for nearly fifteen hundred years to ritual performances staged by the state in today's China.

Indeed, the once-forbidden Confucius temples are now open to anyone who wishes to enter, and the revival of traditional rituals of burning incense in Confucius temples as well as the newly invented ritual practice of praying to Confucius through prayer cards have changed the dynamic of the sacred space. Such creative actions often produce what Hacking calls the "looping effect of human kinds," which refers to the often intense interactions between people and the ways in which they are classified. Hacking states, "*Author* and *brother* are kinds of people, as are *child viewer* and *Zulu*. People of these kinds can become aware that they are classified as such. They can make tacit or even explicit choices, adapt or adopt ways of living so as to fit or get away from the very classification that may be applied to them."[27] And people's social actions in the end affect the classification scheme as well, which is constantly modified and redefined through institutional processes.

If we view the revival of Confucian rituals in this light, it becomes clear that this revival may indeed have transformative effects on the way Confucianism is classified and understood in contemporary Chinese society, as well as on the way we understand what constitutes being a Confucian. For instance, the revival, renewal, and invention of ritual actions related to Confucius worship and ancestral worship in recent years in China have already had an impact on the legitimation of Confucianism as a religion, and it is not inconceivable that Confucianism might be recognized by the state in the future as one of the major religions in China, which would have many significant religious, political, and social consequences.

And one does not need to be a Chinese person to be a Confucian. Indeed, Confucianism has been thriving outside of China for hundreds of years, especially in Korea, Japan, and Vietnam, with South Korea being the country that has perhaps best preserved Confucian ritual practice in the contemporary world.[28] Scholars have long referred to "Confucian East Asia," and now there is also the so-called "Boston Confucianism" represented by Tu Weiming, Robert Neville, and John Berthrong, scholars as well as followers of Confucianism.[29] Through endorsing ongoing Confucian-Christian dialogues, the Boston Confucians have been emphasizing the profound relevance of Confucian ideas and spiritual exercises to the Western world.

The truth is that, like any living religious tradition, Confucianism is ever-changing and ever-evolving, and its future is cast through its transformation in the present. Its current metamorphosis might not be particularly dramatic, yet there are already signs pointing to new developments, indicating adjustment and regeneration. As a result, there will always be new ways of becoming a Confucian.

THE REALITY OF PRACTICES

Is Confucianism a Religion in China Today?

CHAPTER 7

The Emerging Voices of Women in the Revival of Confucianism

IT HAS BEEN DIFFICULT FOR scholars of Confucianism to handle the only direct reference to women in the *Analects*: "Women and small people are hard to deal with" (*Analects*, 17.25).[1] For two thousand years, Confucianism has been known to be a tradition of patriarchal domination, with the male authorities—the ruler in imperial China (*tianzi*, literally meaning "the son of heaven"), the father in the household, and the husband in the marriage—holding indisputable power over women.

Has this really been the case? In recent years, this preconceived notion that Confucianism is inherently patriarchal has been challenged by a growing number of scholars, from historians to philosophers.[2] However, very little attention has been paid to the impact of the current resurgence of Confucianism in contemporary China on the position of women in Confucian tradition. In this chapter, I focus on the role of women in the contemporary revival of Confucianism in Mainland China, and I suggest that, regardless of what has been women's position in Confucian societies in the past, in today's reestablishment and transformation of Confucianism as a lived and living tradition, women have been playing increasingly central roles.

Today the revival of Confucianism in Mainland China takes many forms, from a revival of Confucian education, such as after-school classes focusing on the teaching of the Confucian canon, to the intensification of scholarship on Confucian thought in academia.[3] We also see the popular adaption of Confucian ideas for self-help and business strategies, and the state's effort to promote Confucianism as the dominant Chinese cultural ideology.[4] This myriad development is not surprising, for it corresponds to the many aspects of "Confucianism" as historical, political, institutional, cultural, educational, philosophical, and religious systems of ideas and practices.

In contemporary sociology of religion, the issue of women and religion has long been under scrutiny. Do women play subordinate roles in religious lives? Can we find patriarchal structures across different religions and cultures? When it comes to Confucianism, the common examples involving women are often negative, such as "patrilineal ancestor worship in Chinese society" or "Confucian footbinding, which promotes chastity by making it difficult for women to move about."[5] However, as Fang-Long Shih points out, "the claim that patriarchy is the structuring grammar of all religions is debatable, and there are interpretations and evidence both for and against the idea."[6] Her research on maiden temples in China suggests there are discursive and physical spaces in Chinese religious cultures that allow for creative assertions of identities for women, which are both "reflections of and negotiations with traditional gender relations and wider processes of economic and political change."[7]

Although an outline of Confucian ethics cannot avoid the hierarchical nature of the so-called Five Relations (*wu lun*), which normalize the structure of power of the five dominant social relations in Chinese society—the power the emperor or ruler has over his ministers, the power fathers have over their sons, the power the older brothers have over their younger brothers, the power husbands have over their wives, the equal relation between friends—scholars have been arguing in recent years that women have in fact been able to achieve positions of power within such a hierarchy throughout Chinese history. Historians such as Lisa Raphals, Susan Mann, Yu-yin Cheng, and Annping Chin have examined the complex ways in which women have lived fulfilling lives as intellectuals and moral agents in Confucian society, and the philosopher Li-Hsiang Lisa Rosenlee has tackled explicitly the complex account of gender relations in Confucianism as a philosophy and the most central ethical system in China, proposing a Confucian feminism as "a hybrid identity," combining filial piety as a minimal level of humanity, the virtue of benevolence as the achievement of a relational personhood, and the basic Confucian structure of social relations.[8]

How should we locate these historical and philosophical analyses suggesting the existence and power of women's agency in Confucian China? Joseph Adler, a scholar of Neo-Confucianism, has argued compellingly for the importance of making several sets of distinctions when we speak of women in the two thousand years of gendered history in China; these distinctions are worth repeating here: (1) textual traditions versus social practices; (2) normative texts (such as *Record of Ritual*) versus descriptive texts (such as historical documents); (3) practices of social and cultural elites versus practices of nonelites; (4) women as "ideal symbols" versus women seen as "diverse individuals"; and (5) women portrayed as "objects of a male-centered gaze" versus women as "subjects expressing their own lives and worldviews."[9]

In other words, we need to understand the relationship between women and Confucianism in its complex, multifaceted form, recognizing the many apparent contradictions throughout Chinese history. For instance, although women are not referred to favorably (or often not mentioned at all) in early Confucian texts such as the *Analects* or the *Mencius*, there have been many texts demonstrating Confucian morality and virtues that were specifically written for women, such as *Regulations for the Women's Quarters*, *Biographies of Exemplary Women*, and *Ladies' Classic of Filial Piety*. And the story of the moral education of Mencius by Mencius's honorable and strong-willed mother, a paragon of Confucian virtues, is still a well-known one in China today.

It is also worth remembering that Confucianism is not an essence of Chinese society that remains stable and unchanging. As Adler reminds us, it consists of theories and practices, normative ideas and historical processes, and it is important to always have a historical perspective while examining the changing relations of women to Confucianism. And the shifting social conditions of Chinese society always shape the production and dissemination of Confucian ideas and practices, both through a constant reinterpretation of the cannon and through new ways of relating to Confucian thought and practice in everyday life.

Today's China is a society undergoing a profound social, economic, and political transformation, evolving from a rigid socialist regime into a nominally socialist country with an increasingly successful market economy. With the evaporation of the political and moral authority of communist ideology, contemporary Chinese society has embarked on a quest to rediscover and redefine its Confucian roots. But this is not a rediscovery happening in a social and historical vacuum. For instance, since the founding of socialist China in 1949, significant progress has been made in terms of women's rights, a development made possible by China's socialist feminism. Much has happened since then, including the state-imposed suppression of Confucianism during the Cultural Revolution from 1966 to 1976 and the economic reforms that took off in the 1980s, changing both the economic and political landscape of China.

When Confucian thoughts and practices gradually made a visible return to the center of Chinese life in the 1990s (one could argue that it had never truly gone away), women had already achieved a different, more powerful position in society as a whole. Like the men in society, they have also been struggling with the new challenges posed by the rapid economic development, as well as the fast-changing norms and ethics of behavior, in both the family and society at large. In Daniel Bell's vivid and timely account of the increasing importance of Confucianism in contemporary

Chinese political, social, and cultural life, *China's New Confucianism: Politics and Everyday Life in a Changing Society*, women often take center stage in discussions of pressing social issues ranging from the caring of elderly parents, the treatment of domestic workers, to the societal consequences of prostitution.[10]

Based on research conducted from 2004 to 2010, I suggest that women's voices can be heard in at least three different aspects in the current revival of Confucianism in Mainland China. First, in the popular remaking of Confucianism as a philosophy for everyday life, Yu Dan as a cultural celebrity has been instrumental in promoting Confucius's ideas as relevant to contemporary ways of life. Second, in the scholarly revival of Confucianism, female scholars have made important contributions to the rigorous studies of Confucian thought. Third, in the revival of Confucian rituals preformed in different settings (Confucius temples and the graves of deceased family members), women are active ritual participants, maintaining the continuity of ancient traditions as well as attributing new meaning to them in the fast-evolving modern world.

WOMEN IN THE POPULAR REVIVAL OF CONFUCIANISM: YU DAN AND THE "PEOPLE'S CONFUCIUS"

In *China's New Confucianism*, Bell offers a sharp analysis of the most visible popularizer of Confucianism in China today, Yu Dan, a female college professor and television personality who has appeared on many TV shows and has sold millions of copies of her book about the *Analects*:[11]

> In China, Yu Dan's *Lunyu Xinde* (Reflections on the *Analects* of Confucius) has become a publishing sensation. At the last count, it has sold about ten million copies (including six million pirated copies). The rest of the world is also paying attention: major newspapers and media outlets have reported on the Yu Dan phenomenon. Such headlines as "Confucius Makes a Comeback" in *The Economist* are typical. The last book out of China to attract so much attention has been, well, let me think . . . Mao's *Little Red Book*. If Mao's book erred on the side of excessive politicization of our everyday world, however, Yu Dan's book has the opposite problem.[12]

Bell's critique of Yu Dan is not her charismatic televangelist style of discussing the *Analects* nor her often imprecise or even erroneous interpretations of passages, which have been critiqued or even attacked incessantly by scholars of Confucianism in China, but her depoliticization of Confucianism:

> By telling people they shouldn't complain too much, that they should worry first and foremost about their inner happiness, by downplaying the importance

of social and political commitment, and by informing the critical tradition of Confucianism, Yu Dan deflects attention from the economic and political conditions that actually cause people's misery, as well as the sort of collective solutions needed to bring about substantial improvement to people's lives.[13]

This critical analysis represents many intellectuals' discontent with Yu Dan's feel-good, nonreflective, and nonpolitical reading of Confucianism. Ironically, this might also explain the immense appeal of Yu Dan's message to ordinary Chinese people.

Who is Yu Dan? How did she become so central to the popular revival of Confucianism? She is a professor of media studies at Beijing Normal University, with a master's degree in Chinese literature and a PhD in film and television studies. It is important to note that Yu Dan's academic background is in media studies and that she has not been trained as a scholar of Confucianism. Although she is obviously not an intellectual authority on Confucius, in October 2006 she was offered the opportunity to present a seven-part television lecture series on the *Analects* for the popular prime-time show *Lecture Hall* on the state-owned CCTV (China Central Television). The lectures, broadcast during a golden television time slot, were a sensational success with viewers and made her a household name across China. Her book is based on the transcript of her conversational, light-hearted, and decidedly nonscholarly lectures.

The phenomenon of television lecture series is a unique development in popular culture in China today. After the proliferation of numerous television soap operas in the past thirty years, many people long for more substance in their television viewing experience. But without genuine freedom of the press, the news programs are still very much circumscribed, constrained by written as well as unwritten political rules and regulations. In order to fulfill this void, CCTV, one of the main Chinese television stations, decided to establish a program inviting scholars to discuss traditional Chinese culture in 2001, naming it the *Lecture Hall of One Hundred Scholars*. From the beginning its mission has been to "spread the spirit of traditional Chinese culture," and to "make the specialists and scholars serve the people." Its programming schedule must be the envy of many television executives: daily shows are broadcast first at 12:45 a.m., then are rerun on the same day at 10:40 p.m. and again at 6:40 a.m. the next day.

Today the program is a mainstay of many families' evening entertainment, with professors from history, literature, and philosophy departments lecturing on topics ranging from Confucius (there have been at least two more series of lectures on Confucius since Yu Dan's in 2006: "How Confucius Became Confucius" and "Confucius: His Views of Virtues") to *The Book of Changes*, from women's rights in Tang dynasty to the poetry of Li Bai. Its appeal is at least threefold: first, it is an educational program introducing knowledge that is not usually available to a general audience; second, the lectures are given by professors and experts, whose presence denotes privilege and authority; third, the lectures are usually very accessible, entertaining, and even restorative. Indeed, Yu Dan's lectures had a quasi-self-help and even therapeutic effect; she used passages from the *Analects* to show how one can be a good person, a good friend, a good parent in the complex contemporary world, and how one can be virtuous while being successful in life. Throughout her lectures and book, Yu cited numerous anecdotes from popular culture as well as folk wisdom to demonstrate the points she had supposedly derived from the *Analects*. Here is a typical page from Yu's *The* Analects *from the Heart*:

> Confucius never said that you have to be like any one person in order to be a *junzi*. As he saw it, to be a *junzi* is to be the best possible version of yourself, based on where you are right now, beginning with the things around you, and starting today, so that your mind can achieve a state of perfect balance. For it is only when you are possessed of a truly calm, steady, down-to-earth mind and heart that you can avoid being swayed by the rises and falls, gains and losses of life.
>
> This reminds me of a little story:
>
> Three tailors each opened a shop on the same street. Each of them wanted to attract the most customers.
>
> The first tailor hung up a large sign, on which was written: "I am the best tailor in the province."
>
> When the second tailor saw this, he thought he would go one better, so he made a larger sign that read: "I am the best tailor in the whole country."
>
> The third tailor thought: Am I supposed to say that I'm the best tailor in the whole world? He considered the matter for a very long time, and then put up a very small sign. It drew all the customers on the street to his shop, leaving the other two establishments deserted.
>
> What did the third tailor's sign say? "I am the best tailor on this street."
>
> He turned his eyes back to what was in front to him, starting from the here and now. And this is why it was he who won the customers' approval.[14]

As we can see, there are only vague paraphrases of Confucius's utterances from the *Analects*, and there is no in-depth discussion of any passage, let alone an exegesis. The lesson that is attributed to Confucius's wisdom here—concerning how to become successful in commercial activity—could have come from an episode of *Oprah*, had Oprah Winfrey decided to cite ancient texts by Epictetus or Aristotle to back up her self-empowerment advice.

As Bell has argued, immersion in these lectures is indeed a good way of staying away from pressing social concerns and the anxieties they might bring, while feeling good about one's accumulation of knowledge of traditional Chinese culture. The growing interest in *guoxue* (national learning, meaning traditional knowledge) among ordinary Chinese people is a fairly recent phenomenon; the fervent attention to *guoxue* started much earlier among intellectuals, when Confucianism first moved to the center of academic attention in the 1980s, and this trend has only intensified in the past twenty years. Although Yu Dan's lectures are generally considered to be of questionable quality or worse among intellectuals, a few leading scholars of Confucianism, such as Professor Guo Qiyong, a philosopher and the director of the "Institute of National Learning" at Wuhan University and the vice president of the China Confucius Association, have expressed the view that her popularization of Confucianism has served the purpose of introducing ordinary people to the most important Confucian text, even though one should bear in mind that this is only a preliminary step toward a genuine understanding of Confucianism.[15]

In the preface to Yu Dan's book, Yi Zhongtian, another television personality who made his name giving similar lectures on various aspects of Chinese culture, touched on the secret to her achievement:

> I don't know if Yu Dan's Confucius is the same as the scholars' Confucius, and I don't know if it is the same as the historical Confucius, and I certainly don't know if it is the authentic Confucius. But I do know that this is our Confucius, people's Confucius, masses' Confucius, hence the eternal Confucius. We need such a Confucius. We welcome such a Confucius.[16]

The "People's Confucius": is this a gendered Confucius as well? Although Yu Dan does not speak of gender issues explicitly, and has claimed that "I don't recommend people to view Confucius from the perspective of gender," the fact that she is a woman has certainly played a role in her successes. She has made Confucius accessible and relevant to ordinary people, in a medium in which accessibility is key. She has brought the discussion of Confucius out of the classroom, in which the authority of the teacher has historically been held as absolute, and into the relaxed space of working people's living room, where everyone can comment on whether or not they agree with what's shown on television. She has brought Confucius closer to everyday life in her freewheeling interpretation of the *Analects*, speaking of Confucius's "warmth" rather than his political ideals, and in effect making Confucius a sage of domestic pursuits and self-advocacy. She has used the *Analects* to deal with concerns such as ambition and happiness, love and friendship, not issues of social order. There are now a growing number of female lecturers on the *Lecture Hall* program, attempting to follow in Yu Dan's footsteps.

But is Yu Dan a genuine Confucian? This identification may not interest the most vivacious popular promoter of Chinese tradition and culture at all. After the colossal success of her television show on the *Analects* and the book that followed it in 2006, Yu started a new television series during the spring festival holidays in 2007, this time on the Daoist classic the *Zhuangzi*. The book that followed in March 2007, *The* Zhuangzi *from the Heart*, sold one million copies in the first thirteen days. According to one newspaper article, it was bought in bulk by many corporations and social organizations as the perfect present for the March 8 International Women's Day.[17] A prolific author, Yu became the second wealthiest author in China in 2007, taking in royalty income of roughly $1,660,000 in one year.[18] Scholars may argue about the authenticity of Yu's Confucian cultural identity, but what matters to her viewers and readers is her cultural entrepreneurship. She has become the embodiment of a successful marriage between traditional values and capitalist instinct, between the past and the future.

What the Yu Dan phenomenon represents is a set of tensions that are at the core of the Confucius fever in China today. There is the tension between the long-standing elitist monopoly of Confucian teaching and the emerging popular appropriation of it, in which gender politics plays a notable part. There is also the tension between the rigor of academic knowledge production and the for-profit media use of Confucius as a commercial vehicle and cultural brand. Underneath all the lively, seemingly organic activities is the ever-present hand of the state, constantly weighing the political implications of the popular interest in Confucianism and calibrating its usefulness in maintaining the existing structure of power. It is not an overstatement to say that the singular success of Yu Dan's career as the spokesperson of the "People's Confucius" has confirmed both the need of the people for ethical teaching and the power of popular culture in the revival and redefinition of a Confucian life.

Women in the Scholarly Revival of Confucianism: The Case of Confucius2000 and China Confucius

The revival of scholarly work on Confucianism done by women can be seen clearly in English-language scholarship. Today there are dozens of female scholars doing significant work in fields as diverse as history, philosophy, religious studies, East Asian studies, and sociology. They teach in higher education institutions in the United States, Taiwan, Hong Kong, Singapore, France, and other countries.

However, the situation is less clear in Mainland China. Although there has been a renaissance of academic study of Confucianism since the 1990s, the most prominent scholars in Confucian studies have been men, following a more than two-thousand-year history of Confucian scholarship as exclusively the domain of male intellectuals. Are there female scholars today who are beginning to gain a foothold in this traditionally male-dominated field? Could it be the case that women are achieving success in the popularization of Confucianism only in the general cultural sphere, rather than in the hallowed field of Confucian studies?

A comprehensive analysis of the gender distribution of the authors of all scholarly publications (journal articles as well as books) in the past twenty years that focus on Confucianism would yield a definitive finding regarding the presence of women in the study of Confucianism. However, the scope of such an analysis goes beyond this brief survey. Another systematic approach to determine the presence of women in current Confucian scholarship would be through an analysis of the most prominent websites for the discussion of Confucianism. As I have argued in chapter 3, since the late 1990s, various scholarly as well as politically charged debates over Confucianism have taken place online; a great number of scholars of Confucianism have written short essays engaging other scholars, as well as introducing their own work on the two or three most serious websites devoted to the study of Confucianism. And in many cases the online postings have already been published in print form, such as in journals or newspapers. Websites such as Confucius2000 (www.Confucius2000.com) and China Confucius (*zhongguo kongzi*) (www.chinakongzi.org) offer respectable as well as necessary intellectual spaces for ongoing vibrant dialogue, for they reach a wide readership, bypass bureaucratic (and sometimes political) red tapes, and have the advantage of sharing publications in journal articles with people who do not have easy access to them and can quickly update and make comments on current events relating to Confucianism in China.

Among the half dozen or so major websites focusing on serious discussions about Confucianism, Confucius2000, which was founded in 2001 by a group of young intellectuals, and China Confucius, a website founded by the Chinese Confucius Foundation, the most prominent foundation in China devoted to Confucianism, are the two most visible and possibly most visited sites.[19] Each site offers a list of their most important scholars; for Confucius2000, it is a list of "Editorial Consultants," and for China Confucius, it is a list of "Celebrated Contemporary Scholars [of Confucianism]." In addition, Confucius2000 has a long list of scholars who are frequent contributors to the website.

Not surprisingly, both lists include the most eminent scholars of Confucianism today; also not surprisingly, both lists are heavily dominated by male scholars (see table 7.1).

It is important to note that the proportion of women among Confucian scholars seen through this example is still considerably lower than the proportion of women among all academics in China today. However, we can still be cautiously optimistic about the growing presence of

TABLE 7.1. The Online Presence of Women Scholars of Confucianism

	Number of Scholars	Female Scholars	Percentage of Women
Confucius2000	"Editorial consultants": 41	1	2.4
China Confucius	"Celebrated contemporary scholars": 45	1	2.2
Confucius2000	Most frequent contributors: 205	10	4.9

Source: www.Confucius2000.com; www.chinakongzi.org (October 2010).

TABLE 7.2. Profiles of Women Scholars of Confucianism with an Online Presence

Total Female Frequent Contributors to Confucius2000	PhD Degree	PhD Degree Fields	Academic Positions	Birth Date after 1970	Total Postings
10	7	5 in philosophy; 1 in economics; 1 in history	10	4	93 (articles, essays)

Source: www.Confucius2000.com (October 2010).

women in the traditionally male-dominated field of Confucian studies. Based on the brief biographical sketches available on the website, we learn a few interesting things about the women who contribute to these highly esteemed online academic forums (see table 7.2).

As we can see, this is an extremely accomplished group of women, and their accomplishments are intellectual as well as academic. Indeed, according to the latest data from the Chinese Ministry of Education, among recipients of PhD degrees in all academic fields in 2009, 36 percent were women. Among professors who can supervise PhD students, 12.6 percent are women, and among professors who can supervise master's students, 29 percent are women.[20] The increase in female academics in higher education signals a profound institutional shift in today's China. The rising presence of women in academic institutions, especially in the traditionally male-dominated discipline of philosophy, where most scholars of Confucianism are trained, is a very welcoming change.

And the relative youth (40 percent under the age of forty) of the female scholars who contributed to Confucius2000 as well as the active participation they have demonstrated (an average nine postings of articles and essays per person) might be signs of a broader generational transformation. Members of this younger generation of female scholars are ready to be as visible and vocal as their male counterparts, and one hopes that they will become role models for students who are entering academic training. No paradigmatic change can take place overnight; in this case, such changes might take place one online posting at a time.

However, it is important to note that having more female scholars in the study of Confucianism does not necessarily mean that they will automatically engage in topics related to women's lives or feminist issues. In other words, they will not necessarily speak in an intellectual voice different from that of their male colleagues. A quick search using the keyword "women" (*nu*) reveals that, among thousands of articles on Confucius2000, only thirteen have "women" in their titles, and none of these articles were written by female scholars who are in the group of regular contributors analyzed here.

It seems that it is still too early to assess the intellectual impact of having more female scholars in the field of Confucian studies. In recent years, most monographs presenting genuinely feminist engagements with Confucianism have been written not by scholars in Mainland China but by scholars in the West, such as Lisa Li-Hsiang Rosenlee, author of *Confucianism and Women: A Philosophical Interpretation*, and Chenyang Li, author of *The Sage and the Second Sex: Confucianism, Ethics, and Gender*. It remains to be seen how the growing presence of women in the study of Confucianism in China today might transform the actual scholarship being produced on the teachings of the Sage.

WOMEN IN THE RELIGIOUS REVIVAL OF CONFUCIANISM: CONFUCIUS WORSHIP AND ANCESTRAL WORSHIP

Women have been central to the conduct of many contemporary religious practices in China, from the Mazu cult to the Ciji Merit Compassionate Relief Association in Taiwan.[21] Indeed, it is often remarked upon that women are essential transmitters of religious rites. In "Cultural and Network Capitals: Chinese Women and the 'Religious' Industry in South China," Kuah-Pearce notes that "women play an extremely important role in the reproduction of religious rituals. It is they who 'remembered' and negotiated the types of rituals that are required for domestic rituals and communal religious fairs. It is also they who are primarily involved in the preparation of the food offerings and religious paraphernalia for these occasions."[22] Do women play important roles in ritual practices related to Confucianism in today's China? Can we assess the situation empirically?

The revival of ritual practice related to Confucianism takes at least three forms today, and women play important roles in all of them. The first form consists of formal ceremonies conducted in Confucius temples. As Michael Nylan and Thomas Wilson have argued, since the tenth century "Confucius [has] figured in two overlapping cults": the imperial cult of Confucius, in which the Sage is venerated by the court and civil bureaucracy, and the ancestral cult of Confucius, in which Confucius is venerated as a "founding ancestor."[23]

The most notable ceremony in Confucius temples today is the official rites honoring the spirit of Confucius on his birthday, carried out in many newly renovated Confucius temples throughout China. It can be argued that this is a variation and continuation of the imperial and bureaucratic cult of Confucius. The most formal and prominent of such ceremonies takes place in the Confucius Temple in Qufu, Confucius's birthplace.[24] Since the official revival of these rites in 2004, women have been participating in the ceremonies, including female local officials attending the ceremony and young female students partaking in the rituals with their male counterparts. This is radically different from the traditional Confucius temple ceremonies in imperial China, which were restricted to court officials and Confucian literati, who were strictly male.[25]

Such new acceptance of women in ritual ceremonies can also be detected in the ancestral rites conducted by descendents of Confucius in recent years. These descendents belong to the privileged Kong ancestral clan ("Confucius" is *Kong-zi* in Chinese), a clan with a two-thousand-year genealogy and whose members reside in China as well as other parts of the world. Although the ancestral clan historically follows only the male lineage, today women can be seen at ancestral events, such as in the April 5, 2009, Spring Ancestral Rites that took place at the Qufu Confucius temple and the Confucius tomb nearby.[26] Even though men still dominate these ritual events, with women very much in the minority, the inclusion of women represents an enormous break from tradition.

Other formal ceremonies take place in Confucius temples today, such as the Opening the Brush Ceremony (for children about to start formal education in elementary school) and the Adulthood Ceremony (for adolescents about to enter young adulthood). These are not traditional rites, but rather newly invented rituals making use of the symbolic and cultural aspects of Confucian tradition to fulfill the needs of contemporary society, especially those of parents and schools trying to install a Confucian emphasis on learning and ethical values in the young. These events are attended by both girls and boys, young men and women; there is no discernable gender difference.

The second ritual form is what I call "personal rites" taking place in Confucius temples. These are mostly ritual practices performed by people who pray to Confucius for blessings on their exams, including exams and tests for professional certification. When entering a Confucius temple in China today, one might be surprised by how diverse and innovative the ritual practices are, a contrast to the austere and hierarchical place that Confucius temples have historically been.[27] There is incense to be burned in front of the statue of Confucius; there are prayer mats in front of the tablet of Confucius in the main hall, for people to kneel on and pray; there are also prayer cards for sale, little red note cards on which people write their wishes before hanging them either in trees or on designated wooden hangers outside the main hall of the temple.

At the Confucius temples I have studied, I have noted two groups of people who participate in the rituals taking place there: students who are about to take an important exam (especially the national university entrance exam) and parents and grandparents—mostly mothers and grandmothers—who go to the temple to pray for their children or grandchildren. In the first group of students, there isn't a clear gender difference; I have seen about the same number of each gender at the temples to pray. However, among the people who are not there to ask for blessings with one's own exam or job interview, women are in the majority. Women are at the temple to pray on behalf of their children or grandchildren, burn incense, donate money, and kneel in prayer. This is a radical departure from the traditional use and function of Confucius temples throughout imperial China, a "sacred ground" for Confucian cultural and social elites, consisting only of men.

The third form of ritual practice is what is generally referred to as ancestral worship, which takes place in ancestral shrines, at home in front of an ancestral alter, or at the grave site of a deceased family member. Now let us turn to the broad snapshot of religious practice offered by the 2007 Horizon Spiritual Life in China survey. Although we cannot answer the question of how ancestral rituals are conducted today without data from fieldwork, we can at least get a sense of whether people are participating in the rituals. Table 7.3 offers a summary of the answers to the question "In the past year, which ones of the following activities did you participate in?" That people did participate in the ancestral ritual of venerating the spirit of deceased ancestors by their graves is not surprising; however, what is surprising is the extraordinarily high percentage of people who traveled to the graves of their deceased family members—often back in their ancestral hometowns—in the past year. And there are about equal numbers of men and women who have participated in this ritual practice.

TABLE 7.3. The Horizon Survey: Religious Practice In China

Question: In the Past Year, Which of the Following Activities Did You Participate In?

Response	Gender		Total
	Male	Female	
Venerate ancestral spirits by their graves	2,383	2,360	4,743
Attend church services	36	61	97
Attend services in mosques	9	13	22
Attend formal services in Buddhist temples	8	12	20
Pray, worship, and/or burn incense in Buddhist temples	61	130	191
Attend formal services in Daoist temples	4	1	5
Pray, worship, and/or burn incense in Daoist temples	7	10	17
Pray, worship, and/or burn incense in Confucian temples	3	3	6
Pray, worship, and/or burn incense in ancestral temples	11	13	24
Pray, worship, and/or burn incense in other temples	19	35	54
Did not attend any such activities	814	963	1,777
Refused to answer	12	14	26
Don't know	14	25	39
Total	3,381	3,640	7,021

Source: Spiritual Life Study of Chinese Residents Survey, Horizon 2007.

CONCLUSION

Has Confucianism become a tradition in which women are occupying an increasing visible space and their voices are beginning to be heard? Scholars often view Confucian tradition as conservative, even detecting fundamentalism in Song and Ming Neo-Confucianism.[28] Are we seeing a transformation of the Confucian tradition in China today, based on these snapshots of women's presence in different areas of contemporary Confucian life?

And how do we account for the increasing presence of women in these spheres? Is Confucianism coming to terms with feminism in a postsocialist, postfeminist China? In his edited volume *The Sage and the Second Sex: Confucianism, Ethics, and Gender*, Chenyang Li suggests that there might be "important convergence between Confucian ethical thinking and feminist ethical thinking."[29] Li argues that Confucian ethics is a form of care ethics, which share many affinities with feminist ethics of care, and that "given that Confucianism and feminism are not essentially opposed, we have reason to think that feminism may encounter no more, or perhaps even less, resistance in the Confucian world than in the West."[30] Regardless of whether one agrees with his interpretation of Confucian ethics, this is an important question to consider, especially since the current revival of Confucianism is still a relatively new phenomenon in China and is very likely the beginning of a long-term development.

This is a question that scholars in other East Asian Confucian cultures have been considering as well. In "Gender Issues and Confucian Scriptures: Is Confucianism Incompatible with Gender Equality in South Korea?," Eunkang Koh shows that this is an ongoing debate that is necessary for a fruitful interpretation of Confucian texts, as well as for addressing adequately concerns regarding women's rights in a traditionally male-dominated society.[31] In today's China, with more women participating in the interpretation of the Confucian canon, the transformation of Confucian ideas into everyday life, and the practice of traditional Confucian rituals, will Confucianism eventually become a source of empowerment for women?

In her insightful article "Aristotelian Resources for Feminist Thinking," Deborah Achtenberg speaks of the importance of making use of Aristotle—regardless of the fact that he is "a paradigmatically sexist thinker":

> We find sources for feminist thought in surprising places, for many thinkers who in other respects are sexist nonetheless do not dichotomize reason and passion, or separateness and connectedness. In this essay, I will argue that Aristotle is a philosopher to whose work we may look for such resources for feminist thinking. This is, of course, in a way odd, since Aristotle is a paradigmatically sexist thinker. According to him, women are naturally inferior in the ability that is most definitively human, namely, the capacity for rational activity. Women have reason, he maintains, but it is not sovereign in them—that is, it does not govern their action. Hence, women must be ruled by their husbands (*Pol* I. 5 1254b13–14, I. 13 1260a12–13). Still, if we look to Aristotle's discussion of male development, we find him arguing for the centrality both of reason and passion for human development and for the importance both of relatedness and separation in human flourishing.[32]

And similar things may indeed be said about Confucius, as well as the many Confucian thinkers who came after the Master. After all, in our contemporary society the emphasis on the virtues of justice and benevolence is not reserved for men in Confucianism, nor in the cultural, academic, and social forums in which these ideas are discussed, nor in the ritual veneration of ancestors' spirits at the grave site of a beloved family member, a ritual of reverence revived and treasured, performed in the fresh air of the beginning of April, during the Festival of *Qingming*.[33]

CHAPTER 8

The Contemporary Revival and Reinvention of Confucian Ritual Practices

THE FOCUS OF THIS CHAPTER IS the personal rites performed in Confucius temples (*kongmao* or *wenmiao*) in different regions of China. In addition, I also briefly discuss the revival of graveside ancestral worship and certain Confucian social rituals. My primary methods are ethnographical, involving interviews and participant observations at Confucius temples. I have conducted interviews with visitors to a dozen Confucius temples in Mainland China, focusing on several regions: north (four temples in Beijing, Tianjin, Jinan, and Qufu), south (five temples in the historically literati Jiangnan region), southwest (three temples in Sichuan Province), and southeast (the ancestral temple complex in Foshan, Guangdong Province, which also houses a Confucius temple).[1] I have particularly followed the changes in the Beijing Confucius Temple, Shanghai Confucius Temple, and Foshan Confucius Temple over the past ten years.

In addition, I have conducted fieldwork at three Confucius temples in Taiwan.[2] The Confucius temple life in Taiwan provides a good comparison case, both echoing many of the practices seen in Mainland China and suggesting possible future directions that Confucius temple life in Mainland China might take. Related fieldwork includes visits to non-Confucius temples in which Confucius is also venerated, in both Mainland China and Taiwan.[3] I have also visited four Confucius temples in Japan, where fewer than ten Confucius temples remain in existence.[4]

At these temple sites, I have observed people's ritual actions and collected material objects related to personal rites, such as prayer cards and different items for blessing. Based on my fieldwork from 2000 to 2011, my conclusion is that ritual worship of Confucius is indeed undergoing a significant and diverse revival in temple settings in contemporary Mainland China. There are differences as well as similarities among the temples I have studied; this revival process is by no means uniform but is shaped by differences in local religious history, regional economic development, and the historical status of the temples.

The Revival of Ritual Practices in Confucius Temples

One of the most interesting historical accounts of Confucius temples is given by Matteo Ricci (1552–1610), the great Jesuit missionary of the seventeenth century:

> The real temple of the literati is that of Confucius, which by law is built for him in every city, in the place we call the school (*scuola*); it is very sumptuous, and attached to it was the palace of the magistrate who governs those who have already attained the first degree in letters. In the most prominent place in the temple stands the statue of Confucius, or his name excellently worked into a plaque in gold letters, and at his side the statues or names of his other disciples, who are moreover considered to be saints. To that place at every new moon and full noon come the magistrates of the city, with the above-mentioned graduates, to do honor to him with the usual genuflections, and they light candles to him and place incense in the censer placed before the altar. And likewise on the anniversary of his birth and at certain [other] times of the year, they offer him with great solemnity dead animals and other items to eat to thank him for the fine teachings which he left them in his books, by means of which they attained their magistracies or degrees; [they do this] without reciting any prayers to him or asking anything of him, just as we said concerning their dead.[5]

This account is typical of the Jesuits' position regarding the rites of Confucius and ancestral worship, which is that they are civil rather than religious rituals. Their opponents, such as Bishop Charles Maigrot, who participated in a General Congregation of the Holy Roman and Universal Inquisition in 1693, viewed it differently:

> In every city Confucius had buildings dedicated to him. These are not classrooms nor do they seem to be auditoriums, but rather chapels. In Chinese they are called *Miao*, which means temples of the idols. Some authors call these buildings temples or shrines.[6]

In other words, the Vatican saw Confucius temples as sites of idol worship and the rituals performed at the sites as pagan and religious rituals. What exactly are Confucius temples, and what kinds of rituals are performed there today?

In this section, I first give a brief history of Confucius temples in China, followed by an analysis of the current administrative status of the temples. I then offer an account of the spatial structure of the temple buildings and grounds. Next I give a detailed analysis of the rituals performed in Confucius temples in today's Mainland China, offering a typology of the rituals based on interviews and participant observations, with special attention paid to what I call "reinvented rituals." I end this section with a brief analysis of what I call the "religious ecology" of Confucius temples.

A Brief History of Confucius Temples in China

The first Confucius temple came into being in 479 BCE, when the Duke Ai of Lu, the ruler of the home state of Confucius, ordered Confucius's home in Qufu to be preserved and used as a temple for venerating the spirit of Confucius. There were only three simple rooms, fitting for a teacher who taught his students the importance of living a life of benevolence, justice, ritual, wisdom, and trust. Over the years, however, the temple became larger and more ornate, for rulers were gradually adopting the so-called cult of Confucius as a state cult, and the veneration and worship of Confucius became imperial events, with rulers and later emperors leading the ceremonies. Several hundred years later, in 489 AD, the first Confucius temple outside of Qufu was built by King Xiaowen of Northern Wei, marking the start of the practice of establishing temples for Confucius beyond Confucius's home state.

Throughout imperial China, especially after the incorporation of the Confucian canon into the foundation of state cultural and political ideology through the long-standing (605–1905) institution of civil examinations, Confucius temples became a key sacred site in imperial ritual practice, for the worship of Confucius had become an indispensible part of the legitimation of imperial rule.[7] Ceremonies honoring the spirit of Confucius were conducted in the original Confucius temple in Qufu—now a magnificent and imposing temple complex, a far cry from the original three simple rooms—by the emperors. And because of the close connection between Confucius worship and education, very often Confucian temples were attached to Confucian academies, following the tradition of *zuomiao youxue* (Confucius temple on the left, the academy on the right). The best-known example of such a structure is the Imperial Academy in Beijing (*guozijian*), built on the right side of the Confucius Temple in Beijing in 1306, a few years after the temple was built.

There were at least fifteen hundred Confucius temples spread throughout China by the end of the Qing dynasty in 1911. After the Republican Revolution in 1911, there was a failed attempt to make Confucianism into a national religion, which faded away by the end of the 1920s. Today there are only a few hundred Confucius temples left, following the destruction of religious sites during the Cultural Revolution (1966–76), during which many local Confucius temples either were destroyed or fell into disrepair.

Although the Chinese government included the Qufu Confucius Temple on the First National Cultural Heritage Sites List in 1961, it was not until 1988 that the second most important Confucius temple in the country, the Beijing Confucius Temple, was assigned similar status. Now there are at least thirty-nine Confucius temples that are protected as "national cultural heritage sites":

1961 First Cultural Heritage Sites List: Qufu Confucius Temple
1982 Second Cultural Heritage Sites List: no Confucius temples
1988 Third Cultural Heritage Sites List: Beijing Confucius Temple
1995 Forth Cultural Heritage Sites List: five Confucius temples
2001 Fifth Cultural Heritage Sites List: twelve Confucius temples
2006 Sixth Cultural Heritage Sites List: twenty Confucius temples

Once the temples are designated as national cultural heritage sites, there are strict regulations on construction and renovation, which are crucial in protecting the integrity of the original architecture. The designation also opens up more opportunities for the local governments to promote tourism.

To summarize, these are the key stages in the development of Confucius temples:

479 BCE

The Duke Ai of Lu, the ruler of the home state of Confucius, ordered Confucius's home in Qufu to be preserved and used as a temple venerating the spirit of Confucius.

489 CE

The first Confucius temple outside of Qufu was built by King Xiaowen of Northern Wei, which began the practice of establishing temples for Confucius beyond Confucius's home state.

605–1905

During this era of the civil examinations, temple structures became *zuomiao youxue*: Confucius Temple on the left, the academy on the right.

1911

At the end of the Qing dynasty and imperial China, there were about fifteen hundred Confucius temples throughout China.

1961

The Qu Fu Confucius Temple became the first to be on the National Cultural Heritage Sites List. In 1988 the Beijing Confucius Temple was added to the list.

2011

Now there are thirty-nine Confucius temples that are designated "national cultural heritage sites."

But even without the "national cultural heritage" designation, Confucius temples today are already tourist attractions in many provinces. The two most important ones, the Qufu and Beijing Temples, are routinely on popular tourist schedules for both domestic tourists and visitors from abroad, and in the past decade many provincial governments have been renovating their local Confucius temples in the hopes of attracting tourists to their regions. Such efforts have been financially supported by the state, for they serve both the economic purpose of generating new revenue for local governments through traditional cultural sites and the political goal of establishing Confucianism as the most visible Chinese cultural and social heritage. This is part of the larger endeavor undertaken by the state to promote Confucianism, which arguably started in 2004.

The Administrative Status of Confucius Temples

Administratively, Confucius temples are the property of the state and controlled by the State Administration of Cultural Heritage (SACH), which is an agency under the Ministry of Culture. In 1995, the Chinese National Association for the Protection of Confucius Temples, an organization managed by SACH, was established. Although it only had thirty-one members at its inception; as of 2011 it counted ninety Confucius temples as its members, which testifies to the rapid growth of newly renovated and reopened Confucius temples. The purpose of the association is to promote interactions among Confucius temples that are officially open to the public. The association holds annual meetings as well as training workshops for the temple management, and it also publishes books and journals related to the protection of Confucius temples and the general study of Confucianism.

SACH has numerous local branches in most provinces and cities, and the bureaucratic ties between these local branches and the local municipal governments are myriad and often complex. As a result, many of the temples I studied answer to both the local branches of SACH and one or more local agencies that are part of the municipal government, even though officially the temples are only under the auspices of SACH.

There is a surprising amount of variation in the organization of the financial structure of the temples. What is constant is the basic funding for the administration, maintenance, and renovation of the temple, which always comes from the state (both the central and the local governments). However, the day-to-day management of the temples seems to follow different trajectories of development, with certain temples following more strictly the so-called museum system (*bowuguanzhi*), which means that the temples are uninterested in how many visitors they attract since they receive fixed amounts of funding and salaries from the state regardless of how popular (or unpopular) the temple is (such as Suzhou Confucius Temple), whereas certain temples follow a more entrepreneurial model (*shiye danwei*), promoting individual ritual practice in the temples (such as incense burning and prayer cards) and group ritual activities (such as Adulthood Ceremony) for the sake of attracting more visitors as well as bringing in additional income for the temple. The best example of a temple following the entrepreneurial model is the Nanjing Confucius Temple, which will be analyzed in detail.

Based on my interviews, the differences seem to come from the ways the temples are defined by the local SACH and the local municipal agencies in charge of it; in other words, some local governments define Confucius temples as purely museum sites, whereas others are more open about its financial possibilities. Among the twelve temples in Mainland China I have studied, about 25 percent are quite openly entrepreneurial, which includes the Nanjing Confucius Temple, the Foshan Confucius Temple, and the Shanghai Confucius Temple.

It is very interesting that these temples also happen to be the more vibrant sites for ritual practices. The degree of promotion of old as well as new rituals by the temples has much to do with the financial structure of the individual temples; the temples with a more flexible financial structure (i.e., with the freedom to keep extra temple income for the temple employees instead of turning it over to the government) have a stronger incentive to sell incense and prayer cards, and as a result employees encourage more ritual practices.

Among the temples I studied, besides the one outliner (the Wujiang Confucius Temple that is now housed in a high school and does not have a formal museum status), there are only two temples that are managed as purely museum sites, which are the Suzhou Confucius Temple (it doubles as a museum for an extensive art collection of stone-engraved calligraphy) and the Zizhong Confucius Temple (it is located in a very remote part of Sichuan Province and has virtually no visitors). There is little or no ritual practice promoted in these two temples.

The majority of temples—about 50 percent—I studied, including the most famous ones such as the Qufu and Beijing Confucius Temples, fall into the middle of the two models, meaning that they are interested in promoting ritual practice and group ritual activities, yet they are also required by the administrative agencies to sustain the appearance of a museum site.[8] They must maintain a delicate balance, especially when it comes to the selling of incenses, prayer cards, and other ritual objects, and the promotion of group ritual activities.

Since all Confucius temples belong to SACH, the temples are officially classified not as religious sites but as cultural ones, charging a modest entrance fee at the gate the way museums do. But this status does not necessarily hinder either the official ritual ceremonies or the personal ritual practices taking place in Confucius temples. In fact, since they are not managed by the State Administration of Religious Affairs, the temples are relatively free to develop new ways of increasing visitor traffic and income, as long as they can retain the right balance between their museum status and entrepreneurial support of ritual activities.

THE STRUCTURE OF CONFUCIUS TEMPLES

Where and how are rituals performed at a Confucius Temple? It is important to have a sense of the spatial layout of the temples in order to comprehend the ritual practices that take place. The general layout of Confucius temples follows a template based on the original Confucius Temple in Qufu. However, since the Qufu Temple is one of the three largest existing historical architectural complexes in China today, having been expanded and renovated numerous times throughout history (its scale is second only to the Forbidden City in Beijing), it is impossible for local temples to emulate its grandeur.

Most surviving Confucius temples today are not enormous complexes, and as such they are able to keep only the key components as dictated by the Qufu Temple, imitating its structure rather than scale. For instance, while the Qufu Temple has nine courtyards following a central line, most Confucius temples only have two or three courtyards, maintaining only the most crucial elements.

When one enters a Confucius temple, one has to walk though the main gate into the temple complex, named the Lingxing Gate, which leads to the main courtyard, where Dacheng Hall, the main ceremonial hall, is the architectural focal point of both the courtyard and the entire temple. When one enters Dacheng Hall, which is a traditional temple space with an elaborately carved high wooden altar in the center, one usually sees inside the altar a wooden tablet that bears the venerated formal title of Confucius, representing Confucius himself, as in the Beijing Confucius Temple. However, there are variations on this tradition; for instance, a large stone statue replaces the traditional tablet and altar in the Zizhong Confucius Temple in Sichuan, which is a very exceptional case; in the Foshan Confucius Temple, a dark stone relief depicting the image of Confucius stands behind the tablet. Only in the Qufu Confucius Temple do we find both the tablet and a statue: an ornate statue of Confucius is placed right behind the wooden tablet.

On each side of the Confucius tablet and/or statue are tablets of Mencius (often referred to as the "Second Sage" of Confucianism), Yan Hui and Zengzi (two of the most important students of Confucius's; Zengzi is also believed to have written *The Classic of Filial Piety*), and Zishi (Confucius's grandson, whose importance lies in the fact that Mencius might have studied with his students).

The Dacheng Hall is generally where the worship of Confucius takes place, along with the open space in the courtyard right in front of the hall, where a large incense burner is always placed. The open courtyard is often also the space in which the prayer cards are hung on wooden shelves right outside of the Dacheng Hall.

There are usually two smaller halls flanking Dacheng Hall that serve as additional ceremonial spaces in the same rectangular courtyard, often for the altars of the most important students of Confucius's and the most revered scholars of Confucianism from later dynasties. There are usually another one or two courtyards surrounding the main courtyard, frequently used for exhibition spaces, offices, and the temple shop; the temple shops have played an unexpected yet important role in the revival and reinvention of rituals. Very often the temples also have a man-made pond (*banchi*), a high, grand, outer brick wall painted crimson (*wanren gongqiang*), and other architectural features with references to Confucius's life as well as traditions from the long history of Confucius temples in imperial China.

In the open spaces between these sets of buildings, one can often see well-designed gardens with ancient trees growing by the ceremonial halls. This is where one can usually find a tall statue of Confucius made of stone, in a standing pose known as Confucius Teaching (*kongzi xingjiao*). The statue is placed in different locations in different temples (for example, in the center of the courtyard in Shanghai Confucius Temple, and beside the temple in Foshan), and generally has an incense burner right in front of it.

RITUAL PRACTICES IN CONFUCIUS TEMPLES

I have observed at least three main forms of ritual practices performed by individuals in Confucius temples in Mainland China:

1. Burning incense;
2. Praying to the tablet, the statue, or the portrait of Confucius (bowing or kneeling);
3. Writing prayers on prayer cards (*xuyuan qian*) that hang in the trees or on special shelves within the temple.

The frequency of the performance of these rituals varies greatly from temple to temple, mostly due to their locations and visitor traffic. Among the sites I have studied, the ones where the most rituals are performed are in the center of urban areas, such as the Beijing, Nanjing, Foshan, and Shanghai Temples. The Qufu Temple in Confucius's birthplace also receives a tremendous amount of visitors every year, which leads to constant performances of rituals. The ones with the least ritual activity are in general located in remote regions, such as the Zizhong Temple in Sichuan Province, which is in a small town a two-hour drive outside of a cosmopolitan area.

Among the twelve temples in Mainland China I've studied, in only two temples did I not detect any ritual activity. The first is the Bishan Confucius Temple in the small city of Bishan in Sichuan Province, which I visited in May 2010. It was a temple with fading paint and deteriorating roof in need of extensive restoration. Unlike the other temples I've studied, it was no longer a museum site but a site housing several local cultural institutions: the Bishan Bureau of Culture Heritage, the Bishan City Museum, and the Bishan Association of Literature and History.

Most unexpectedly, Dacheng Hall, the main ceremonial hall, had been rented out as the site for a traditional teahouse, a popular gathering place for local men—more than half of whom were retired or elderly—to meet, talk, play Chinese chess, and read newspapers. During my visit, I counted at least sixty men in the teahouse on a weekday afternoon, which had the relaxed atmosphere of an old-time men's social club. The hall also served as a space for public lectures on local culture and history, an innovative measure of bringing in extra income, according to Mr. He, the manager of the teahouse. It was unclear when the temple would be renovated and restored to its proper status as a temple for Confucius.

The second temple that displayed no ritual activity was the Wujiang Confucius Temple in Zhejiang Province, which I visited in December 2010. The small Confucius temple was difficult to find, for it was entirely enclosed within Wujiang High School, an elite high school in the region and a compound of modern buildings built around the temple site. The temple itself was used as a reading room and library, with tables and chairs in Dacheng Hall, although it seemed quite underutilized by students and teachers. The temple grounds were fairly well preserved, but it was not open to the public, and I observed no ritual practice.

RITUAL APPARATUS IN CONFUCIUS TEMPLES

So how do people carry out rituals in these temples? In the interior ceremonial space of Dacheng Hall, the following ritual apparatus can be found in most Confucius temples, listed in descending order of distance from the entrance of the ceremonial hall, which corresponds to specific rituals performed:

1. A narrow high table for offerings to Confucius, placed right in front of the altar of Confucius, which is used for official sacrifices during

formal ceremonies, and personal offerings of flowers, fruits, and other items during private rituals, which today include prayer cards sold in temple shops. Such offerings are usually presented after a person bows to the altar and says a silent prayer.
2. An incense burner for the offering of incense (in almost all temples the incense cannot be lighted due to fire regulations). People usually buy incense from the temple shop or from the ticketing agent at the temple gate.
3. A few prayer mats for people who wish to kneel in prayer and/or touch their forehead to the ground in prayer.

Outside of the interior spaces, there are other opportunities for ritual practices in the temples:

1. The incense burner in front of the standing statue of Confucius in the courtyard.
2. The wooden shelves right outside of Dacheng Hall, or the trees in the courtyards (such as in Foshan), where people hang their prayer cards.

In other words, there are multiple religious spaces as well as apparatus that make the ritual practices possible; these spaces and equipment are important aspects of the revival and reinvention of religious rituals, which is true not only in Confucius temples, but in other temples as well.

The Invention of Prayer Cards

The prayer cards in Confucius temples are a new phenomenon. They did not exist in Confucius temples in imperial China, and they did not exist in Confucius temples until the beginning of the twenty-first century. My fieldwork suggests that they are indeed a newly invented ritual apparatus, and their origin can be traced back to influences from Japan. The prayer cards seen in different Confucius temples in China today look strikingly similar to the *ema* found in most Shinto temples in Japan. Ema are wooden tablets bearing the name of the Shinto temple or god on one side and written wishes desired from the god on the other. They are of comparable size (a prayer card and an ema is roughly the size of one's palm) and function (an object on which wishes desired from a god are written). There are two notable differences between the Confucius temple prayer cards and the Shinto ema: First, the Confucius ones are made of paper, whereas the Shinto ones are made of wood; second, the Confucius temple cards are usually red, whereas the Shinto ema are the natural color of wood.

According to Ms. Ai-Zhen Wang, the director of the Shanghai Confucian Temple Administration Office, whom I interviewed on December 24, 2010, the prayer cards were in fact invented in 2002. After taking a trip to Japan in early 2000, Ms. Wang was inspired by the prayer cards (ema in Japanese) she saw in Japanese Shinto temples and brought the idea back to the Confucius Temple in Shanghai, where she had worked since 1999. She believed that the Shanghai Confucius Temple was the first of all Confucius temples in China to provide and sell such prayer cards, for in 2002 she was asked to give a presentation about the innovative ways the Shanghai temple attracted visitors at the annual conference of the Chinese National Association for the Protection of Confucius Temples.

I suggest that these prayer cards are different from what are often called "paper offerings" in Chinese ritual practice, which refer to "objects made of paper, many of them handmade and one of a kind, which are offered to the beings residing beyond the world of the living: the gods, the ghosts, and the ancestors," according to anthropologist Janet Lee Scott. In her research, Scott shows that "nearly all these paper items are burned in order to reach their destination in the other world. This burning is a vital component of both public and private worship during religious holidays and during everyday life."[9] Unlike the items burned in "paper offerings," the paper-made prayer cards in Confucius temples are meticulously displayed in public, either on wooden shelves made for this specific purpose right outside of the main temple hall (very similar to the way ema prayer cards are hung in Shinto temples) or on tree branches.

Several Confucius temple managers remarked in interviews that they have to carefully take down the prayer cards every few months in order to free up space on the wooden shelves as well as in the trees. When there are too many cards on trees, such as right after the Chinese New Year, which is a popular time for visits to temples, there are also concerns about the safety of the trees: the branches might break off under the weight of thousands of prayer cards. This is especially the case at the Foshan Confucius Temple.

One temple manager mentioned that the cards that have been taken down (tens of thousands of them) are stored in a back room of the temple. Such a statement signifies the importance of the physical existence of the prayer cards; unlike paper offerings, they seem to function as ritual objects only when they are displayed in the temples, or at least stored on temple ground.

PRAYERS TO CONFUCIUS

What do people ask for in their prayers? Do they come to temples merely to pay respect to Confucius, the ancient sage of virtue and wisdom?

Among the visitors I have interviewed, many were indeed at the temples to pay respect to the Master and to admire the classical architecture that the Confucius temples are justifiably known for. For the most part they are tourists, for whom the Confucius temple is a regular stop on a tour of Beijing or Nanjing. However, the people who actually perform rituals—such as burning incense, bowing or kowtowing in front of the tablet or statue of Confucius, and writing and hanging prayer cards—are carrying out these acts with a different purpose in mind: to ask for blessings from Confucius, the god of learning and examinations and, by extension, career advancement and general good fortune.

Many tourists do in fact perform such rituals as well; there is a long-standing tradition in China of carrying out ritual practices during travels, which brings people to religious sites in cities or mountains—often they are famous cultural sites as well—that they otherwise would not have easy access to.[10] The frequency of the performance of these rituals varies greatly not only from temple to temple but also according to the time of the year; the most popular period is right before the very competitive national university entrance examinations in early June, a time when many students and their parents and grandparents visit temples to ask for blessings.

It is important to note that there is a common thread that runs through prayers uttered at Confucius temples and temples in other traditions. Making a request to a god and thanking the god for fulfilling a wish afterward—"the making and repaying of vows" (*xuyuan huanyuan*)—is a practice found not only at Confucius temples, which I have observed, but also at Buddhist temples as well as temples for local deities, such as the Hanzu (Patriarch Han) temple in north China studied by Overmyer.[11] As Overmyer remarks, this is in fact one of the most important ritual practices in Chinese religious life:

> [F]or ordinary people one of the most basic rituals carried out at festivals is the making and repaying of vows to a deity (*xu yuan, huan huan*) by a worshipper making a requite for aid and promising a grateful response if the request is granted. The requests can be for healing, success in farming, business or school, or for the birth of a child. The god is promised that he or she will be given a gift if the petition is granted, such as a new robe, repair of its shrine or new gilding for its image. For such a ritual the worshiper offers sticks of incense before the god's image, then bows to pray for aid, and promises a specific response if the request is granted.[12]

Among the prayers offered on prayer cards, the most typical ones are the following:[13]

> Dear Confucius, please help me be successful in my college entrance examination, and help me attend such and such university.[14]

> Dear Confucius, please help me be successful in my graduate school examination (or law school examination, or TOFEL examination, or GRE examination, or professional licensing such as electrician's license examination).[15]
>
> Dear Confucius, please help my child be successful in his/her college entrance examination.
>
> Dear Confucius, please help me (or my child) be a good student, and be successful in student life.
>
> Dear Confucius, I will offer thanks to you [by returning here with symbolic gifts such as incense] if I am successful in my examination.
>
> Dear Confucius, Please bless my family with good health, great fortunate, and longevity.

In fact, the prayers can be quite uniform, the result of people copying each other's prayer cards by reading the existing prayer cards before submitting their own. In one instance, the uniformity of prayers on prayer cards at Shanghai Confucius temple apparently resulted from the coaching of the elderly sales woman in the gift shop who sold prayer cards; she had been instructing people how to write their prayers to Confucius.

There are some variations to these prayers, such as prayers asking for success in romantic love ("Dear Confucius, please bless us and let us be together forever"), although these are quite atypical.

To summarize, based on my interviews and content analysis of prayer cards, I have found generally two types of people who perform rituals at Confucius temples:

1. People who go to the temples specifically for the purpose of asking for blessings from Confucius, especially blessings on their exams, such as students who are about to take the national university entrance examination and their parents, or people who are about to take other exams for professional reasons (such as the graduate school exam, the civil servant exam, or even the exam for an electrician's license). These people are mostly residents of the areas where the temples are located.

2. People who perform rituals when they are visiting a temple as tourists; they ask not only for blessings for exams but also for more general blessings, such as good health, happy relationships, and financial fortune.

Interestingly, according to my interviews, people who perform rituals and ask for blessings in Confucius temples do not in general consider themselves to be "Confucians" (*rujiaotu*). This category is alien to them, and it is a moot one anyway: people frequently go to other temples to ask for blessings as well, especially the temples in which another god of learning from the Daoist tradition, Wenchang Dijun, can be worshipped; this is an even more popular phenomenon in Taiwan.

The truth is that people do not find it problematic at all to ask for blessings from different gods and deities, a common attitude toward ritual practice in China. In fact, people might be more likely to go to a Confucius temple to ask for blessings if there are other temples in its vicinity, such as in Foshan, where the Confucius temple is housed within a Daoist temple complex, making it easy for people to ask for blessings from different deities during a single outing or at festival time, such as on the day of the Chinese New Year.

Do People Believe in the Existence of the Spirit of Confucius?

One of the most intriguing discoveries of my interviews at Confucius temples is that, when people performing different rituals for blessings they are asked whether they think Confucius is a god or spirit or whether they "believe in" the power of Confucius, the most common type of answer is "I don't know" or "I am an ordinary person, and these are things I don't know much about." Only on rare occasions did people say, "I think Confucius might be a god and might have supernatural power, otherwise people wouldn't build temples and pray to him." Another typical answer is "Confucius is a great teacher, and that's why I'm here asking the Sage for help," which seems to be contradictory: if Confucius has no supernatural power, why would one pray to him in the first place? Surely one doesn't usually pray to someone who is merely a virtuous teacher? There have also been people who claim "Confucius is not a god; I am here to pay the Sage respect, not to worship him," even when they have just been observed offering incense or a prayer card for blessings.

What is the rationale behind the ritual actions in Confucius temples? It seems to be unnecessary to debate whether these actions are "veneration" or "worship," for these are secondary labels that hinder rather than help us with a nuanced understanding of the actual ritual practices being performed. The issue here is the fact that people appear to be surprisingly uninterested in having a firm belief in the divinity or supernatural power of Confucius. Do people actually believe in the existence of the spirit of Confucius when they pray to him? The apparent gap between the lack of avowed belief and the actual ritual practice indeed makes it difficult to understand the nature of prayers to Confucius; no wonder Catholic missionaries in China in the sixteenth and seventeenth centuries had very different interpretations of the meaning of ritual practice in Confucius temples, with the Jesuits emphasizing its "civil" nature and the others seeing it as clearly pagan idolatry.

This is an issue that bothers not only scholars of Confucianism, but also scholars of Chinese religions in general. In his extensive study of popular religion in contemporary China, *Miraculous Response*, Adam Chau addressed "the problem of religious belief" before discussing the culturally and sociopolitically embedded religious habitus of the Shaanbei people he studied: "Rodney Needham has famously asserted that unless a culture has a set of vocabulary to express and talk about religious belief we cannot assume that this culture has such things as belief or the people actually 'experience belief.' To all of these I would add that even if the natives have a language for belief and really believe what they say they believe, we might still have the problem of explicating the nature of that belief."[16]

The historian Paul Veyne famously asked, "Did the Greeks believe in their mythology?" His own reply: "The answer is difficult, for 'believe' means so many things."[17] Do the Chinese believe in the power of Confucius in helping them with academic examinations? How could someone not believe in the existence of the spirit of Confucius yet still ask for blessings from him? Is it possible to half-believe?

> How is it possible to half-believe, or believe in contradictory things? . . . It is necessary to recognize that, instead of speaking of beliefs, one must actually speak of truth, and that these truths were themselves products of the imagination. . . . There was a time when poets and historians invented royal dynasties all of a piece, complete with the name of each potentate and his genealogy. They were not forgers, nor were they acting in bad faith. They were simply following what was, at the time, the normal way of arriving at the truth.[18]

And the "normal way of arriving at the truth" is a historical and social reality, similar to the "regime of truth" described by Foucault.[19] Truth is a product of complex social, cultural, institutional, political, economic, and material realities; what is considered "true" is always part of the "regime of truth" that makes it possible.

In the case of ritual life in Confucius temples, there has indeed been a particular "normal way of arriving at the truth" at work, made possible by the thousand-year-old legacy of the civil examination system in imperial China, which consisted of a particular institutional and cultural structure in which ascendant social mobility was gained through Confucian learning and rigorous examination. It was in this context that Confucius became a kind of patron saint to people who sought success in the highly competitive examinations. The ritual practice seen in Confucius temples today is the revival of the long-standing social practice of seeking and finding reassurance and solace from traditional rituals such as offering incense and prayers to Confucius.

Do people who pray to Confucius actually have belief in the supernatural power of Confucius's spirit? This is indeed a wrong question to ask; the right question is, does it make sense to people who pray to Confucius that they are offering their prayers without having a firm or clearly articulated belief in the divinity or supernatural power of Confucius? The answer seems to be an unqualified yes.

THE ECOLOGY OF CONFUCIUS TEMPLES

How do we explain the different levels of intensity of ritual practice in different Confucius temples? Why do certain temples have a more robust ritual life? Many factors seem to be at work: the physical location of the temple (urban center vs. rural location); whether the temple is a popular tourist site (the confluence of tourist sites and religious sites);[20] the availability of ritual apparatus (which varies greatly from temple to temple); the structure of temple finances (whether it is run as purely a museum site or more of an entrepreneurial site); the existence of local religious custom and religious habitus (whether there is a strong tradition in the region to pray to various deities for blessings); and the existence of other temples nearby (whether there are temples in the surrounding area of the Confucius temple that allow for similar ritual practices).

In order to make sense of this complex dynamic, a metaphor of ecology is needed, instead of a metaphor of rigid structures and boundaries. As Vincent Goossaert and David Palmer have suggested, the religious ecology model "takes a holistic view to describe all forms of religiosity with a community, from communal temples to the Three Teachings of Confucianism, Taoism, and Buddhism; Christianity; and Islam. Such an approach is a significant advance, breaking out of the narrow definitions that have long constrained the discourse on religion in China, and looking at the interrelations between different forms of religious practice and social organization."[21]

There are many possible ways to utilize the ecological metaphor in understanding religious practice; here I mention only the two that are connected to my study of Confucius temples. The first is the ecology of temple life: the ways religious organizations and sites coexist through competition as well as codependence and interdependence. This may lead to studies of ecologies of local temple life, which examine not only how temples coexist and thrive (or fail) together in a region but also the linked ecologies of local social, political, and cultural life.[22]

The second is the ecology of religious traditions: the ways beliefs, rituals, and ritual apparatus are circulated in different religious traditions throughout Chinese society. A study of the ecology of Chinese religious traditions will lead to a more nuanced understanding of the way different religious and ritual traditions coexist in Chinese society. The emphasis here is on the coexistence and interdependence of temples, shrines, ritual practices, and ritual apparatus since people do not need to choose between one or the other in their religious life, but can practice many different things at once.

Indeed, as the philosopher Daniel Garber, who specializes in the relations among philosophy, science, and society during the Scientific Revolution, once remarked, the matter with ritual practice is not "why," but "why not."

From Traditions and Orthodoxy to Reinventions and Creativity

In this analysis, I emphasize personal ritual practices taking place in Confucius temples today, paying close attention to the actual rituals performed by people who visit the temples, without making value judgments about whether these are "original" or "authentic" or "correct" ritual practices. Although the complex issue of authenticity is a meaningful one in philosophical, theological, and historical contexts, the purpose of this sociological study is different; I am trying to capture the existence of actual practices carried out by real people in the real world, without judging whether they conform to any criteria of "authentic Confucian rituals."

In fact, since I do not hold an essentialist position regarding ritual performances, which regards only certain rituals as authentic and treats others as false or problematic, I view all rituals performed by people as legitimate, and I accept their own interpretations for the meaning of these rituals as legitimate. If a prayer is offered to Confucius in a temple devoted to Confucius, regardless of whether the prayer takes the form of either traditional incense burning or a prayer written on a newly invented prayer card, I view it as a Confucian prayer. Since such rituals do not conform to the historical ceremonial practices performed in temples controlled by literary and political elites in imperial China, some observers have been inclined to demean them as merely folk rituals and deny them the status of being Confucian. Such judgments assume that there is a correct or orthodox form of Confucius temple life as opposed to the constantly changing and developing character of any living religious tradition.

But how significant are these reinventions of Confucian ritual? While it is true that only the future will tell if they can survive in the hurly-burly world of modern Confucianism in China, they nevertheless have much to tell us about people's growing need for a life that is made meaningful by connecting with traditions that belong to the past as well as the future.

The Revival of Confucian Social Rituals

In addition to ancestral worship and ritual activities at Confucius temples, a surprising array of new rituals related to Confucianism is practiced in today's China. These new practices, which I call social rituals, range from the teaching of the classical Confucian canon to the teaching of Confucian behavior on the basis of an ancient manual for students, and from the revival of traditional ways of dressing to the invention of Confucian weddings. Here I offer only a few examples of this diverse and vibrant movement.

The emergence of after-school courses that teach children the basic texts of the Confucian canon as well as small, private Confucian academies that aim to replace the standard, state-run elementary and high school education are two noticeable recent developments that carry ritual components, for there are specific social rituals related to Confucian teacher-student relations, which emphasize the utmost respect for the teacher through manners and speech, as well as the veneration of Confucius.[23]

The classical text *Rules for Students and Children* (*dizi gui*), written by a seventeenth-century scholar as a simple manual for cultivating Confucian virtues such as filial piety, moderation, and benevolence in children, has been gaining a startling amount of popularity in China today. The *Rules* list clearly how one should act in the following social situations: expressing filial piety toward one's parents; interacting with one's siblings and elders with respect; behaving responsibly in everyday routines, such as having the correct behavior when one sits, walks, and speaks; interacting with others in society according to the virtues of trust, charity, and benevolence; approaching study and learning with the correct social manners as well as the correct state of mind. The *Rules* are now widely read in elementary schools, and there are various versions available in bookstores and online, from cartoon renditions to video clips with musical accompaniment, all for the purpose of getting the Confucian message across to children and teaching them how to behave properly in relation to their elders, superiors, and peers in everyday life.

However, the *Rules* are meant not just for children; there are also articles, books, and lectures for adults who are interested in a more rigorous and upright moral life. Interestingly, discussions of the *Rules* are more often than not found in forums promoting Buddhism. In this context, the *Rules* seem to be used for self-control—a handbook or code for learning how to behave in an appropriately moral way—with Buddhism as the ultimate religious teaching.

Other newly developed social rituals are a bit more surprising, such as the recent invention of Confucian wedding rituals, which seem to be gaining popularity among young people. In such a wedding ceremony, couples bow to a large portrait of Confucius hanging in the banquet hall and repeat their vows in front of the portrait, with the portrait serving as the functional equivalent of an altar in a religious wedding ceremony. Also, the attendants wear ancient robes, giving the ceremony a historical flair. This is certainly something new in China; no portrait of Confucius is ever present in traditional Chinese wedding ceremonies, even though many of the social rituals taking place—such as bowing or kowtowing to the parents during traditional wedding ceremonies—can be seen as expressions of Confucian virtues, such as filial piety.

Another innovation is a Confucian-themed ceremony for the renewal of marriage vows. As mentioned in chapter 3, in 2004, 180 married couples participated in a marriage renewal ceremony in Beijing, organized by the Chinese Association for the Study of Confucius. The couples, attired in formal jackets and white wedding dresses, recited a written Manifesto of True Marital Love in front of the statue of Confucius, vowing they would always be faithful to each other and never divorce. The event attracted media attention as well as online commentary, which ranged from incredulous to admiring.[24]

A more recent example of this new tradition is a wedding that took place on May 22, 2010, in Shenzhen, a high-tech and financial center near Hong Kong, which received a great deal of media attention. About eighty people were involved in the Confucian ceremonial performance, including a professional "Confucian sacred music choir," performing music composed for the occasion, and "Confucian ritual attendants" wearing lavish traditional "Confucian costumes" guiding the wedding procession through the most fashionable streets of the city. The newlyweds exchanged their vows in front of a shrine to Confucius, against the background of a large portrait of Confucius, which had a tablet placed in the center. The couple received a "Confucian marriage certificate" at the ceremony.

These two events share at least two remarkable aspects. First, as in the renewal of marital vows ceremony in 2004, all the so-called Confucian rituals in the 2010 wedding, including the music, the choir, the attendants, the procession, the actual wedding ceremony with offerings to Confucius, and even the style of the costume, are new inventions. They were made up for the occasion from various cultural, social, and religious sources, from classical Confucian texts to images of classical China in popular culture, from the structure of Christian weddings to elements from traditional Chinese weddings (the new couple's bowing to heaven, earth, ancestral spirits, and their parents).

Second, both ceremonies were spearheaded by institutions actively involved in the revival of Confucian tradition as well as the invention of new ways to make Confucianism an essential part of contemporary Chinese life. The 2004 renewal of marital vows ceremony was organized by the Chinese Association for the Study of Confucius, and the 2010 wedding was organized by Shenzhen *kongsheng tang* (Confucius Hall), a new and innovative Confucian institution founded in 2009. Its website introduces the institution as a "sacred space" for promoting Confucianism; it has a Confucius temple as well as lecture space, and it intends to hold classes, organize associations for Confucian Merchants, and eventually build a Confucian academy.[25] Among the ritual ceremonies it organizes (or plans to organize) are Confucian weddings, funerals, naming ceremonies, and inauguration ceremonies. Most strikingly, it has a weekly formal Confucian service, which consists of the singing of "sacred songs," a sermon, and the "reading of sacred text." This is clearly modeled on formal services in the Christian tradition, a very new and intriguing development for Confucianism indeed.

In Sébastien Billioud's recent study of Confucian revival in China, he discovered a nonprofit association in Beijing, Yidan Xuetang, which "engaged in the promotion of self-cultivation teachings based on traditional culture and Confucianism."[26] He defines such associations as *jiaohua* (transformation of the self and of the others by teaching) organizations, which is a category beyond the religious and secular distinction of social groups. His research points out that there is the "possible emergence of larger-scale organizations," such as Confucian NGOs, in China's future.[27]

Where is Confucianism going from here? When I first began conducting research on Confucian ritual practice in 2000, it was an obscure subject. At the time there were only a few signs of the revival of ritual life in the Confucian tradition. That was then. Today, when heated debates on Confucianism rage among Chinese intellectuals, when Confucianism has become a tool of the state, and when ordinary people are actively reviving Confucian rituals in Confucius temples, what is clear is that something powerful is emerging in the newly dynamic Confucian tradition in China.

As the intellectual debates gradually fade, popular Confucian rituals are dramatically on the rise. Nor has this popularity of multiple Confucian revivals escaped the attention of the state. We have seen how state-sponsored Confucianism has five basic dimensions—cultural, ideological, ritualistic, symbolic, and political—of which domestic politics may in the long run prove to be the most important. It may fairly be asked whether Confucianism might not develop in a comparatively weak political direction, as a de facto civil religion, as a cultural resource for nationalism, and as a form of life for people I have called "cultural Confucians," that is, people who endorse Confucian moral values and Confucian social practices. These developments make it not implausible to suppose that, for China, the twenty-first century may prove to be the Confucian century.

CHAPTER 9

The Politics of the Future of Confucianism

HERE ARE THREE SNAPSHOTS OF recent events related to Confucianism that might hold the key to our understanding of the future of Confucianism in China.

The first snapshot is the latest edition of the *Annual Report on China's Religions* (2010). It is published annually by the prestigious Social Sciences Academic Press as part of an official series on the state of religion in China. Here is what the "Table of Contents" page presents:

Reports on the Major Religions:

The Development of Buddhism and Its Dilemma in a Commercial Age
Chinese Taoist Culture and Education in 2009
A Survey of Chinese Islam in 2009
Observations on Chinese Catholicism in 2009
The State of Chinese Protestant Christianity in 2009
Report on Confucianism (*rujiao*): Forms of Confucianism in Folk
    Culture
The Revival of Traditions and Beliefs in Chinese Folk Religions[1]

Although this is not the first time Confucianism has been listed under "Major Religions," it is the most recent and the most noticeable. Is this a sign that Confucianism is under consideration by the Chinese state to become "a major religion," joining the other Five Major Religions, which are all represented in the report?

The second snapshot is the thirty-one-foot bronze statue of Confucius that was erected in front of the National History Museum on Tiananmen Square in Beijing in January 2011. According to the *Economist*, "A week before President Hu Jintao's visit to America on January 18th [2011] the appearance of a giant bronze statue of Confucius on the east side of Tiananmen Square caused a stir in the Chinese capital. He is the first non-revolutionary to be commemorated on the hallowed ground of Chinese communism. The party, having once vilified the ancient sage, now depends on him in its attempts at global rebranding. . . . During his trip to America, Mr. Hu hopes Confucius will help him connect with ordinary Americans."[2]

On April 21, 2011, however, the giant bronze statue suddenly disappeared overnight. Everyone was in shock. In an article titled "Confucius Stood Here, but Not for Very Long," the *New York Times* reported, "[A] spokesman for the museum, which had unveiled the statue with great fanfare, said he had no idea what had happened."[3] A day later, on April 22, *Beijing Evening News* reported that the statue had been moved inside the National Museum, which will be displayed "along with other statues of celebrities." In the same article, a researcher at the Institute of Literature at the Chinese Academy of Social Sciences was interviewed and called the move "the right step to take": "Although Confucianism is an essential part of Chinese culture, it cannot sum up all the values and ideals that modern China represents and aspires for."[4]

The third snapshot is the so-called "Qufu Church Controversy." On December 12, 2010, Xinhua News Agency reported that a new Protestant church was about to be built in Qufu. An article titled "Jesus to Join Confucius as Qufu Plans Church" stated that this would be the first "real church" for the nearly ten thousand Christians in Qufu, since they have had only a "makeshift building," capable of seating only seven to eight hundred people. The new church would be able to hold three thousand and would cost about $3 million to build. Its foundation had already been laid in July 2010, and the planning of the building had been going on for years, with the church receiving government land use permission in 2001. Kong Xiangling, a pastor for the Qufu Protestant Church and a seventy-fifth-generation descendent of Confucius, said that "although building a church in China is nothing new, it means a lot since the Christian church is to be built in Confucius' hometown, a symbol of Chinese civilization."[5]

On December 22, 2010, ten well-known Confucian scholars, known as the Confucian Ten Scholars, published an open letter protesting the building of the church in what they called "the sacred city" of Qufu, Confucius's birthplace and home to the most majestic Confucius temple in the world. The letter was supported by ten Confucian associations and ten Confucian websites. Written in a learned half-classical, half-colloquial style, the letter stated, "When we hear that there is going to be a 40-meter-high [130 feet] church built for three thousand people near the Qufu Confucius Temple, we are shocked and dismayed as Confucian scholars and associations. We beseech you to respect this sacred land of Chinese culture, and stop the building of the Christina church at once."[6]

Two days later, there was an official response from the government in the form of an editorial from the Xinhua News Agency, which stated that there was historical precedence for the building of Christian churches in

Qufu. This response did nothing to calm the gathering storm. Numerous online postings appeared, some supporting the Confucian Ten (with titles such as "Qufu Is Not Jerusalem," and "They Are Nailing Confucius on the Cross"), some supporting the Christians (with titles such as "Render unto God the things which are *God's*, and unto Confucians the things that are Confucians'"). Many held the position that although the church should be built, its proposed grand scale would in the end dominate the cityscape, and the fact that it could hold three thousand people was too powerful an allusion to the legend that Confucius had taught three thousand disciples, and would in effect overshadow the cherished Confucian tradition in Qufu.

Each of these events can be seen as corresponding to key issues involved in the future development of Confucianism in China. The first one might be called the "politics of epistemology," the second the "politics of the religion question," and the third the "politics of Confucian nationalism." I will address each briefly, before ending the discussion with an assessment of recent debates over whether Confucian might, could, or should become the civil religion of China.

THE POLITICS OF EPISTEMOLOGY

Is Confucianism on its way to being classified as a "major religion" in China, as the official *Annual Report on China's Religions* seems to suggest? What is at stake in the "religion" classification for scholars of Confucianism today? As Wilfred Cantwell Smith remarked perceptively in 1963, "'Is Confucianism a religion?' is one [question] that the West has never been able to answer, and China never able to ask."[7] Do we have to answer this question today? What is at stake?

I suggest that there are at least two reasons why this question has to be addressed. First, we have to deal with the "epistemological ignorance," which is the problematic nature of the existing classifications of Chinese religious traditions. We need to examine these classifications through historical analysis as well as a critical reflection of methodologies used in social scientific studies. As we have seen in our historical case study of the birth of Confucianism as a world religion in late nineteenth-century Europe and in twentieth-century China, the normalizing force of the world religion discourse has been very much at work.

The second reason is that the institutionalization of the discourse in popular imagination, in textbooks, in academic disciplines, and in domestic and international politics has made these classifications "real." They are real as categories in knowledge production as well as policy making. Indeed, statistical data have become a crucial part of the statecraft of contemporary nation-states, as well as international and transnational organizations. They have become the foundation of the self-understanding and self-knowledge of modern societies.

Scholarship is always conditioned by history. And the question "Is Confucianism a religion?" has become a question to which contemporary scholars have to provide an answer. It is a question made possible by a specific set of historical conditions, and the "looping effect" of emerging historical categories through classification and knowledge production, as Ian Hacking suggests, has made it into an empirical question about social practice as well.[8] It remains to be seen whether Confucianism will eventually be classified as a "major religion" by the Chinese state, which would have significant consequences for the development of contemporary Chinese cultural and religious politics.

The Politics of the Religion Question

What is at stake for the Chinese state to start calling something a religion? Why would the Chinese state be interested in classifying Confucianism as a religion in the first place? Indeed, why this sudden interest in Confucianism and Confucius, whose ideas were much maligned by the socialist ideologues for forty years until the recent rehabilitation, which did not take place until the 1990s? The appearance and disappearance of the Confucius statue on Tiananmen Square is a telling example of the complex and often ambiguous relationship the Chinese state has with Confucianism and the Sage.

There exist many contradictions within the Chinese state. Today it is ideologically atheist, politically antireligion, institutionally secular, socially increasingly tolerant toward ritual practice, culturally Han-centric (which means Confucian-centric for cultural nationalists), and ethically rooted in Confucian ethics. The pressure of conforming to the perceived norms of modernity, intensified through international comparison with Western nation-states, seems to suggest that modernity equals secularism and the separation of church and state. But how can a society be considered secular when there isn't a strong, singular, monotheistic religion to be separated from? China has been trying hard to deal with the "religion question," or perhaps the "religion complex," since the beginning of the twentieth century, and the issues are becoming more pressing.

The historian Rebecca Nedostup has detailed the uneasy and fascinating institutional and political processes through which the category of "religion"—and along with it the category of "superstition"—was introduced into Chinese life by politicians, intellectuals, and census takers during Nationalist rule in the 1920s and 1930s.[9] Is it more modern to have "religion" instead of "superstition"? Indeed, this complex situation regarding religion has informed many aspects of the politics of religion in modern China: from the Confucianity Movement of the 1910s and 1920s, right after the Chinese Republican Revolution, to the establishment of the Five Major Religions classification in socialist China in the 1950s, on which basis the State Administration of Religious Affairs was founded, to today's numerous attempts to present and normalize diverse Chinese religious practices along the lines of the "norms" of major world religions.

Here is a good example of the international pressure China is experiencing today. Tony Blair wrote an essay for the *Washington Post* on April 11, 2011, titled "How Will Religion's Growth in China Impact Its Relations with the West?"

> China's growing willingness to engage with religious ideas and institutions will greatly assist East-West relations. . . . It is above all this quest for a harmonious (we would probably say fair or just) society that engages the Chinese leadership with religion. . . . The rise of interest in religious studies and their proliferation in China's universities is bi-product of religious revival. Thomas Aquinas' concept of the organic society and the need for virtue fits well with aspects of Confucian ethics. There are a lot more budding Thomists in China than in Britain and a genuine intellectual excitement with themes in Christian thought. . . . So where is this all going? "Never impose on others what you would not choose for yourself," Confucius counseled. We may have a lot to learn from China's evolving experience of religion, just as we are learning from its spectacular purchase on the global economy.[10]

As I have shown, such strong pressure for China to engage the West in terms of the category of "religion" is nothing new; it has only intensified in recent years, as religious conflicts worsen in many parts of the world, including China itself (especially in the case of Tibetan Buddhism and Islam).

In order to present the world with a "religion" that is compatible with the political and cultural agendas of the state, China has rediscovered Confucianism, with the hope that it is something that can be used and controlled at will, a perfect cultural symbol and political tool on the international stage, with an aura of "religion" yet without any actual religious organization that the state has to deal with. After all, unlike Christianity, Islam, Buddhism, and Daoism, there is neither a clergy nor a priesthood in Confucianism. In contemporary China, it has become a diffused tradition without a core Confucian stratum fighting for its own interests. Or is this no longer the case?

The Politics of Confucian Nationalism

The so-called Qufu Church Controversy has been much discussed among Chinese intellectuals, and the staunch position taken by many well-respected scholars of Confucianism has sparked criticism of their lack of religious tolerance. This is an event that demonstrates well both the positive and negative sides of the emergence of a powerful Confucian cultural and religious identity. These Confucian activists—to use Stephen Angle's term—are now making use of Confucian tradition to forge a strong sense of self-identity and group solidarity, which could become a cause of religious conflict, as in the case of the proposed church in Qufu. Indeed, the combative and intolerant tone of many online posts is disturbing, signaling a hardening of ideological commitments of emerging cultural nationalists.

However, not all Confucian activists are Confucian nationalists. The emerging Confucian commitment to political activism could also become a source of positive political resistance and change. Indeed, as Angle remarks, "recent developments suggest a more confident attitude that is reminiscent of the traditional Confucian responsibility of intellectuals to remonstrate with superiors (be they parents or rulers) who deviate from the Way."[11]

There are several possibilities for future conflicts between Confucian activists and the state. First, there might be more tensions between the Confucian nationalists and the state. For instance, Confucian fundamentalist activists such as Jiang Qing and Kang Xiaoguang insist on the necessity of installing Confucianism as a state religion, which could become grounds for future conflicts with the state. Second, the tension between Confucianism and other religious traditions might intensify. Besides the existing conflicts between Confucian nationalist activists and Christians in China, Confucianism could also be used by the state to oppose the growth of other religious groups, which is a genuine concern long held by many Christians as well as scholars of Chinese religions.[12] Third, there is a remote possibility that the state might try to mold Confucianism into a form of "State Confucianism," like "State Shinto" in Japan, which could lead to further conflicts with Confucian activists, who would not accept the way the state makes use of Confucianism for its own political purposes.[13]

THE POLITICS OF CONFUCIANISM AS A CIVIL RELIGION

The possibility of Confucianism as a civil religion has been a recurring theme among Chinese intellectuals who are interested not only in the fate of Confucianism in contemporary China but also in the fate of contemporary China itself. Many have been searching for a solution to the moral and ethical crisis in contemporary Chinese society, and Confucianism as a civil religion seems to hold great promise for a "moral reconstruction" of China, which is urgently needed at the beginning of the twenty-first century.[14]

For scholars as well as activists of Confucianism, this approach also allows them to speak of Confucianism without getting into multifarious debates over whether Confucianism is a religion. Instead they can focus on the historical and philosophical development of Confucianism and emphasize its relevance in the contemporary world as an important moral, cultural, and political force. In some ways we may say that the most pressing and relevant question about Confucianism in today's China might be moving from "Is Confucianism a religion?" to "Is Confucianism a civil religion?"

As we will see, the discussion of whether Confucianism is a civil religion has moved beyond the realm of the descriptive—how and why Confucianism has religious elements—and into the realm of the prescriptive—whether and should Confucianism be a civil religion, and whether it is compatible with democracy. This important transformation of the debate over Confucianism from issues regarding history and religion to ideas of political theory signals a shift, one that is consistent with the deep concern with politics and social order that has long been one of the fundamental elements of Confucian thought since its very beginning.

In his insightful essay "Revival of Confucianism in the Sphere of the Mores and Reactivation of Civil Religion Debate in China," Sébastien Billioud summarizes three main positions regarding Confucianism as a civil religion.[15] The first is represented by Chen Ming, a scholar of Confucianism and leading public intellectual who is the editor of a journal promoting "the original [Confucian] *dao*" (*yuandao*). It might be useful to call him a "cultural conservative and political liberal Confucian." He makes the distinction between civil religion and political ideology, and believes that Confucianism is compatible with democracy.[16] In Billioud's analysis, Chen Ming's position is different in an important way from those of other prominent Confucian public intellectuals, Jiang Qing and Kang Xiaoguang, who want to promote a political Confucianism as the sole source of Chinese state ideology and establish Confucianism as a state religion. It might be useful to term them "cultural conservative and political nationalist Confucians," for whom it is unimportant whether Confucianism is a civil religion.

The second position is represented by Ji Zhe, a scholar of Chinese religion teaching in Paris who emphasizes civil religion as "a non-religious expression of the sacredness of modern society, and that it should be based on a rule-of-law state and a civil society. . . . According to this view, republican values should be insisted on, and national morality should be compatible with humanity's morality."[17] Billioud characterizes his position as not using civil religion as a tool of political legitimation, but "a secular belief" developed by "citizens of a 'civilized society.'"[18]

The third position is represented by Fenggang Yang, a leading sociologist of Chinese religions teaching in the United States. Billioud notes Yang's concern, based on empirical evidence, that Confucianism "could also turn into some nationalistic form of political religion." In the latest, most detailed articulation of his position, Yang speaks of his hope that "instead of establishing Confucianism as the state religion, which would result in grave consequences, . . . it is perhaps feasible and more helpful to develop some kind of civil religion based on Confucianism, as most Chinese people share the common cultural heritage and most of Confucian values. The Chinese notion of *Tian* is so readily available for civil religion, which can be interpreted by different religions in reference to their own divinity, thus affirming the inclusive spirit since the ancient time of the Chinese civilization." He further suggests "a kind of civil religion based on Confucianism and Christianity, if successfully constructed or developed."[19]

It seems clear that both Ji and Yang believe Confucianism should be the civil religion of China; where they differ seems to be how to construct or develop Confucianism as a civil religion. Here we need to return to Bellah's conception of the idea of "civil religion" in his 1967 essay "Civil Religion in America" as well as his later modifications of the concept in order to respond to these scholars' diverse visions.

It is a well-known fact that the idea of "civil religion" has long been used for different political purposes since the publication of the essay during the years of the Vietnam War. In fact, Bellah refrained from using the term "civil religion" after it was constantly misunderstood to be a concept affiliated with nationalism; he mentions in his essay "Civil Religion: Term and Concept" that the misuse would not have happened had he used more neutral terms such as "political religion," "religion of the republic," or "political piety."[20]

In his article "Return to Durkheim: Civil Religion and the Moral Reconstruction in China," Ji offers an excellent analysis of the Durkheimian and Rousseauian roots of Bellah's concept. It touches on two key components of the idea of civil religion: civil religion as religious collective conscience without association with a specific religion, and civil religion as the political conscience of a democratic, republican society.

Here are the key aspects of these two components according to Ji's analysis, the first religious and moral, the second political:

1. As formulated by Bellah, showing great affinities with Durkheim's view on morality and society, civil religion is a generic form of moral life that expresses the sacredness of modern society, which contains essential moral ideals that hold a society together.
   a. It is not associated with specific religions, although it could come from specific existing historical religions.

    b. It is "diffused collective sentiments that express more or less explicitly the general will of a society."

    c. It resides in "habits, customs and public opinion as vehicles of simple but fundamental values."[21]

2. As formulated by Rousseau and Bellah, civil religion is "the moral content of the social contract, the sacred expression of general will, and the fundamental conscience of the Republic."

    a. Civil religion is "set by the Sovereign," and "this sovereignty is in the hand of the people."

    b. Civil religion can exist only in a democratic, republican society.

    c. Civil religion "is not aimed at legitimizing the existing government"; it judges society with moral standards, pursues civil rights, and defends civil society.[22]

If we accept Ji's formulation, how do we envision a civil religion for China? Ji ends his discussion with a call for the emergence of prophets in today's moral crisis in Chinese society, people who can forge a civil religion of universal humanity rather than a nationalistic civil religion of Chinese "traditional" values and culture. And he suggests that Confucianism, especially the moral philosophy of Mencius, might be the source we need.

There are two separate points that I would like to make regarding Ji's superb analysis. The first is normative, which is that, for all its nuance and depth, Ji's articulation of Bellah's concept of civil religion does not pay enough attention to the dynamic nature of the formation of civil religion. In order for the sacredness of morality to express itself through habits, customs, and public opinions, it must be a dynamic process of discords and reconciliations, disagreements and collaborations, actualized temporally through history. If civil religion is the fundamental conscience of the citizens of a republic, a dynamic process of democratic conflicts ought to be its modus operandi. Indeed, civil religion in Bellah's conception is not something that can be established; it has to emerge gradually and organically from the people, as with civil religion in America since the beginning of the republic, where disagreements have been constantly settled and resettled through complex historical processes of conflicts, consensus, and compromises. What we hope to see in China today is precisely the beginning of this process of the democratic emergence of civil religion. No group of people or institution can "establish" a civil religion in China, for it has to come from the sovereign power of the people.

The second point is descriptive. It seems that a more difficult, perhaps even antagonistic, path might be awaiting the rise of civil religion in China. I contend that it is not a foregone conclusion that Confucianism—or any other religious tradition—can be the single source of morality for Chinese people. And it is not a given either that the process of the emergence of a civil religion in China, which is a social, cultural, institutional, and political process, would not be an intensely contested one. Instead of peaceful dialogue and serene cooperation, what is waiting ahead might be a long process of conflict and divergence among scholars, activists, religious practitioners, many different religious and cultural institutions, and the state.

Consider the religious and moral aspect of civil religion. What does it mean to have a civil religion that expresses the sacredness of modern China, which contains the essential moral ideals that are shared by everyone in society? In the case of the United States, Christianity, more specifically Protestantism, has been the dominating source of essential ideals throughout the history of the country; no other religious tradition has seriously challenged the fact that Protestant values, symbols, and rituals are shared by most citizens of the republic.[23] A similar case can be argued for France, replacing Protestantism with Catholicism; only in recent years has Islam been posing a challenge to the French civil religion and its sacred ideal of republican secularism (laicite). What was difficult for the transformation of a specific religion to civil religion was separating the particular religious institutions from the state; what was not difficult was identifying the sources from which collective moral sentiments and moral ideals were borrowed.

However, due to the pluralistic and ecological nature of Chinese religious practices and the multiple sources of Chinese moral teachings, it is not a given that Confucianism is the de facto main source of contemporary Chinese morality. Will the moral and ethical ideals of Confucianism eventually fill the spiritual vacuum? There is conflicting evidence, and it remains to be seen whether other religious traditions, such as Christianity, Buddhism, or Daoism, might contest its claim, or whether a syncretic, truly diffused version of moral teaching might eventually emerge. As Billioud has shown in his illuminating fieldwork on Confucian-inspired organizations, many Confucian classics and ideas are in fact disseminated in Buddhist and sectarian groups. We might have to ask, when does something cease to be Confucian and become something else?

Furthermore, in terms of ritual practice, as I have learned through my fieldwork in Confucius temples as well as survey research on religious life in China, although Confucianism does have a clear religious dimension, it is certainly not the dominant one in most ordinary people's live. People who pray to Confucius also pray to a variety of gods, and most people have a rich and diverse repertoire of things whose existence they believe in, including ancestral spirits, karma, the god of fortune, as well as the spirit of Confucius.[24] In such a diverse sphere of rituals and beliefs, does it still make sense for us to speak of someone being Confucian rather than Buddhist or Daoist?

The other aspect of dynamic conflict is the potential political conflict over the development of civil religion in China. If we consider the cases of the disappearing Confucius statue on Tiananmen Square and the Qufu Church Controversy, both occurring in 2011, we can see that these are emerging conflicts that might only intensify as different groups—religious, cultural, political—compete for public attention, cultural authority, economic resources, and religious legitimation, and, eventually, fight over the important role of being the leading source of a Chinese civil religion.

Pluralism is rarely about peace and consensus. But conflicts are welcome news, for one could argue that this is the essence of true pluralism and democracy. As China becomes more democratic, many more conflicts will be fought openly, in the public sphere, as in the case of the Qufu Church Controversy, which made national news with its many stages of petitions and protests, unlike the case of the disappearing Confucius statue, which took place literally behind closed doors, in the darkness of the night.

We have seen how the question "Is Confucianism a religion" is indeed a question "the West has never been able to answer, and China never able to ask." Here is how the question of "Is Confucianism a civil religion?" is fundamentally different. This is a question that China *has been able to answer*, for the asking comes not from perplexed early comparative religionists who were unable to grasp the complexity and uniqueness of Asian traditions, but from Robert Bellah, a comparativist whose sharp insights about the United States are rooted in his understanding of other cultures, such as Japan. His deep insights into history—as shown splendidly in *Religion in Human Evolution*, his magnum opus—allow him to speak of a grand narrative not only of the past, but also of the future, which is a future of unfoldings and becomings rooted in the ethical ideals of diverse religious traditions of the axial age, the political ideals of different philosophical traditions, and the dialectical movement that is history, carrying forward the many antagonistic elements from which we can never separate our ideals—all the material, institutional, cultural, religious, as well as political forces—that constitute the very essence of modernity.

There are still uncertainties in the politics of the future of Confucianism. However, we can be sure of one thing, that Confucianism—as ritual practice, as cultural identity, as political identity, as possible foundation of morality, as possible source of civil religion—will never go away. So much has already happened in the first decade of the twenty-first century; the future of the revival of Confucianism no doubt holds for us anxiety, but also great hope.

Notes

Preface

1. I thank one of the anonymous readers of my manuscript for suggesting an account of my personal journey behind this project.

2. "Mind, Faith and Spirit," *Princeton Weekly Bulletin* 88, no. 25 (April 26, 1999).

3. Max Weber, *The Religion of China: Confucianism and Taoism*, trans. Hans H. Gerth and Don Martindale (New York: Free Press, 1951 [1915]).

4. See Richard Hughes Seager, *The World's Parliament of Religions: The East/West Encounter, Chicago 1893* (Bloomington: Indiana University Press, 1995). After the first parliament in 1893, six more parliaments have been held in the past one hundred years, the latest in 2009 in Melbourne, Australia, with nearly ten thousand people attending. According to the website for the Council for a Parliament of the World's Religion, there is one representative of Chinese religious traditions serving on the International Advisory Committee, alongside the Dalai Lama and Archbishop Desmond Tutu; Professor Tu Weiming represents "Taoist/Confucianist" teaching, and his short biography states that "as a renowned international scholar and thinker, he is committed to the study of Confucian teachings in the modern age."

5. "Mind, Faith and Spirit."

6. Anna Sun, "Confusions over Confucianism: Controversies over the Religious Nature of Confucianism, 1870–2007" (PhD diss., Princeton University, 2008).

7. Fenggang Yang, Victor Yuan, Anna Sun, Lu Yengfang, Rodney Stark, Byron Johnson, Eric Liu, Carson Mencken, and Chiu Heu-Yuan, *Spiritual Life Study of Chinese Residents* (University Park, Pa.: Association of Religion Data Archives, 2007).

8. I thank Fenggang Yang for drawing my attention to the distinction between "national religion" and "state religion." As Yang points out, most sociologists of religion in the West use "state religion" when discussing religions that are officially endorsed by the state, such as Anglicanism as the official religion of England, and Islam as the official religion of Egypt. However, the situation in the Chinese case has additional complications. The Chinese term *guojiao* literally means "state/national religion." Since *guo* can be used to refer to the political regime of a state as well as the cultural identity of a nation, there is inherent uncertainty in the usage of the term. For Confucian activists who wish to turn Confucianism into a religion endorsed by the Chinese state, their usage of *guojiao*

allows them to present themselves as political Confucians as well as cultural Confucians. I suggest that *guojia zongjiao* (which explicitly means "state religion") might be a better Chinese term to describe their real position than *guojiao*. However, *guojiao*, the more ambiguous term, is still the most commonly used. In the rest of this book, I shall translate the term *guojiao* into "state religion" when it refers to a religion endorsed by the state, and "national religion" when it refers to a religious ethos shared by the people of a nation. The translation should be a case-by-case judgment based on specific contexts.

9. According to the *New York Times*, "Foxconn, founded by the Taiwanese industrialist Terry Gou, is a $60 billion manufacturer with a reputation for military-style efficiency that includes mapping out assembly line workers' movements in great detail and monitoring tasks with a stopwatch" ("After Suicides, Scrutiny of China's Grim Factories," *New York Times*, June 6, 2010).

10. The Sacred Hall of Confucius is managed by Zhou Beichen, a longtime disciple of Jiang Qing. Zhou has published several books on Confucianism as a religion, including *Rujiao yaoyi* [The Essentials of Confucian Religions] (Hong Kong: China International Culture Press, 2009), in which he details the principle beliefs, ritual acts, and history of Confucian as a religion, with a structure that is not dissimilar to Christian catechism. Following Jiang, he also emphasizes the importance of making Confucianism into the national religion of China.

11. Jiang's latest book, *The Politics of Kingly Government and Confucian Constitutionalism: Confucian Reflections on the Future Development of Chinese Politics*, was self-published in 2010, after he was notified that the book would not be allowed to be published by any official publishers; Jiang Qing, *Wangdao Zhengzhi Yu Rujiao Xianzheng: Weilai Zhongguo Zhengzhi Fazhande Ruxuesikao* [The Politics of Kingly Government and Confucian Constitutionalism: Confucian Reflections on the Future Development of Chinese Politics] (Guizhou: Yangming Academy, 2010). The first volume of English translation of Jiang's writing, edited by Daniel Bell and Ruiping Fan, has recently been published; see *A Confucian Constitutional Order: How China's Ancient Past Can Shape Its Political Future* (Princeton: Princeton University Press, 2012). Jiang and Bell coauthored a much-read op-ed piece on July 10, 2012, in the *New York Times*, laying out the main ideas of Jiang's Confucian constitutionalism. Citing an ancient Confucian commentary text, the *Gongyang Zhuan*, the authors declared that "political power can be justified through three sources: the legitimacy of heaven (a sacred, transcendent sense of natural morality), the legitimacy of earth (wisdom from history and culture), and the legitimacy of the human (political obedience through popular will)." Based on this Confucian notion of "Humane Authority," the authors stated the ideals of a Confucian constitutional order: "In modern China, Humane Authority should be exercised by a tricameral legislature: a House of Exemplary Persons that represents sacred legitimacy; a House of the Nation that represents historical and cultural legitimacy; and a House of the People that represents popular legitimacy" ("A Confucian Constitution for China," *New York Times*, July 10, 2012).

Introduction

1. Ann-ping Chin, *The Authentic Confucius: A Life of Thought and Politics* (New York: Scribner, 2007); Michael Nylan and Thomas A. Wilson, *Lives of*

Confucius: Civilization's Greatest Sage through the Ages (New York: Doubleday, 2010); Daniel Bell, *China's New Confucianism: Politics and Everyday Life in a Changing Society* (Princeton: Princeton University Press, 2008).

2. Talal Asad, *Genealogies of Religion: Discipline and Reasons of Power in Christianity and Islam* (Baltimore: Johns Hopkins University Press, 1993); Tomoko Masuzawa, *The Invention of World Religions* (Chicago: University of Chicago Press, 2005).

3. Bell, *China's New Confucianism*.

4. Peter Steinfels, "Globally, Religion Defies Easily Identified Patterns," *New York Times*, October 23, 2009.

5. Tom W. Smith, "Religious Change around the World" (NORC/University of Chicago, October 23, 2009).

6. Ibid., 3.

7. Ibid., 15–16.

8. Regrettably the "Religious Change around the World" report has little to say about trends in non-Western societies, especially Asian countries; it simply concludes that "no simple generalization adequately captures the complexity and nuance of the religious change that has been occurring" (15). Part of this is due to the lack of access to data on religion from certain regions (for instance, the report does not have access to the Horizon data on Chinese religions, which were used exclusively by the Empirical Study of Religions in China project until 2010), and part of this is due to the complexity of the very task of defining what constitutes religion and religious life in societies with non-monotheistic and/or syncretic religious traditions.

9. Ian Johnson, "China Gets Religion!," *New York Review of Books*, December 22, 2011.

10. Confucius temples in Taiwan, such as the Taipei Confucius Temple and the Tainan Confucius Temple, are not religious organizations either; both are organizationally part of the municipal city government. There are very few Confucius temples left in Japan; the ones I visited, including Yushima Seido in Tokyo, Shizutani Shrine in the Shizutani School in Okayama, and the Confucian Temple in Nagasaki, are all administratively cultural institutions rather than religious ones.

11. C. K. Yang, *Religion in Chinese Society: A Study of Contemporary Social Functions of Religion and Some of Their Historical Factors* (Berkeley: University of California Press, 1961).

12. James A. Beckford and N. J. Demerath, *The Sage Handbook of the Sociology of Religion* (Thousand Oaks, Calif.: Sage, 2007); Nancy Tatom Ammerman, *Everyday Religion: Observing Modern Religious Lives* (Oxford: Oxford University Press, 2007); Lynn Davidman, *Tradition in a Rootless World: Women Turn to Orthodox Judaism* (Berkeley: University of California Press, 1993).

13. Adam Yuet Chau, *Miraculous Response: Doing Popular Religion in Contemporary China* (Stanford, Calif.: Stanford University Press, 2006); Vincent Goossaert and David A. Palmer, *The Religious Question in Modern China* (Chicago: University of Chicago Press, 2011).

14. Richard Madsen, *Meaning and Modernity: Religion, Polity, and Self* (Berkeley: University of California Press, 2001); Mayfair Mei-hui Yang, ed., *Chinese Religiosities: Afflictions of Modernity and State Formation*, Global,

Area, and International Archive (Berkeley: University of California Press, 2008); Xun Liu, *Daoist Modern: Innovation, Lay Practice, and the Community of Inner Alchemy in Republican Shanghai*, Harvard East Asian Monographs (Cambridge, Mass.: Harvard University Asia Center, 2009); Rebecca Nedostup, *Superstitious Regimes: Religion and the Politics of Chinese Modernity*, Harvard East Asian Monographs (Cambridge, Mass.: Harvard University Asia Center, 2009).

15. For recent accounts of Confucianism as spiritual exercise, see Barry C. Keenan, *Neo-Confucian Self-Cultivation*, part of the "Dimensions of Asian Spirituality" book series (Honolulu: University of Hawaii Press, 2011). Also see P. J. Ivanhoe, *Confucian Moral Self Cultivation* (Indianapolis: Hackett, 2000).

16. I intend to explore this comparison further in my future research. Based on my preliminary reading, there are indeed a great deal of similarities between ancient Roman religions and contemporary Chinese religious life, from the worship of multiple gods to the importance of local deities, from hero cults to the centrality of rituals.

17. I thank my colleagues in the Secularism Seminar at the Institute for Advanced Study in May 2011 for their excellent challenges and suggestions.

18. Adam B. Seligman et al., *Ritual and Its Consequences: An Essay on the Limits of Sincerity* (Oxford: Oxford University Press, 2008).

19. Fenggang Yang, *Religion in China: Survival and Revival under Communist Rule* (Oxford: Oxford University Press, 2012), 27.

20. Ibid.

21. Ian Hacking, *The Social Construction of What?* (Cambridge, Mass.: Harvard University Press, 1999), 31–32.

22. I thank Jeffrey Stout for this suggestion.

23. Friedrich Nietzsche, *On the Genealogy of Morality*, trans. Carol Diethe (1887; repr., Cambridge: Cambridge University Press, 1994), 53.

24. As of December 12, 2010, there were 133,647 mentions of "harmonious society" on the website for *People's Daily* (www.people.com.cn), the official Chinese government newspaper. Interestingly, there are 2,506 mentions of "Confucius temples" (*kongmiao*) in the same database, but only 1,191 mentions of "Confucian religion" (*rujiao*). For detailed discussions of "harmonious society" and current development of diverse schools of Confucian political thought, see Stephen C. Angle, *Contemporary Confucian Political Philosophy: Toward Progressive Confucianism* (Cambridge: Polity, 2012).

25. "About Confucius Institutes," Confucius Institute Headquarters, http://english.hanban.org/node_7716.htm.

26. D. D. Guttenplan, "Critics Worry about Influence of Chinese Institute on U.S. Campuses," *New York Times*, March 4, 2012.

27. I will discuss this incident in more detail in chapter 9.

28. For an in-depth analysis of the revival of formal ceremonies taking place in Confucius temples in China, see Sébastien Billioud and Joël Thoraval's "*Lijiao*: The Return of Ceremonies Honouring Confucius in Mainland China," *China Perspectives* 4 (2009): 82–100. One of their fascinating findings is that there is now beginning to emerge a new trend of what they call "grassroots Confucianism and Confucian ceremonies," which are ceremonies organized not by government

officials but by local associations promoting Confucianism and "ancient ritualis-tic culture and music" (91).

Chapter 1
Four Controversies over the Religious Nature of Confucianism

1. Lothar von Falkenhausen, *Chinese Society in the Age of Confucius (1000–250 BC): The Archaeological Evidence* (Los Angeles: Cotsen Institute of Archae-ology, University of California, Los Angeles, 2006).

2. Cho-Yun Hsu, *Ancient China in Transition: An Analysis of Social Mobil-ity, 722–222 B.C.* (Stanford, Calif.: Stanford University Press, 1965), 66. Also see Mark Lewis, *Sanctioned Violence in Early China* (Albany: State University of New York Press, 1990) and Yang Xiao, "Ethical Thought in China," in *The Rout-ledge Companion to Ethics*, ed. John Skorupsi (London and New York: Rout-ledge, 2010).

3. The *Analects* quotations are mostly from Simon Leys's translation, with modification. See Simon Leys, trans., *The Analects of Confucius* (New York: Nor-ton, 1997).

4. P. J. Ivanhoe, "Heaven as a Source for Ethnical Warrant in Early Confu-cianism," *Dao: A Journal of Comparative Philosophy* 6 (2007): 211–20.

5. Thomas A. Wilson, *Genealogy of the Way: The Construction and Use of the Confucian Tradition in Late Imperial China* (Stanford, Calif.: Stanford Uni-versity Press, 1995); Thomas A. Wilson, *On Sacred Grounds: Culture, Society, Politics, and the Formation of the Cult of Confucius*, Harvard East Asian Mono-graphs 217 (Cambridge, Mass.: Harvard University Asia Center, 2002); Thomas A. Wilson, "The Ritual Formation of Confucian Orthodoxy and the Descendants of the Sage," *Journal of Asian Studies* 55, no. 3 (1996): 559–84.

6. Wilson, *On Sacred Grounds*; Wilson, "Ritual Formation."

7. Benjamin A. Elman, *A Cultural History of Civil Examinations in Late Imperial China* (Berkeley: University of California Press, 2000).

8. Daniel K. Gardner, *The Four Books: The Basic Teachings of the Later Confucian Tradition* (Indianapolis: Hackett, 2007).

9. For a detailed analysis, please see Lionel M. Jensen, *Manufacturing Con-fucianism: Chinese Traditions and Universal Civilization* (Durham, N.C.: Duke University Press, 1998). In his 1999 dissertation "Confucianism Encounters Re-ligion: The Formation of Religious Discourse and the Confucian Movement in China," Hsi-Yuan Chen divided the movement and its aftermath into the fol-lowing four stages: Kang Youwei's "Reformation" and the Evangelization of Confucianism, the Confucian Religion Association, the Making of the Constitu-tion and the State Religion Campaign, and the Anti-religious Movement and the De-religionization of Confucianism. Please see Hsi-Yuan Chen, "Confucianism Encounters Religion: The Formation of Religious Discourse and the Confucian Movement in China" (PhD diss., Harvard University, 1999).

10. For detailed accounts of the May Fourth Movement and the New Culture Movement, see Charlotte Furth, "Intellectual Change: From the Reform Move-ment to the May Fourth Movement, 1895–1920," in *Republican China 1912–1949, Part 1. The Cambridge History of China*, ed. John K. Fairbank (Cambridge:

Cambridge University Press, 1983), 322–405, and Kai-wing Chow, et al., ed., *Beyond the May Fourth Paradigm: In Search of Chinese Modernity* (Lanham, Md.: Lexington Books/Rowman & Littlefield, 2008).

11. Suzanne Pepper, *Radicalism and Education Reform in 20th-Century China: The Search for an Ideal Development Model* (Cambridge: Cambridge University Press, 1996), 469.

12. "Confucianism," in *Oxford English Dictionary* (Oxford: Oxford University Press, 2012).

13. James Legge, *The Religions of China: Confucianism and Taoism Described and Compared with Christianity* (London: Hodder and Stoughton, 1880), 4.

14. See Federico Masini, "The Formation of Modern Chinese Lexicon and Its Evolution toward a National Language: The Period from 1840 to 1898," *Journal of Chinese Linguistics*, monograph no. 6 (1993).

15. T. H. Barrett and Francesca Tarocco, "Terminology and Religious Identity: Buddhism and the Genealogy of the Term *Zongjiao*," in *Dynamics in the History of Religions between Asia and Europe: Encounters, Notions, and Comparative Perspectives*, ed. Volkharde Krech and Marion Steineke (Leiden and Boston: Brill, 2012), 311.

16. Ibid., 317. See also Lydia Liu, *Translingual Practice: Literature, National Culture, and Translated Modernity, China 1900–1937* (Stanford, Calif.: Stanford University Press, 1995), 301.

17. Sarah Thal, "A Religion That Was Not a Religion: The Creation of Modern Shinto in Nineteenth-Century Japan," in *The Invention of Religion: Rethinking Belief in Politics and History*, ed. Derek R. Peterson and Darren R. Walhof (New Brunswick, N.J.: Rutgers University Press, 2002), 101.

18. Nedostup, *Superstitious Regimes*, 8.

19. Liu, *Daoist Modern*, 55.

20. Carine Defoort, "Is There Such a Thing as Chinese Philosophy? Arguments of an Implicit Debate," *Philosophy East & West* 51, no. 3 (2001): 394.

21. Feng Youlan, *A History of Chinese Philosophy*, trans. Derk Bodde (Princeton: Princeton University Press, 1952). The Chinese version was published in 1931.

22. Wing-Tsit Chan, *A Source Book in Chinese Philosophy* (Princeton: Princeton University Press, 1963).

23. Ibid., 15.

24. See, for instance, Ivanhoe, *Confucian Moral Self Cultivation*; and Kwong-loi Shun, *Mencius and Early Chinese Thought* (Stanford, Calif.: Stanford University Press, 1997).

25. Benjamin I. Schwartz, *The World of Thought in Ancient China* (Cambridge, Mass.: Belknap, 1985).

26. Hoyt Cleveland Tillman, "The Use of Neo-Confucianism, Revisited: A Reply to Professor de Bary," *Philosophy East and West* 44, no. 1 (1994): 135–42; Peter Bol, *This Culture of Ours* (Palo Alto, Calif.: Stanford University Press, 1992).

27. Yu Ying-Shi, *The Historical World of Zhu Xi: A Study of the Political Culture of Song Literati (Zhuxi De Lishi Shijie)* (Taipei: Runchen, 2003).

28. Gilbert Rozman, ed., *The East Asian Region: Confucian Heritage and Its Modern Adaptation* (Princeton: Princeton University Press, 1991); Joseph B.

Tamney and Linda Hsueh-Ling Chiang, *Modernization, Globalization, and Confucianism in Chinese Societies* (Westport, Conn.: Praeger, 2002).

29. See Daniel Bell, *East Meets West: Human Rights and Democracy in East Asia* (Princeton: Princeton University Press, 2000); Daniel Bell, *Beyond Liberal Democracy: Political Thinking for an East Asian Context* (Princeton: Princeton University Press, 2006); Daniel Bell and Chaibong Hahm, *Confucianism for the Modern World* (New York: Cambridge University Press, 2003); Daniel Bell and Joanne Bauer, eds., *The East Asian Challenge for Human Rights* (New York: Cambridge University Press, 1999); Bell, *China's New Confucianism.*

30. Wm. Theodore de Bary and Tu Weiming, eds., *Confucianism and Human Rights* (New York: Columbia University Press, 1998); Irena Bloom and Wayne L. Proudfoot, eds., *Religious Diversity and Human Rights* (New York: Columbia University Press, 1996).

31. Tu Weiming, *Centrality and Commonality: An Essay on Chung-Yung* (Honolulu: University Press of Hawaii, 1976).

32. Tu, *Lunruxue De Zongjiaoxing: Dui Zhongyong De Xiandai Chanshi* [The Religiosity of Confucianism: Modern Interpretation of Zhongyong] (Wuhan: Wuhan University Press, 1999).

33. Robert C. Neville, *Boston Confucianism: Portable Tradition in the Late-Modern World* (Albany: State University of New York Press, 2000), xxi.

34. Mary Evelyn Tucker and Tu Weiming, eds., *Confucian Spirituality* (New York: Crossroad, 2003–4); Neville, *Boston Confucianism.*

35. Neville, *Boston Confucianism*, 57.

36. Rodney Leon Taylor, *The Religious Dimensions of Confucianism* (Albany: State University of New York Press, 1990); Rodney Leon Taylor, *The Cultivation of Sagehood as a Religious Goal in Neo-Confucianism* (Missoula, Mont.: Scholars Press, 1978); Rodney Leon Taylor, *The Way of Heaven: An Introduction to the Confucian Religious Life* (Leiden: Brill, 1986).

37. Wilson, *Genealogy of the Way*; Wilson, *On Sacred Grounds*; Wilson, "Ritual Formation."

38. Benjamin A. Elman, "Rethinking Confucianism: Past and Present in China, Japan, Korea, and Vietnam," in Elman, Duncan, and Ooms, *Rethinking Confucianism*, 527.

39. Benjamin Elman, "Benjamin Elman Interview," http://www.princeton.edu/history/people/display_person.xml?netid=elman&interview=yes.

40. Michael Nylan, "A Problematic Model: The Han 'Orthodox Synthesis,' Then and Now," in *Imagining Boundaries: Changing Confucian Doctrines*, ed. K. Chow, O. Ng, and J. B. Henderson (Albany: State University of New York Press, 1999); Michael Nylan, *Five "Confucian" Classics* (New Haven: Yale University Press, 2002).

41. This is a paraphrased version of his ideas; see Stephen F. Teiser, "Introduction: The Spirits of Chinese Religion," in *Religions of China in Practice*, ed. Donald Lopez, Jr. (Princeton: Princeton University Press, 1996), 6.

42. Susan Naquin, *Peking: Temples and City Life, 1400–1900* (Berkeley: University of California Press, 2000); Jun Jing, *The Temple of Memories: History, Power, and Morality in a Chinese Village* (Stanford, Calif.: Stanford University Press, 1996).

43. G.E.R. Lloyd, *Disciplines in the Making: Cross-Cultural Perspectives on Elites, Learning, and Innovation* (Oxford: Oxford University Press, 2009), 1.

44. For more details about the controversy, see J. S. Cummins, *A Question of Rites: Friar Domingo Navarrete and the Jesuits in China* (Aldershot: Scolar Press, 1993); Charles E. Ronan and Bonnie B. C. Oh, eds., *East Meets West: The Jesuits in China, 1582–1773* (Chicago: Loyola University Press, 1988); David Mungello, ed., *The Chinese Rites Controversy: Its History and Meaning* (Nettetal: Steyler Verlag, 1994); and George Minamiki, *The Chinese Rites Controversy: From Its Beginning to Modern Times* (Chicago: Loyola University Press, 1985). The latest take on the controversy is Liam Matthew Brockey, *Journey to the East: The Jesuit Mission to China, 1579–1724* (Cambridge, Mass.: Belknap, 2007).

45. Jonathan D. Spence, *The Memory Palace of Matteo Ricci* (New York: Penguin, 1985).

46. Jonathan D. Spence, "Claims and Counter-Claims: The Kangxi Emperor and the Europeans (1661–1722)," in Mungello, *Chinese Rites Controversy*, 16.

47. Spence, *Memory Palace of Matteo Ricci*, 9.

48. Ibid., 114–15.

49. David Mungello, *Curious Land: Jesuit Accommodation and the Origins of Sinology* (Stuttgart: Franz Steiner Werlag Wiesbaden GMBH, 1985), 15, 62–63.

50. D. E. Mungello, "An Introduction to the Chinese Rites Controversy," in Mungello, *Chinese Rites Controversy*, 3.

51. Ray R. Noll, ed., *100 Roman Documents Concerning the Chinese Rites Controversy (1645–1941)* (San Francisco: Ricci Institute for Chinese-Western Cultural History, University of San Francisco, 1992), vi–vii.

52. Li Tiangang, "Examining the Origin of the Religious Nature of Confucianism through Two Documents," in *Quawenha de chanshi* [Cross-Cultural Interpretation] (Beijing: New Star Press, 2007), 293–327.

53. "Brevis Relatio eorum, quae spectant ad Declarationem Sinarum Imperatoris Kam Hi," cited in Li, "Examining the Origin," 305–7.

54. Guy G. Stroumsa, *A New Science: The Discovery of Religion in the Age of Reason* (Cambridge, Mass.: Harvard University Press, 2010), 145.

55. Mungello, "Introduction to the Chinese Rites Controversy," 3–4.

56. The Kangxi Emperor enjoyed discussing science and philosophy with the learned Jesuit missionaries; apparently he also became very fond of European wine, which was given as gifts by the French and Italian Jesuits; see Li Tiangang, *Zhongguo Liyi Zhizheng: Lishi, Wenxian He Yiyi* [Chinese Rites Controversy: History, Documents and Meaning] (Shanghai: Shanghai guji chubanshe, 1998), 102–3.

57. Minamiki, *Chinese Rites Controversy*, 54.

58. Ibid., 67.

59. Spence, "Claims and Counter-Claims," 15.

60. Stroumsa, *New Science*, 149.

61. For detailed accounts of Enlightenment intellectuals' fascination with China, see Jonathan I. Israel, *Enlightenment Contested: Philosophy, Modernity, and the Emancipation of Man, 1670–1752* (Oxford: Oxford University Press, 2008) and Franklin Perkins, *Leibniz and China: A Commerce of Light* (Cambridge: Cambridge University Press, 2004).

62. Cardinal Pietro Biondi-Fumasoni and Archbishop Celso Constantini, "The Sacred Congregation for the Propagation of the Faith: Instruction Concerning Certain Ceremonies and the Oath about the Chinese Rites," in Noll, *100 Roman Documents*, 87–88.

63. Pope John Paul II, "In Quest of Dialogue with China," Fidelio 10, no. 3 (Fall 2001), http://www.schillerinstitute.org/fid_97-01/013_invite_dialogue_JPII .html.

64. For a detailed account of Jesuits' translation or creation of "Confucius," see Jensen, *Manufacturing Confucianism*, 31–77.

65. Ibid., 5.

66. Ibid., 7.

67. Recently there have been many discussions about the meaning of *ru* among sinologists. Michael Nylan, a historian, believes that *ru* should be translated as "professional classicists," rather than "Confucians." See her article "Problematic Model."

68. Nicolas Standaert, "The Jesuits Did Not Manufacture 'Confucianism,'" *East Asian Science, Technology, and Medicine* 16 (1999): 129.

69. Wilfred Cantwell Smith, *The Meaning and End of Religion: A New Approach to the Religious Traditions of Mankind* (New York: Macmillan, 1963), 254n37.

70. Norman J. Girardot, *The Victorian Translation of China: James Legge's Oriental Pilgrimage* (Berkeley: University of California Press, 2002), 214.

71. Ibid., 30–31.

72. Andrew F. Walls, "The Eighteenth-Century Protestant Missionary Awakening in Its European Context," in *Christian Missions and the Enlightenment*, ed. Brian Stanley (Surrey: Curzon Press, 2001), 36. For a general account of the British Protestant Missions in the nineteenth century, see Andrew Porter, ed., *The Imperial Horizons of British Protestant Missions, 1880–1914* (Cambridge: Eerdmans, 2003).

73. Girardot, *Victorian Translation of China*, 36.

74. In his review of Girardot's biography of Legge, John Berthrong notes,

Although obviously dated by the passage of time and scholarly advances in East Asia and the West, Legge's massive translation project has fared remarkably well. China scholars still consult Legge's translations, exegetical notes, and interpretations not only for antiquarian fascination with the bygone scholarship of the Victorian age but also because Legge was such an accurate and perceptive scholar.

See John H. Berthrong, "Review of the Victorian Translation of China," *Journal of Chinese Philosophy* 31, no. 3 (2004): 412. For reprints of Legge's translations, see, for instance, Friedrich Max Müller, *Sacred Books of the East*, 50 vols. (London: Routledge, 2007), and James Legge, trans., *The Shu King, or Book of Historical Documents* (Whitefish, Mont.: Kessinger, 2004).

75. Girardot, *Victorian Translation of China*, 142.

76. Donald W. Treadgold, *The West in Russia and China: Religious and Secular Thought in Modern Times, Volume 2: China, 1582–1949* (Cambridge: Cambridge University Press, 1973), 42–43.

77. Girardot, *Victorian Translation of China*, 217. For a more detailed analysis of the Shanghai Missionary Conference, please see 214–34.

78. Treadgold, *West in Russia and China*, 43–44.

79. Jensen, *Manufacturing Confucianism*, 142.

80. Academia Sinica, Institute of Modern History, *Jiaowu Jiaoan Dang* [Archival Materials Related to Religious Affairs, 1871–1878] (Taipei: Academia Sinica, 1976), 1.

81. Ibid., 2.

82. See vol. 1 of Kang Youwei, *Kang Youwei Zhenglunji* [Collective Political Writings of Kang Youwei] (Beijing: Zhonghua shuju, 1981), 233.

83. Please see Zhang Wei-Bo, *Minguo Chuqi Zunkong Sichao Yanjiu* [Study of Confucianity Thoughts in Early Republic China] (Beijing: Renmin Chubanshe, 2006), 28–53.

84. The petition was denied by the Constitution Committee. Although Liang was one of the signers of the petition, his own view on Confucianism was quite complex; it's possible that his interpretation of Confucianism was national morality, rather than the national religion of the Chinese people. For a nuanced discussion, please see Marianne Bastid-Bruguiere, "Liang Qichao and the Question of Religion (Liang Qichao Et Le Problème De La Religion)," in *Liang Qichao, Meiji Riben, Xifang* [Liang Qichao, Meiji Japan and the West], ed. Hazama Naoki (Beijing: Shehui kexue wenxian chubanshe, 2001), 443.

85. For comprehensive accounts of the Confucianity Movement, see Hsi-Yuan Chen, "Confucian Encounters Religion" and Zhang, *Minguo Chuqi Zunkong Sichao Yanjiu*. Hsi-Yuan Chen's analysis focuses on the collision between the Chinese traditional discourse on *jiao* and the Western modern discourse on religion from late Qing to early Republican China; Zhang Weibo's book examines the intellectual currents that run underneath the short-lived Confucianity Movement.

86. Goossaert and Palmer, *Religious Question in Modern China*, 87.

87. Ibid., 93.

88. Ibid., 107. It is fascinating that redemptive societies such as Yiguandao are now making a return to Mainland China; see Sébastien Billioud, "Carrying the Confucian Torch to the Masses: The Challenge of Structuring the Confucian Revival in the People's Republic of China," *Oriens Extremus* 49 (2010); Sébastien Billioud, "Confucian Revival and the Emergence of 'Jiaohua Organizations': A Case Study of the Yidan Xuetang," *Modern China* 37, no. 3 (2011).

Chapter 2
The Making of a World Religion

1. Girardot, *Victorian Translation of China*, 216.

2. Ibid., 219.

3. Ibid., 228–29.

4. Eric J. Sharpe, *Comparative Religion: A History* (London: Duckworth, 1986), 35–36.

5. "The Science of Religion: Lecture One," from *Lectures on the Science of Religion* (1870), in Friedrich Max Müller and Jon R. Stone, *The Essential Max*

Müller: On Language, Mythology, and Religion (New York: Palgrave Macmillan, 2002), 110.

6. Steven Shapin, "Here and Everywhere: Sociology of Scientific Knowledge," *Annual Review of Sociology* 21 (1995): 300.

7. Ibid., 289.

8. Bruno Latour, *Science in Action: How to Follow Scientists and Engineers through Society* (Cambridge, Mass.: Harvard University Press, 1987), 29.

9. Ibid., 30.

10. Ibid., 31.

11. Ibid., 62.

12. Bruno Latour, *The Pasteurization of France* (Cambridge, Mass.: Harvard University Press, 1988).

13. See Ruth Macklin's "The Forms and Norms of Closure" in H. Tristram Engelhardt Jr. and Arthur L. Caplan, eds., *Scientific Controversies: Case Studies in the Resolution and Closure of Disputes in Science and Technology* (Cambridge: Cambridge University Press, 1987). For other examples of studies on the sociology of scientific controversies, see Dorothy Nelkin, ed., *Controversy: Politics of Technical Decision* (London: Sage, 1979); Harry M. Collins, *Changing Order: Replication and Induction in Scientific Practice* (London: Sage, 1985); and Brian Martin, *Scientific Knowledge in Controversy: The Social Dynamics of the Fluoridation Debate* (Albany: State University of New York Press, 1991).

14. Thomas Gieryn, "Boundary-Work and the Demarcation of Science from Non-Science: Strains and Interests in Professional Interests of Scientists," *American Sociological Review* 48 (1983): 781.

15. Michèle Lamont and Virág Molnár, "The Study of Boundaries in the Social Sciences," *American Sociological Review* 28 (2002): 179.

16. Mario L. Small, "Departmental Conditions and the Emergence of New Disciplines: Two Cases in the Legitimation of African-American Studies," *Theory and Society* 28 (1999).

17. Donald Wiebe, *The Politics of Religious Studies: The Continuing Conflict with Theology in the Academy* (New York: St. Martin's, 1999), 12.

18. See, for instance, Joseph M. Kitagawa and John S. Strong, "Friedrich Max Müller and the Comparative Study of Religion," in *Nineteenth Century Religious Thought in the West*, ed. Ninian Smart et al. (Cambridge: Cambridge University Press, 1985); Maurice Olender, *The Language of Paradise: Race, Religion, and Philology in the Nineteenth Century*, trans. Arthur Goldhammer (Cambridge, Mass.: Harvard University Press, 1992); Adrian Cunningham, "Religious Studies in the Universities: England," in King, *Turning Points in Religious Studies*; and Masuzawa, *Invention of World Religions*.

19. Russell T. McCutcheon, *Manufacturing Religion: The Discourse on Sui Generis Religion and the Politics of Nostalgia* (New York: Oxford University Press, 1997), 58–59.

20. Besides being considered the founder of comparative religion, Max Müller is also remembered today as a colorful and somewhat controversial figure in the history of Oxford University. In *The History of the University of Oxford*, there are more references to Max Müller than to Henry Liddell, the powerful dean of Christ Church and later vice-chancellor; see M. G. Brock and M. C. Curthoys,

eds., *The History of the University of Oxford, Volume VII: Nineteenth-Century Oxford, Part 2* (Oxford: Clarendon, 2000).

21. Paul Rabinow, ed., *The Foucault Reader* (New York: Pantheon Books, 1984), 114.

22. Ibid., 114.

23. For a history of Sanskrit study in Germany, see Douglas T. McGetchin, Peter K. J. Park, and Damodar SarDesai, eds., *Sanskrit and "Orientalism": Indology and Comparative Linguistics in Germany, 1750–1958* (New Delhi: Manohar, 2004). See also Lourens van den Bosch, *Friedrich Max Müller: A Life Devoted to Humanities* (Leiden: Brill, 2002).

24. See Bosch, *Friedrich Max Müller*; Nirad C. Chaudhuri, *Scholar Extraordinary: The Life of Professor the Rt. Hon. Friedrich Max Müller* (London: Chatto & Windus, 1974); and Friedrich Max Müller, *Chips from a German Workshop* (New York: Scribner, 1869).

25. Chaudhuri, *Scholar Extraordinary*, 142–43.

26. It is ironic that the Goethe Institutes sponsored by the German government were renamed the Max Müller Institute in India. According to the German Embassy in New Delhi,

> In India, it is the Culture Department of the German Embassy and the six branches of the Goethe-Institut, named Max Mueller Bhawans after the famed German Indologist Max Mueller, that deal with bilateral cultural affairs—each complementing the other. The Culture Department is responsible for fundamental and policy matters of cultural affairs, whereas the Max Mueller Bhavans are involved in art practice, concentrating on executing cultural programmes and projects, mostly on a bilateral basis.

See German Embassy, New Delhi, "Bilateral Cultural Relations, " http://www .india.diplo.de/Vertretung/indien/en/13__Culture/Bilaterals/Bilateral__Relations .html.

27. Chaudhuri, *Scholar Extraordinary*, 109.

28. Peter Sutcliffe, *The Oxford University Press: An Informal History* (Oxford: Oxford University Press, 1978), 42.

29. Chaudhuri, *Scholar Extraordinary*, 221.

30. Arthur Anthony Macdonell, "Max Müller, Friedrich 1823–1900," in *The Dictionary of National Biography*, ed. Leslie Stephen and Sidney Lee (London: Smith, Elder & Co., 1901), 1024–25.

31. Chaudhuri, *Scholar Extraordinary*, 200–222.

32. Friedrich Max Müller, "List of Testimonials: In Favour of Max Müller, Fellow of All Souls College, M.A. Christ Church," in *Max Müller Papers* (Oxford: Bodleian Library, 1860).

33. Max Müller, "Boden Sanskrit Professorship, Dec. 1, 1860," in *Max Müller Papers* (Oxford: Bodleian Library, 1860). The emphases and the capitalization are original.

34. One could indeed argue that, throughout his life, Max Müller's work was intimately connected to his Christian evangelical mentality. Maurice Olender writes, "If Max Müller fought hard for recognition of 'the legitimate place of the religions of those called uncivilized,' the logic of his argument simultaneously

assured the immense superiority of Christianity 'over all other religions'"; see Olender, *Language of Paradise*, 91. For a comprehensive analysis of the relationship between the world religion discourse and Christianity, please see ibid. and Masuzawa, *Invention of World Religions*.

35. Macdonell, "Max Müller, Friedrich 1823–1900."

36. Max Müller, *Lectures on the Science of Religion, with a Paper on Buddhist Nihilism, and a Translation of the Dhammapada or "Path of Virtue"* (New York: Scribner, 1872).

37. William Dwight Whitney, "Müller's Rig-Veda and Commentary," *The New Englander* 35 (1876): 772, 791.

38. Cited in Stephen G. Alter, *William Dwight Whitney and the Science of Language* (Baltimore: Johns Hopkins University Press, 2005), 4. For a comprehensive account of the birth of the science of language and the centrality of the idea of language in modern intellectual history, see Geoffrey Galt Harpham, *Language Alone: The Critical Fetish of Modernity* (New York: Routledge, 2002).

39. Alter, *William Dwight Whitney*, 174–75.

40. Kitagawa and Strong, "Friedrich Max Müller," 208–9.

41. Max Müller, "The Sub-Librarianship of the Bodleian Library," in *Max Müller Papers* (Oxford: Bodleian Library, 1865).

42. Max Müller, "Letters on Various Controversies in Which Müller Was Involved, 1845–91," in *The Papers of Friedrich Max Müller* (Oxford: Bodleian Library, University of Oxford, 1845–91).

43. Girardot, *Victorian Translation of China*, 161. Legge's *Chinese Classics* was published by Trübner between 1861 and 1872; see James Legge, *The Chinese Classics: With a Translation, Critical and Exegetical Notes, Prolegomena, and Copious Indexes* (London: Trübner, 1861–72).

44. Georgina Max Müller, *The Life and Letters of the Right Honourable Friedrich Max Müller* (London: Longmans, Green, and Co., 1902), 510.

45. Max Müller and Stone, *Essential Max Müller*, 115.

46. Max Müller, "The Religions of China," in *Last Essays: Essays on the Science of Religion* (New York: Longmans, Green, and Co., 1901), 262.

47. James Legge, *Confucianism in Relation to Christianity: A Paper Read before the Missionary Conference in Shanghai on May 11th, 1877* (Shanghai: Kelly and Walsh, 1877).

48. Legge, *Religions of China*, 4.

49. Ibid., 5–6.

50. Ibid., 5.

51. Ibid., 6.

52. I had the good fortune of examining the Oxford University Press Archive after it was reorganized by Dr. Martin Maw, the archivist of the press, and I was able to obtain records that were previously thought to be unavailable. Norman J. Girardot noted in his 2002 biography of James Legge, "The Oxford University Press archive has only recently been professionalized. Years of neglect have taken their toll on the existence and condition of material. . . . The Oxford University Press archive (i.e. contained in the separate Sacred Books of the East files) have no documents specially relating to the approval and Delegates' vote on the Sacred Books"; see Girardot, *Victorian Translation of China*, 646–47. I did find

documents relating to the delegates' vote on the Sacred Books in the archive, which are in the "Minutes of the Delegates, 1876." Max Müller first "offers translation of the Sacred Books of the Five Great Oriental Religions" on January 28, 1876, and the delegates "accepted generally" on February 3, 1876, with the condition that "[t]he Dean of Christ Church to communicate with the India Office with a view of obtaining assistance" ("Minutes of the Delegates, 1976," Oxford University Press Archive, Oxford).

53. For instance, Arie L. Molendijk, *The Emergence of the Science of Religion in the Netherlands* (Leiden: Brill, 2005).

54. Jonathan Z. Smith, "A Matter of Class: Taxonomies of Religion," *Harvard Theological Review* 89, no. 4 (1996): 401.

55. C. P. Tiele, *Outline of the History of Religion to the Spread of Universal Religions*, trans. J. Estlin Carpenter (London: Kegan Paul, Trench, Trübner, 1877).

56. Masuzawa, *Invention of World Religions*, 109. For detailed discussions of Tiele's classification system, please ibid., 107–20, and Smith, "Matter of Class," 394–95.

57. Quoted in Masuzawa, *Invention of World Religions*, 110.

58. Please see "Preface," in Müller, *Sacred Books of the East*, 2.

59. Max Müller, *Natural Religion: The Gifford Lectures Delivered before the University of Glasgow in 1888* (London: Longmans, Green, and Co., 1889), 549.

60. "Orders of the Delegates of the Press, 1876" (1876, Oxford University Press Archive, Oxford).

61. "Agreement, the Delegates of the Clarendon Press, Oxford and F. Max Müller" October 19, 1877, Oxford University Press Archive, Oxford).

62. Sutcliffe, *Oxford University Press*, 45.

63. "Letter to the Council of India," in *OS/1/2/5* (April 29, 1876, Oxford University Press Archive, Oxford).

64. Max Müller, "Letter of Resignation to the Vice-Chancellor," in *Max Müller Papers* (Oxford: Bodleian Library, December 1, 1875).

65. Chaudhuri, *Scholar Extraordinary*, 233.

66. The one voice of dissent came from the Oxford writer and mathematician Charles Lutwidge Dodgson, best known as Lewis Carroll. According to Chaudhuri, Dodgson suggested that "the deputy would be the real professor, and the retiring Professor would really get a pension, . . . that the university should be able to provide the pension without mulcting the real professor of half of his income." Dodgson stressed that "he was writing in the interest of the unknown future holder of the Chair, thought also in the interest of Max Müller, 'for surely the very proposal to invite the new Professor to do the work for half the present salary, is to say, by implication, that the work has been hitherto overpaid—against which suspicion I, for one, desire to record my protest.'" See ibid., 233–34.

67. Max Müller, "Preface," in Max Müller, *Sacred Books of the East*, 3.

68. Ibid., 27.

69. I have collected several copies of such pirated or copycat editions; for example, Epiphanius Wilson, *Sacred Books of the East*, rev. ed. (New York: Colonial Press, 1900); Charles F. Horne, ed., *The Sacred Books and Early Literature of the East. Vol. 12 Medieval China* (New York: Parke, Austin, and Lipscomb, 1917).

70. Sutcliffe, *Oxford University Press*, 46. As of 2007 the SBE could be found in the United Nations Educational, Scientific, and Cultural Organization

"UNESCO Collection of Representative Works." The current catalogue has about fourteen hundred titles. See UNESCO, "Literature and Translation."

71. Interview, July 4, 2003.

72. "Letter Re 'Legge: Chinese Classics,'" in *OS/1/2/5* (May 9, 1928, Oxford University Press Archive, Oxford).

73. Sutcliffe, *Oxford University Press*, 44.

74. By 1949 there were already seventy-two quires of Legge's *Chinese Classics*. "Letter Re Legge's Chinese Classics from McNeely," in *OS/1/2/5* (June 14, 1927, Oxford University Press Archive, Oxford).

75. "Letter Re 'Back to Confucius' Movement from McNeely" (November 28, 1932, Oxford University Press Archive, Oxford).

76. Sutcliffe, *Oxford University Press*, xiii.

77. Ibid., 4.

78. "Sacred Books of the East Cheap Editions," in *OS/1/2/5* (February 20, 1908, Oxford University Press Archive, Oxford).

79. For discussions of Max Müller's evangelical tendencies, see Olender, *Language of Paradise*.

80. Masuzawa, *Invention of World Religions*, 20.

81. Ibid., 21.

82. Ibid., 21. Similar arguments have been made regarding the discourse of sinology. For discussions of the colonial genealogy of sinology, see T. H. Barrett's eloquent history of British sinology in *Singular Listlessness: A Short History of Chinese Books and British Scholars* (London: Wellsweep, 1989); also see Ho-fung Hung, "Orientalism and Area Studies: The Case of Sinology," in *Overcoming the Two Cultures: Science Versus the Humanities in the Modern World-System*, ed. Richard E. Lee and Immanuel Wallerstein (Boulder, Colo.: Paradigm, 2004).

83. Masuzawa, *Invention of World Religions*, 27.

84. Cunningham, "Religious Studies in the Universities," 22–23.

85. Brock and Curthoys, *History of the University of Oxford*, 103.

86. Manchester College didn't officially become part of the University of Oxford until 1996, when the queen finally granted it college status within the university. Now it is called Harris Manchester College, Oxford.

87. Ruth Watts, "Manchester College and Education, 1786–1853," in Smith, *Truth, Liberty, Religion*, 82.

88. Arthur J. Long, "The Life and Work of J. Estlin Carpenter," in Smith, *Truth, Liberty, Religion*, 274.

89. Brock and Curthoys, *History of the University of Oxford*, 102.

90. Quoted in Chaudhuri, *Scholar Extraordinary*, 361.

91. Ibid., 361.

92. Neil Spurway, *Humanity, Environment and God: Glasgow Centenary Gifford Lectures* (Oxford: Blackwell, 1993).

93. Hibbert Trust, "About the Trust," http://www.thehibberttrust.org.uk/about.htm.

94. Max Müller, *Lectures on the Origin and Growth of Religion, as Illustrated by the Religions of India 1878, Delivered in the Chapter House, Westminster Abbey, in April, May, and June, 1878* (London: Longmans, Green, and Co., 1878).

95. Chaudhuri, *Scholar Extraordinary*, 357.

96. Brock and Curthoys, *History of the University of Oxford*, 103.

97. Louis Henry Jordan, *Comparative Religion: Its Method and Scope* (London: Henry Frowde, 1908), 13–15.

98. Ibid., 16–17.

99. Max Müller and Stone, *Essential Max Müller*, 117–18.

100. Theodore M. Porter and Dorothy Ross, "Introduction: Writing the History of Social Science," in Porter and Ross, *Cambridge History of Science*.

101. George W. Stocking, Jr., *Victorian Anthropology* (New York: Free Press, 1987), 257–73; Adam Kuper, "Anthropology," in Porter and Ross, *Cambridge History of Science*, 355.

102. The growth of academic sociology was slower in Germany, despite the significant contributions of classical theorists such as Marx, Simmel, and Weber, with the first chair of sociology created in 1919. In Britain the first chair of sociology was established in 1907 at the London School of Economics for Leonard Hobhouse, and it was the only chair in sociology until after the World War II; see Robert C. Bannister, "Sociology," in Porter and Ross, *Cambridge History of Science*, 341–43.

103. Cunningham, "Religious Studies in the Universities," 23.

104. Ibid., 23.

105. Joseph M. Kitagawa, "Introduction to the *Essays in the History of Religions* by Joachim Wach," In *Essays in the History of Religions*, edited by Joseph M. Kitagawa and Gregory D. Alles (New York: Macmillan, 1988), vii.

106. J.J.M. De Groot, *Religion in China: Universism: A Key to the Study of Taoism and Confucianism* (New York: Putnam, 1912).

107. Jordan, *Comparative Religion*, 20.

108. Edward Said, *Orientalism* (New York: Vintage, 1979), 3.

109. Randall Collins, *The Sociology of Philosophies: A Global Theory of Intellectual Change* (Cambridge, Mass.: Harvard University Press, 1998), 1–3.

110. Andrew Abbott, *Chaos of Disciplines* (Chicago: University of Chicago Press, 2001), 139.

111. Ibid., 140.

112. Ibid.

Chapter 3
The Confucianism as a Religion Controversy in Contemporary China

1. Robert Wuthnow, *Communities of Discourse: Ideology and Social Structure in the Reformation, the Enlightenment, and European Socialism* (Cambridge, Mass.: Harvard University Press, 1989), 5.

2. Ibid., 5.

3. Although it was officially founded in 1977, CASS was set up on the basis of the Division of Philosophy and the Social Sciences at the Chinese Academy of Sciences, which was created in 1949.

4. From the interview with Mr. Jin Ze, the deputy director of the Institute of World Religions at CASS, January 13, 2004, and from the speech given by the general secretary of CASS on the occasion of the fortieth anniversary of the establishment of the Institute of World Religion, September 24, 2004.

5. Mao Zedong, "Mao Zedong Tongzhi Guanyu Jiaqiang Zongjiao Wenti Yanjiu De Pishi" [Memo from Comrade Mao Zedong Regarding the Strengthening

of Studies of Religions] (December 30, 1963), http://zjwh.qikan.com/Article
View.aspx?titleid=zjwh20040403.

6. For a detailed analysis of the birth of religious research in China, see Fenggang Yang, "Between Secularist Ideology and Desecularizing Reality: The Birth
and Growth of Religious Research in Communist China," *Sociology of Religion*
65, no. 2 (2004).

7. I was turned down repeatedly in my quest to consult the State Administration of Religious Affairs (SARA) archive in 2003–4. In my telephone conversations
with someone knowledgeable about the archival documents at SARA, I was told
that the documents related to the establishment of the category of Five Major Religions were stored in the Central Archive in the National Archive, along with other
classified political documents. The documents are not available for research because "discussions of religion are too sensitive to be open to scholars." The official
also expressed her view that "Confucianism is definitely not counted as a religion
in our thinking, because it doesn't have supernatural beliefs or rituals. It's natural
that it was not included in the Five Major Religions." In the end I did secure an
interview with an official working for the bureau, who shall remain anonymous.

8. Zhu De, the legendary general and a close colleague of Mao's, was at one
point in his youth a Daoist priest before he joined the Communist Party. Zhu De
must have reasoned that the only way to help the Daoists avoid future prosecu-
tion was to make them part of an officially recognized and legitimate religion. But
he didn't expect the onset of the Cultural Revolution, which sought the destruction of anything relating to religion.

9. From my interview with Professor Ren on January 8, 2004, in the Chinese National Library, Beijing. The People's Political Consultative Congress is a
so-called democratic association for national policy consultation; it is run by the
state in an effort to control different religious associations, several "democratic
parties," various mass organizations, and notable individual intellectuals.

10. Ren Jiyu, ed., *Rujiao Wenti Zhenglun Ji* [Confucianism as a Religion De-
bate] (Beijing: Religion and Culture Press, 2000), 1–21.

11. Ibid., 15.

12. Ibid.

13. Ibid., 21.

14. Wen Li, "Guanyu Rujiao Yu Zongjiao De Taolun" [Confucianism and Religion Debate], *Zhongguo zhexue shi* [The History of Chinese Philosophy] 2 (2002).

15. Tu Weiming, ed., *The Triadic Chord: Confucian Ethics, Industrial East
Asia, and Max Weber: Proceedings of the 1987 Singapore Conference on Confu-
cian Ethics and the Modernization of Industrial East Asia* (Singapore: Institute of
East Asian Philosophies, 1991).

16. Julia Ching, *Chinese Religions* (Maryknoll, N.Y.: Orbis Books, 1993).

17. Han Xing, *Rujiao Wenti: Zhengming Yu Fansi* [Question of Confucian
Religion: Controversies and Reflections] (Shaanxi: Shaanxi People's Publishing
House, 2004).

18. Chen Yongming, "Guojiaji De Doufuzha Gongcheng" [The Federal Project Made of Tofu Dregs: Reflections on the First Volume of *History of Confucianism as a Religion in China*] (2001), http://www.confucius2000.com/scholar/
drjshshyg.htm.

19. Li Shen, "Zhongguo Rujiaoshi Zaokong Zhounianji" [Remarks on the First Anniversary of the Attack on History of Confucianism as a Religion in China] (October 16, 2002), http://www.confucius2000.com/confucian/rujiao/zgrjszkznj.htm.

20. Han, *Rujiao Wenti: Zhengming Yu Fansi*.

21. Li now holds a professorship in Shanghai, and he is also affiliated with *Science and Atheism*, a journal published by the Chinese Association of the Study of Atheism.

22. Cao Zhongjian, ed., *Zhongguo Zongjiaoyanjiu Nianjian, 2001–2002* [Annual of Religious Studies in China, 2001–2002] (Beijing: Chinese Academy of Social Sciences Press, 2003).

23. Wang Dasan, "Dalu Xin Rujia Yu Xiandai Xin Rujia" [Mainland China New Confucians and Modern New Confucians] (September 29, 2009), http://www.xici.net/d31196763.htm.

24. Editorial Board, "Zhongguo Rujiao Yangjiu Tongxun Fakanci" [Inaugural Editorial of the Newsletter for the Study of Confucianism in China].

25. China Confucianism Online, "Zhongguo Rujiao Wang" [China Confucianism Online], http://www.chinarujiao.net/.

26. Jiang Qing, ed., *Zhonghua Wenhua Jingdian Jichu Jiaoyu Songben* [The Fundamental Texts of Chinese Culture Classics for Reciting] (Beijing: Gaodeng Jiaoyu Chubanshe, 2004).

27. For instance, see Xue Yong, "Zouxiang Mengmei De Wenhua Baoshou Zhuyi—Chi Dangdai 'Daru' Jiang Qing" [Blind Cultural Conservativism: Refuting the So-Called "Confucian Master" Jiang Qing].

28. Huaxia Fuxing Online, "Yangming Jingshe Huijiang Jianbao" [Yangming Spiritual House Retreat Report] (August 13, 2006), http://www.confucius2000.com/admin/list.asp?id=2574. It is noted in the article that the event was sponsored by the "Confucian Businessmen Zhang Hua and Lai Hongbiao."

29. Naquin, *Peking*.

30. "Qufu Kongmiao Juxing Dadian Jikongzi 2,555 Sui" [Grand Ceremony Venerating Confucius on His 2,555th Birthday Took Place in the Confucius Temple in Qufu], *Xinhua*, September 28, 2004, http://news.xinhuanet.com/photo/2004-09/28/content_2034695.htm.

31. "Quanqiu Jiangban Baisuo Kongzi Xueyuan" [There Will Be 100 Confucius Institutes All over the World], *Xinhua*, November 21, 2004, http://news.xinhuanet.com/newscenter/2004-11/16/content_2222750.htm.

32. Su Shipeng, "Guji Baohu Ying Chuanshi Yu Chutu Bingzhong" [The Preservation of Chinese Classics Should Value Recently Discovered Texts as Well as Received Texts], *People's Daily*, March 27, 2007.

33. "Beijing Yibaibashidui Fuqi Zhongqiu Miandui Kongzi Huaxiang Xuanshi Yongbu Lihun" [180 Couples in Beijing Vowing Never to Divorce before the Portrait of Confucius], *Sina News*, September 29, 2004, http://news.sina.com.cn/s/2004-09-29/08543798162s.shtml.

34. Yang, *Religion in China*, 86–87.

Chapter 4
Confucianism as a World Religion

1. H. H. Gerth and C. Wright Mills, eds., *From Max Weber: Essays in Sociology* (New York: Oxford University Press, 1964), 267.

2. Max Weber, *The Protestant Ethic and the Spirit of Capitalism* (New York: Routledge Classics, 2001 [1904–5]).

3. Weber, *Religion of China*.

4. Max Weber, *The Religion of India: The Sociology of Hinduism and Buddhism*, trans. Hans H. Gerth and Don Martindale (New York: Free Press, 1958 [1916–17]). There is one reference to Max Müller in Weber's discussion of the Vedas (see p. 27), which means that Weber had certainly consulted Max Müller's writing.

5. Max Weber, *Ancient Judaism*, trans. Hans H. Gerth and Don Martindale (New York: Free Press, 1952 [1917–19]).

6. Gerth and Mills, *From Max Weber*, ix.

7. For instance, see Robert Bellah, *Tokugawa Religion: The Cultural Roots of Modern Japan* (New York: Free Press, 1957); Toby E. Huff and Wolfgang Schluchter, eds., *Max Weber and Islam* (New Brunswick, N.J.: Transaction, 1999); Bryan S. Turner, *Weber and Islam* (London: Routledge Kegan Paul, 1978); and David Martin Jones, *The Image of China in Western Social and Political Thought* (Hampshire: Palgrave, 2001). The historian Michael Puett has also addressed Weber's treatment of Confucianism; see Michael Puett, *To Become a God: Cosmology, Sacrifice, and Self-Divinization in Early China* (Cambridge, Mass.: Harvard University Press, 2002), 5–8. Scholars have also been examining the multifaceted historical conditions under which Weber produced his analysis of China. In his remarkable comparative study of the German colonial state, the sociologist George Steinmatz states,

> Weber's *Religion of China* was structured around the premise of Chinese economic stagnation, which he explained in terms of shortcomings of Chinese values or national culture. He drew most heavily on the writings of Jan de Groot, who considered the Chinese to be "semi-civilized" and prone to religious "fanaticism." Weber was ignorant of the growth of Chinese capitalism in the late nineteenth century, including in the region around the future German colony in Shandong Province. He also ignored the fettering impact of Western imperialism on Chinese capitalism and of British opium on the Chinese work ethic. Weber accepted de Groot's sweeping assertion that Confucianism was oriented toward "adjustment to the world" rather than "rational transformation of the world" in ways that prevented the emergence of "those great and methodical business conceptions which are rational in nature."

See *The Devil's Handwriting: Precoloniality and the German Colonial State in Qingdao, Samoa, and Southwest Africa* (Chicago: Chicago Press, 2007), 416.

8. Thomas S. Kuhn, *The Structure of Scientific Revolution* (Chicago: University of Chicago Press, 1962), x.

9. Ibid., 10.

10. Ibid., 19.

11. I briefly discuss the reception of the world religions paradigm in China in chapter 4.

12. Huston Smith, *The World's Religions: Our Great Wisdom Traditions* (San Francisco: Harper, 1991 [1958]).

13. Huston Smith, *The Illustrated World's Religions: Guide to Our Wisdom Traditions* (San Francisco: Harper, 1995).

14. Lewis Hopfe and Mark Woodward, *Religions of the World*, 10th ed. (Upper Saddle River, N.J.: Prentice Hall, 2006); Michael Molloy, *Experiencing the World's Religions: Tradition, Challenge, and Change*, 3rd ed. (New York: McGraw-Hill, 2004).

15. Brandon Toropov and Father Luke Buckles, *The Complete Idiot's Guide to World Religions*, 3rd ed. (New York: Alpha Books, 2004).

16. Philip Novak, *The World's Wisdom: Sacred Texts of the World's Religions* (San Francisco: Harper, 1995).

17. Glenn Masuchika, "Review of The World's Wisdom: Sacred Texts of the World's Religions," *Library Journal* (1994): www.libraryjournal.com.

18. Jacob Neusner, ed., *World Religions in America: An Introduction*, 3rd ed. (Grand Rapids, Mich.: Westminster John Knox, 2003), 157.

19. Jeffrey Moses, *Oneness: Great Principles Shared by All Religions*, rev. ed. (New York: Ballantine Books, 2002).

20. Pope Benedict, *Truth and Tolerance: Christian Belief and World Religions*, trans. Henry Taylor (San Francisco: Ignatius Press, 2004), 40–41.

21. Patrick K. O'Brien, ed., *Atlas of World History* (New York: Oxford University Press, 1999).

22. John McCannon, *How to Prepare for the AP World History* (Hauppauge, N.Y.: Barron's Educational Series, 2005).

23. Mary Pope Osborne, *One World, Many Religions: The Ways We Worship* (New York: Knopf, 1996), front flap.

24. Jennifer Glossop, *The Kids Book of World Religions* (Tonawanda, N.Y.: Kids Can Press, 2003).

25. John Bowker, *World Religions: The Great Faiths Explored & Explained* (New York: DK, 2006).

26. John L. Esposito, Darrell J. Fasching, and Todd Lewis, *World Religions Today* (New York: Oxford University Press, 2005), 437.

27. Here I focus only on English-language books. A discussion of publications on Confucianism in the Chinese language can be found in chapter 4.

28. My first encounter with the copious nineteenth-century texts on world religions was in Firestone Library, Princeton; I'm grateful for the open-stack arrangement that enabled me to step back to see the books as part of a larger picture. My many visits to the Harris Manchester Library, Oxford, especially its Carpenter Collection, one of the best late nineteenth- and early twentieth-century collections of books and pamphlets on comparative religion (especially religions in Asia), made it possible for me to start understanding the patterns. I'm very grateful to Sue Killoran, fellow librarian of Harris Manchester College, for allowing me to sort through the treasures, and for giving me a hard copy of the catalogue of the Carpenter Collection before it was made available online.

29. Although WorldCat offers access to a large number of library catalogs, it is by no means perfect. The three items relating to Confucianism listed on World-Cat for the period between 1800 and 1830 were all misattributed until recently, partly due to the fact that these books are from an earlier time and the so-called copyright pages are not as uniform as today. The first item is *The Rise and Decline of Islam* by William Muir (1819–1905); since he was barely eleven years old in 1830, it's unlikely that his book was published between 1800 and 1830. In fact, his book was published around 1883 by Present Day Tracts. The second

item is *The Ideal Man of Confucianism* by Arnold Foster (1846–1919), who was not even born in 1830 (the information is from the University of Cambridge catalogue, which dates the book as "1800s"). The third and last item is *China's Educational System: What She Studies and What She Needs to Learn*, by a J. L. Stewart. This is most certainly John Leighton Stuart (1876–1962), a missionary and later U.S. ambassador to China, who became the first president of Yenching University in 1919 and had written on Chinese educational issues.

30. These are in fact the reprints of the same 1867 book by James Legge, *The Life and Teachings of Confucius, with Explanatory Notes* (Philadelphia: J.B. Lippincott, 1867).

31. Joseph Edkins, *The Religious Conditions of the Chinese: With Observations on the Prospectors of Christian Conversion Amongst That People* (London: Routledge, Warnes & Routledge, 1859).

32. Louis Henry Jordan, *Comparative Religion: Its Genesis and Growth* (New York: Scribner, 1905).

33. Harvard University, "Committee on the Study of Religion Undergraduate Coursework," http://studyofreligion.fas.harvard.edu/icb/icb.do?keyword=k70796 &tabgroupid=icb.tabgroup108363.

34. Ibid.

35. Yale University, Religious Studies, "Course Listing," http://religiousstudies .yale.edu/course-listings.

36. One may note that Confucianism does not appear in the description of the course "Lecture on World Religions and Ecology: Asian Religions." However, since it is taught by Mary Evelyn Tucker, a well-known scholar on Confucian spirituality (she coedited with Tu Weiming a two-volume book on Confucian spiritual thought and practice) and an expert on Confucianism and ecology, one may infer that Confucianism is very likely to be one of the Asian religions discussed in the course. For Tucker's work, please see Tucker and Weiming, *Confucian Spirituality*, and Mary Evelyn Tucker and John H. Berthrong, *Confucianism and Ecology: The Interrelation of Heaven, Earth, and Humans*, Religions of the World and Ecology (Cambridge, Mass.: Harvard University Center for the Study of World Religions, 1998). The latter is part of a series titled "World Spirituality: An Encyclopedic History of the Religious Quest."

37. Stanford University, "Stanford University Religious Studies Course Bulletin," http://explorecourses.stanford.edu/CourseSearch/search?view=catalog&filter -coursestatus-Active=on&page=0&catalog=&q=introduction+to+chinese+ religions&collapse=.

38. University of Pennsylvania, "Department of Religious Studies Course Offerings," https://www.sas.upenn.edu/religious_studies/pc/course/2012C/RELS001.

39. Duke University, "Religion Department Different Religious Traditions," http://religiondepartment.duke.edu/undergraduate/three-religious-traditions.

40. Duke University, "Religion Department New/Noteworthy Courses," http://religiondepartment.duke.edu/undergraduate/new-courses.

41. Princeton University, "Department of Religion Undergraduate Announcement 2011–12," http://www.princeton.edu/ua/departmentsprograms/rel/.

42. Columbia University course catalogue, http://apps.college.columbia.edu/ unify/bulletinSearch.php?toggleView=open&school=CC&courseIdentifier Var=RELIV2405&header=www.college.columbia.edu%2Finclude%2Fpopup_

header.php&footer=www.college.columbia.edu%2Finclude%2Fpopup_footer
.php.

43. There is no ranking of religious studies or theology programs in *US News & World Report*, nor is there a commonly used ranking of theology PhD programs today. The 1995 National Research Council ranking was the last official one, and it combines religious studies programs with divinity school programs. For a more recent assessment, see R. R. Reno's personal ranking of theology programs. R. R. Reno, "Best Schools for Theology," *First Things: The Journal of Religion, Culture and Public Life*, August 30, 2006.

44. Yale University, "Divinity School Bulletin 2009–2010," Series 105, No. 2, June 20, 2009, 68, http://www.google.com/url?sa=t&rct=j&q=&esrc=s&source=web&cd=4&ved=0CGwQFjAD&url=http%3A%2F%2Fwww.yale.edu%2Fprinter%2Fbulletin%2Farchivepdffiles%2FDivinity%2FDivinity_2009-2010.pdf&ei=kWYRUJPvMcKS0QG0oYCYBQ&usg=AFQjCNFuvkNqJuIA-R7izhaCm2Hv0hv3-g.

45. PrincetonTheological Seminary, "PrincetonTheological Seminary 2007–2008 Catalogue," 65, https://our.ptsem.edu/UploadedFiles/pdf/Catalogue2007-2008.pdf.

46. University of Chicago, Divinity School, "Faculty Profiles," http://divinity.uchicago.edu/faculty/yu.shtml.

47. John H. Berthrong and Evelyn Nagai Berthrong, *Confucianism: A Short Introduction* (Oxford: Oneworld, 2000); John H. Berthrong, *All under Heaven: Transforming Paradigms in Confucian-Christian Dialogue* (Albany: State University of New York Press, 1994).

48. Neville, *Boston Confucianism*.

49. D. G. Hart, *The University Gets Religion: Religious Studies in American Higher Education* (Baltimore: Johns Hopkins University Press, 1999), 10.

50. Hart, *University Gets Religion*, 10. A similar trajectory can be found in the institutionalization of religious studies in Britain, although the growth of the discipline there has not been nearly as swift as in the United States; see King, *Turning Points in Religious Studies*.

51. Hart, *University Gets Religion*, ix.

52. American Academy of Religion, "A Brief History of the American Academy of Religion," http://www.aarweb.org/About_AAR/History/default.asp.

53. Hart, *University Gets Religion*, 10–13.

54. American Academy of Religion, "Brief History," http://www.aarweb.org/about/annualreport/AR2006.pdf. This was very likely posed before the release of new figures on AAR members in 2006.

55. American Academy of Religion, "American Academy of Religion Annual Report 2006," 21, www.aarweb.org/Publications/Annual_Report/2006.pdf.

56. Ibid., 2.

57. American Academy of Religion, "Confucian Traditions Group Program Unit Information," http://www.aarweb.org/meetings/annual_meeting/program_units/PUinformation.asp?PUNum=AARPU016.

58. I was a participant in the Religious Status of Confucianism panel at the 2007 AAR meeting; my paper was titled "Is Confucianism a Religion in China?"

59. I thank Keith Knapp, cochair of the Confucian Traditions Group, for this valuable information.

60. As a sociologist who studies Confucianism, I have attended all of these conferences. Most of the time I have been either the only one studying Confucianism as a religion among sociologists of religion (at the ASA, SSSR, and ASR) or the only sociologist among scholars from other disciplines who study Confucianism as a religion (AAR and AAS).

Chapter 5
Counting Confucians through Social Scientific Research

1. I thank Dr. Jibum Kim of NORC at the University of Chicago for directing me to census data on Confucianism in South Korea, and I'm grateful to Prof. Edward Y. J. Chung of the University of Prince Edward Island for helping me with Confucian rituals in Korea. I also thank Prof. Mark MacWilliams at St. Lawrence University for helpful references on Confucianism in Japan.

2. Tu Weiming, *Confucian Traditions in East Asian Modernity: Moral Education and Economic Culture in Japan and the Four Mini-Dragons* (Cambridge, Mass.: Harvard University Press, 1996); Tamney and Chiang, *Modernization, Globalization, and Confucianism.*

3. Elman, Duncan, and Ooms, *Rethinking Confucianism.*

4. Hongkyung Kim, "A Party for the Spirits: Ritual Practice in Confucianism," in *Religions of Korea in Practice*, ed. Robert E. Buswell Jr. (Princeton: Princeton University Press, 2007).

5. Bellah, *Tokugawa Religion*; Edwin O. Reischauer, *The Japanese* (Cambridge, Mass: Harvard University Press, 1977).

6. Kazuo Kasahara, ed., *A History of Japanese Religion* (Tokyo: Kosei, 2001), 475–76.

7. Ian Reader, *Religion in Contemporary Japan* (Honolulu: University of Hawaii Press, 1991), 30.

8. M. Fournier De Flaix, "Development of Statistics of Religion," *Publications of the American Statistical Association* 3, no. 17 (1892): 32.

9. Jordan, *Comparative Religion.*

10. World Values Survey, "World Values Survey: China," http://www.world valuessurvey.org/index_surveys. The World Values Survey is a leading comparative data set; the research is conducted by an international network of social scientists, who survey the values and belief of people in more than eighty societies on six continents. Because of its comparative nature, the questions regarding religion are similar in surveys conducted in different countries.

11. The emphases in this section are mine.

12. This is the only question of the Taiwan survey that addresses Confucianism or Confucian rituals.

13. The Spiritual Life Study of Chinese Residents survey has a national probability sample of 7,021 adults in fifty-six locations in China. It was administrated by Horizonkey Information and Consulting Co. between May and July 2007. The survey is also referred to as the 2007 Horizon Survey in this chapter. The data set is now available on the website of the Association of Religion Data Archives; see http://www.thearda.com/Archive/Files/Descriptions/SPRTCHNA .asp.

14. Jan Swyngedouw, "Religion in Contemporary Japanese Society," in *Religion and Society in Modern Japan*, ed. Mark R. Mullins, Shimazono Susumu, and Paul L. Swanson (Berkeley, Calif.: Asian Humanities Press, 1993), 55.

15. This idea of the "tool kit" is borrowed from the work of sociologist of culture Ann Swidler; see Ann Swidler, "Culture in Action: Symbols and Strategies," *American Sociological Review* 51 (1986) and Robert Ford Company, "On the Very Idea of Religions (in the Modern West and in Early Medieval China)," *History of Religions* 42, no. 4 (2003): 287–319.

16. Mu-chou Poo, *In Search of Personal Welfare: A View of Ancient Chinese Religion* (Albany: State University of New York Press, 1998), and von Falkenhausen, *Chinese Society in the Age of Confucius*.

17. Nylan and Wilson, *Lives of Confucius*, 145.

18. Lyle B. Steadman and Craig T. Palmer, *The Supernatural and Natural Selection: The Evolution of Religion* (Boulder, Colo.: Paradigm, 2008), 55, 70.

19. Ibid., 68.

20. Robert Smith, *Ancestor Worship in Contemporary Japan* (Stanford, Calif.: Stanford University Press, 1974).

21. Ibid., 1.

22. Martina Deuchler, *The Confucian Transformation of Korea: A Study of Society and Ideology* (Cambridge, Mass.: Harvard University Press, 1992), 284–85.

23. Edward Y. J. Chung, "Confucian *Li* and Family Spirituality: Reflections on the Contemporary Korean Tradition of Ancestral Rites" (paper, annual meeting of the American Academy of Religion, Washington, D.C., 2006).

24. Kim, "Party for the Spirits," 166–67.

Chapter 6
To Become a Confucian

1. Diane Austin-Broos, "The Anthropology of Conversion: An Introduction," in *The Anthropology of Religious Conversion*, ed. Andrew Buckser and Stephen Glazier (Lanham, Md.: Rowman & Littlefield, 2003), 2.

2. William James, *The Varieties of Religious Experience* (New York: Penguin, 1982), 189.

3. Torkel Brekke, "Conversion in Buddhism?" in *Religious Conversions in India: Modes, Motivations, and Meanings*, ed. Rowena Robinson and Sathianathan Clarke (New Delhi: Oxford University Press, 2003), 181–91, 183.

4. See, for instance, David Yamane and Sarah MacMillen, *Real Stories of Christian Initiation: Lessons for and from the RCIA* (Collegeville, Minn.: Liturgical Press, 2006); Anna Mansson-McGinty, *Becoming Muslim: Western Women's Conversions to Islam* (New York: Palgrave Macmillan, 2006).

5. Yang, *Religion in Chinese Society*.

6. Joseph A. Adler, "Confucianism as Religion/Religious Tradition/Neither: Still Hazy after All These Years" (paper, annual meeting of the American Academy of Religion, Washington, D.C., 2006), 10.

7. Wilson, *On Sacred Grounds*.

8. Nylan and Wilson, *Lives of Confucius*, 149–50.

9. Poo, *In Search of Personal Welfare*; and von Falkenhausen, *Chinese Society in the Age of Confucius*.

10. Chin-shing Huang, *Shengxian yu Shengtu* [Sages and Saints: Collected Essays on History and Religion] (Taipei: Asian Culture Press, 2001), 143–44.

11. Brockey, *Journey to the East*, 106–7.

12. Ibid., 107.

13. Ibid., 105.

14. Ibid., 107.

15. Lewis R. Rambo, *Understanding Religious Conversion* (New Haven: Yale University Press, 1993), 13.

16. I intentionally use the term "social rituals" rather than "civil rituals" for the reason that the term "civil rituals" was used by the Jesuits during the Chinese Rites Controversy to refer to rituals that they considered nonreligious, such as the veneration of Confucius and ancestors, but that are seen as religious rites in this analysis.

17. Jiang Qing, *Zhengzhi Ruxue* [Political Confucianism] (Beijing: Sanlian Shudian, 2004); Kang Xiaoguang, *Benevolent Government (Ren Zheng): The Third Path of China's Political Development* (Singapore: World Scientific, 2005).

18. Bell, *China's New Confucianism*.

19. Prasenjit Duara, "Religion and Citizenship in China and the Diaspora," in Yang, *Chinese Religiosities*, 43.

20. Angle, *Contemporary Confucian Political Philosophy*, 7–8.

21. Pierre Hadot, *Philosophy as a Way of Life: Spiritual Exercises from Socrates to Foucault* (Oxford: Blackwell, 1995), 109.

22. Tu Weiming, *Humanity and Self-Cultivation* (Berkeley: University of California Press, 1979); Tu Weiming, *Confucian Thought: Selfhood as Creative Transformation* (Albany: State University of New York Press, 1985); Robert Eno, *The Confucian Creation of Heaven: Philosophy and the Defense of Ritual Mastery* (Albany: State University of New York Press, 1990).

23. Ivanhoe, *Confucian Moral Self Cultivation*, and Xiao, "Ethical Thought in China."

24. Patricia B. Ebrey, ed. and trans., *Chu Hsi's Family Rituals* (Albany: State University of New York Press, 1991), 3–4.

25. Lorraine Daston, "The Moral Economy of Science," *Osiris* 10 (1995): 4.

26. Sharon Lafraniere, "China Might Force Visits to Mom and Dad," *New York Times*, January 29, 2011. I am grateful to Didier Fassin for introducing me to the concept of moral economy.

27. Ian Hacking, "Why Ask What?," in *Social Construction of What?*, 33–34.

28. Elman, Duncan, and Ooms, *Rethinking Confucianism*; and Deuchler, *Confucian Transformation*.

29. Neville, *Boston Confucianism*.

Chapter 7
The Emerging Voices of Women in the Revival of Confucianism

1. This single line from 17.25 of the *Analects* invites several possible interpretations. Contemporary scholars have employed various philological techniques in

order to explain away its unfortunate sexist meaning. For instance, some have interpreted the word *nu* (women) as referring to "women servants" or girls who are underage. Another theory—not as plausible—is that the character *nu* here is in fact a different character, a "borrowed word" (*tongjiazi*) meaning "you." The debate is still ongoing; the China Academic Journals Full-Texts Database contains twenty-two articles dealing with the different interpretations of this sentence published between 1994 and 2010.

2. See, for instance, Li-Hsiang Lisa Rosenlee, *Confucianism and Women: A Philosophical Interpretation* (Albany: State University of New York Press, 2006); Susan Mann and Yu-Yin Cheng, *Under Confucian Eyes: Writings on Gender in Chinese History* (Berkeley: University of California Press, 2001); Ellen Widmer and Kang-i Sun Chang, *Writing Women in Late Imperial China* (Stanford, Calif.: Stanford University Press, 1997). For a more detailed list and analysis, see Joseph Adler, "Daughter/Wife/Mother or Sage/Immortal/Bodhisattva? Women in the Teaching of Chinese Religions," *ASIANetwork Exchange* 14, no. 2 (2006).

3. See John Makeham, *Lost Soul: "Confucianism" in Contemporary Chinese Academic Discourse*, Harvard-Yenching Institute Monographs (Cambridge, Mass.: Harvard University Asia Center for the Harvard-Yenching Institute, 2008).

4. According to the official website for Confucius Institutes, "by the end of August, 2011, 353 Confucius Institutes and 473 Confucius Classrooms had been established in 104 countries and regions in the world." http://english.hanban.org/node_7716.htm.

5. See, for example, Fang-long Shih, "Women, Religions, and Feminism," in *The Sociology of Religion*, ed. Bryan S. Turner (Oxford: Blackwell, 2010), 221–22.

6. Ibid.

7. Ibid., 238.

8. Lisa Ann Raphals, *Sharing the Light: Representations of Women and Virtue in Early China*, SUNY Series in Chinese Philosophy and Culture (Albany, N.Y.: State University of New York Press, 1998); Mann and Cheng, *Under Confucian Eyes*; Rosenlee, *Confucianism and Women*; and Chin, *Authentic Confucius*.

9. Adler, "Daughter/Wife/Mother."

10. Bell, *China's New Confucianism*.

11. Yu Dan's *Lunyu Xinde* now has an English translation, published in October 2009. Yu Dan and Esther Tyldesley, *Confucius from the Heart* (New York: Atria Books, 2009).

12. Bell, *China's New Confucianism*, 163.

13. Ibid., 174.

14. Yu Dan, *The* Analects *from the Heart* (Beijing: Zhonghua Shuju, 2006), 56–57. My edition is the fifteenth printing, in 2007, with three million copies already published. The English translation here is from *Confucius from the Heart*, 82–83.

15. "Guo Qiyong: 'Lunyu Benlai Jiushi Jiachuan Husong Zhixue'" [Guo Qiyong: "The *Analects* Is Meant to Be Read in Every Household"], *Guangming Daily*, April 1, 2008, http://book.people.com.cn/GB/69362/7070134.html.

16. Yu Dan, *Lunyu Xinde* (Beijing: Zhonghua, 2006), 2.

17. "Yu Dan's *The* Zhuangzi *from the Heart* Sold One Million Copies Ahead of Schedule," *Sina News*, March 19, 2007, http://cul.book.sina.com.cn/o/2007-03-19/1025168163.html.

18. "The 2007 List of Wealthiest Writers in China," *Xinhua News*, November 6, 2007, http://news.xinhuanet.com/book/2007-11/06/content_7018276.htm.

19. According to statistics kept by Motigo Webstats, which monitors traffic to websites, on October 29, 2010, there had been 158,920 visits to Confucius2000 .com in the previous week, with an average of 22,703 visits per day.

20. According to statistics available on the website of the Ministry of Education of the People's Republic of China, http://www.moe.edu.cn/publicfiles/business/htmlfiles/moe/s4960/index.html.

21. Yang, *Chinese Religiosities*.

22. Khun Eng Kuah-Pearce, "Cultural and Network Capitals: Chinese Women and the 'Religious' Industry in South China," in *Chinese Women and Their Cultural and Network Capitals*, ed. Khun Eng Kuah (Singapore: Marshall Cavendish Academic, 2004), 124.

23. Nylan and Wilson, *Lives of Confucius*, 165.

24. Billioud and Thoraval, "*Lijiao*."

25. For detailed discussions of traditional rituals in Confucius temples, see Nylan and Wilson, *Lives of Confucius*.

26. A few women can be seen as members of the Kong clan delegation in news pictures of the events. They wear the same formal attire as the men in the clan: dark jackets and yellow silk scarves.

27. Wilson, *On Sacred Grounds*.

28. Vivian-Lee Nyitray, "Fundamentalism and the Position of Women in Confucianism," in *Fundamentalism and Women in World Religions*, ed. Arvind Sharma and Katherine K. Young (New York: T&T Clark, 2007).

29. Chenyang Li, *The Sage and the Second Sex: Confucianism, Ethics, and Gender* (Chicago: Open Court, 2000).

30. Ibid., 39.

31. Eunkang Koh, "Gender Issues and Confucian Scriptures: Is Confucianism Incompatible with Gender Equality in South Korea?," *Bulletin of SOAS* 71, no. 2 (2008).

32. Deborah Achtenberg, "Aristotelian Resources for Feminist Thinking," in *Feminism and Ancient Philosophy*, ed. Julie K. Ward (London: Routledge, 1996), 97.

33. The Day of Qingming, which falls on April 5, is the traditional day for graveside veneration of ancestral spirits. It was declared a national holiday by the state in 2008, allowing people to travel back to their ancestral hometown to perform the ritual.

Chapter 8
The Contemporary Revival and Reinvention of Confucian Ritual Practices

1. The thirteen Confucius temples in Mainland China on which I have conducted research are Beijing Confucius Temple; Tianjin Confucius Temple, city of Tianjin; Qufu Confucius Temple, Shandong Province; Jinan Confucius temple, Shandong Province; Deyang Confucius Temple, Sichuan Province; Bishan Confucius Temple, Sichuan Province; Zizhong Confucius Temple, Sichuan Province; Suzhou Confucius Temple, Jiangsu Province; Nanjing Confucius Temple, Jiangsu

Province; Hangzhou Confucius Temple, Zhejiang Province; Wujiang Confucius Temple, Zhejiang Province; Shanghai Confucius Temple, city of Shanghai; and Foshan Confucius Temple, Guangdong Province. In addition, I visited the Mencius Temple in Zoucheng, Shandong Province.

2. The Confucius temples in Taiwan on which I have conducted research are Taipei Confucius Temple, Taipei; Tainan Confucius Temple, Tainan; and Zhanghua Confucius Temple, Zhanghua.

3. The non-Confucius temple sites are White Cloud Temple, Beijing; Wumiao Temple, Tainan; Baoan Gong, Taipei; and Qingan Gong, Zhanghua.

4. The temple sites in Japan are Yushima Seido, Tokyo; Shizutani Shrine in the Shizutani School, Okayama; Confucius Shrine, Nagasaki; and Confucian Temple, Nagasaki. A related site I visited during fieldwork is the Shinto Tenmangū Shrine in Tokyo, which is a shrine for a god of learning and exams.

5. Matteo Ricci, *Fonti Ricciane*, vol. 1, N. 178, translated by and cited in Minamiki, *Chinese Rites Controversy*, 19–20.

6. Vatican, "1704, Nov. 20: Rome's Evaluation of Maigrot's 1693 Edict," in Noll, *100 Roman Documents*, 13.

7. For a history of the civil examinations, particularly from the twelfth century to the nineteenth century, see Elman, *Cultural History*.

8. The Mencius Temple in Zoucheng, Shandong Province also belongs to this category.

9. Janet Lee Scott, *For Gods, Ghosts and Ancestors: The Chinese Tradition of Paper Offerings* (Seattle: University of Washington Press, 2007), 2.

10. For a discussion of the connection between tourist sites and religious sites in China, see James Robson, "Faith in Museums: On the Confluence of Museums and Religious Sites in Asia," *PMLA* 125, no. 1 (2010).

11. Daniel L. Overmyer, *Local Religion in North China in the Twentieth Century: The Structure and Organization of Community Rituals and Beliefs*, Handbook of Oriental Studies, Section 4, China (Leiden: Brill, 2009), 124.

12. Ibid., 175.

13. These are prayers that I have seen in all Confucius temples in Mainland China, as well as in Taiwan.

14. This is the most commonly seen prayer.

15. Sometimes the prayers are quite complex, such as the following one from the Shanghai Confucius temple: "Dear Confucius, let me offer a wish for myself. Although I feel you may not be powerful (*lingguang*), it is always good to offer as many wishes as possible. My wish is the following: I want to get into a culinary high school, which means my exam score has to be high enough! I want to be the best chef in the future! P.S. By the way, I've been seriously considering Christianity in the past few years, but there is no boundary between beliefs (*xinyang wu guojie*)! Amen. May 28, 2011."

16. Chau offered the following example: "During the course of my fieldwork in Shaanbei, however, I seldom encountered any explicit talk of 'belief in deities.' Shaanbei people do have the word for the verb 'believe' (*xiangxin*) as used in 'I believe what you are saying,' but they do not say 'I believe in the Black Dragon King' or 'I believe in gods and goddesses.' Most important, they do not have the noun 'belief' (as in 'you have the right to hold your religious beliefs') or 'faith'

to refer to the totality of their 'beliefs.' In contemporary elite discourse in China there is the word 'belief' or 'conviction' (*xinyang*), but I have never heard Shaanbei people use it." Chau, *Miraculous Response*, 59–61.

17. Paul Veyne, *Did the Greeks Believe in Their Myths? An Essay on the Constitutive Imagination* (Chicago: University of Chicago Press, 1988), 1.

18. Ibid., xi.

19. Michel Foucault, "Truth and Power," in Rabinow, *Foucault Reader*, 74.

20. Robson, "Faith in Museums."

21. Goossaert and Palmer, *Religious Question in Modern China*, 12–13.

22. Andrew Abbott, "Linked Ecologies: States and Universities as Environments for Professions," *Sociological Theory* 23, no. 3 (2005).

23. Several scholars have produced research examining the revival of Confucian education, including Joy Lam's dissertation in progress on after-school Confucian "sacred text reading" courses (*dujing ban*) and Guillaume Dutournier's work on the emergence of private Confucian schools, or "family schools," such the "Academy of the Mother of Mencius" (*mengmu yuan*), in contemporary China.

24. "Beijing Yibaibashidui Fuqi Zhongqiu Miandui Kongzi Huaxiang Xuanshi Yongbu Lihun" [180 Couples in Beijing Vowing Never to Divorce before the Portrait of Confucius], *Sina News*, September 29, 2004, http://news.sina.com .cn/s/2004-09-29/08543798162s.shtml.

25. See the website for Shenzhen Confucius Hall (*kongsheng tang*) at http:// www.kongshengtang.org/about.asp. The Confucius Hall is partially financed by the Hong Kong Confucian philanthropist Tang Enjia, who has been very active and visible in the current revival of Confucianism in Mainland China. Zhou Beichen, the founder of Confucius Hall, is a Confucian scholar who resigned his university teaching post to be the master (*tangzhu*) of Confucius Hall. He is a student and follower of Jiang Qing, the leading figure in the ongoing movement aiming to reshape Confucianism as a state religion.

26. Billioud, "Confucian Revival," 286.

27. Billioud, "Carrying the Confucian Torch," 220.

Chapter 9
The Politics of the Future of Confucianism

1. Jin Ze and Yonghui Qiu, *Zhongguo Zongjiao Baogao 2010* [Annual Report on China's Religions 2010] (Beijing: Social Sciences Academic Press, 2010).

2. "Rectification of Statues," *Economist*, January 20, 2011.

3. "Confucius Stood Here, but Not for Very Long," *New York Times*, April 23, 2011.

4. "Statue Moved Inside," *China Daily*, April 22, 2011.

5. Xinhua News Agency, "Jesus to Join Confucius as Qufu Plans Church," *China Daily*, December 12, 2010, http://www.chinadaily.com.cn/china/2010-12/13/content_11695800.htm.

6. Confucian Ten Scholars, "Zunzhong Zhonghua Wenhua Shengdi, Tingjian Qufu Jejiao Jiaotang" [Respect the Sacred Ground of Chinese Culture, Stop the Building of the Christian Church in Qufu] (2010), http://www.hxwm.net/view thread.php?tid=51619. It is consigned by the Confucian Ten Scholars, with the

support of ten international and domestic Confucian cultural organizations, as well as ten Confucian websites, including Confucius2000.com and Chinarujiao.net.

7. Smith, *Meaning and End of Religion*, 69.

8. Hacking, *Social Construction of What?*

9. Nedostup, *Superstitious Regimes*.

10. Tony Blair, "How Will Religion's Growth in China Impact Its Relations with the West?," *Washington Post*, April 11, 2011.

11. Angle, *Contemporary Confucian Political Philosophy*, 8.

12. Fenggang Yang, "A Sociological Perspective on Confucianism as Religion" [in Chinese], *Journal of Lanzhou University (Social Sciences)* 36, no. 2 (2008).

13. Helen Hardacre, *Shinto and the State, 1868–1988* (Princeton: Princeton University Press, 1989).

14. This urgency for moral reconstruction is felt strongly in China, intensified by several scandals that have enraged the nation in recent years and have signified for many the final collapse of the moral and ethical order in today's China, where now the brute desire for profit and extreme selfishness have been justified and legitimized by China's tremendous economic success and seem to have in effect become the unspoken law of the land. The scandals include popular milk products with poisonous ingredients that led to the deaths of infants (2008), the disastrous collapse of poorly constructed school buildings in the Sichuan earthquake that led to the deaths of many young children (2008), and the death of a two-year-old girl in a car accident on a city street, in which eighteen bystanders walked past the injured child without stopping to help (2011).

15. Sébastien Billioud, "Revival of Confucianism in the Sphere of the Mores and Reactivation of Civil Religion Debate in China" (paper, City University of Hong Kong Habit of the Heart Conference, December 2011).

16. Ibid., 11.

17. Ji Zhe, "Return to Durkheim: Civil Religion and the Moral Reconstruction in China" (paper, Elementary Forms of Religious Life: A Dialogue between the Disciplines workshop, University of Oxford, July 2011).

18. Billioud, "Revival of Confucianism," 11–12.

19. Fenggang Yang, "Confucianism as Civil Religion" (paper, City University of Hong Kong Habit of the Heart Conference, December 2011), 14.

20. Robert Bellah, "Civil Religion: Term and Concept," in *The Robert Bellah Reader*, ed. Robert N. Bellah and Steven M. Tipton (Durham, N.C.: Duke University Press, 2006), 246.

21. Ji, "Return to Durkheim," 6.

22. Ibid., 8–9.

23. According to Diane Eck's "Pluralism" project, although there are a great number of religions being practiced in contemporary America, only 6 percent of the population practices non-Christian religions, i.e., "diverse religious traditions within the U.S.," not counting diversity within Christianity. See The Pluralism Project, "Statistics," http://pluralism.org/resources/statistics/index.php.

24. See the Horizon Spiritual Life of Chinese Residents survey, 2007.

Bibliography

Abbott, Andrew. *Chaos of Disciplines*. Chicago: University of Chicago Press, 2001.
———. "Linked Ecologies: States and Universities as Environments for Professions." *Sociological Theory* 23, no. 3 (2005): 245–74.
Academia Sinica, Institute of Modern History. *Jiaowu Jiaoan Dang* [Archival Materials Related to Religious Affairs, 1871–78]. Taipei: Academia Sinica, 1976.
Achtenberg, Deborah. "Aristotelian Resources for Feminist Thinking." In *Feminism and Ancient Philosophy*, edited by Julie K. Ward, 95–117. London: Routledge, 1996.
Adler, Joseph A. "Confucianism as Religion/Religious Tradition/Neither: Still Hazy after All These Years." Paper presented at the annual meeting of the American Academy of Religion, Washington, D.C., 2006.
———. "Daughter/Wife/Mother or Sage/Immortal/Bodhisattva? Women in the Teaching of Chinese Religions." *ASIANetwork Exchange* 14, no. 2 (2006): 11–16.
Alter, Stephen G. *William Dwight Whitney and the Science of Language*. Baltimore: Johns Hopkins University Press, 2005.
American Academy of Religion. "American Academy of Religion Annual Report 2006." www.aarweb.org/Publications/Annual_Report/2006.pdf.
———. "A Brief History of the American Academy of Religion." http://www.aarweb.org/about/annualreport/AR2006.pdf.
———. "Confucian Traditions Group Program Unit Information." http://www.aarweb.org/meetings/annual_meeting/program_units/PUinformation.asp?PUNum=AARPU016.
Ammerman, Nancy Tatom. *Everyday Religion: Observing Modern Religious Lives*. Oxford: Oxford University Press, 2007.
Angle, Stephen C. *Sagehood: The Contemporary Significance of Neo-Confucian Philosophy*. Oxford: Oxford University Press, 2009.
———. *Contemporary Confucian Political Philosophy: Toward Progressive Confucianism*. Cambridge: Polity, 2012.
Asad, Talal. *Genealogies of Religion: Discipline and Reasons of Power in Christianity and Islam*. Baltimore: Johns Hopkins University Press, 1993.
Austin-Broos, Diane. "The Anthropology of Conversion: An Introduction." In *The Anthropology of Religious Conversion*, edited by Andrew Buckser and Stephen Glazier, 1–14. Lanham, Md.: Rowman & Littlefield, 2003.
Bannister, Robert C. "Sociology." In Porter and Ross, *Cambridge History of Science*, 329–53.

Barboza, David. "After Suicides, Scrutiny of China's Grim Factories." *New York Times*, June 6, 2010.

Barrett, T. H. *Singular Listlessness: A Short History of Chinese Books and British Scholars*. London: Wellsweep, 1989.

Barrett, T. H. and Francesca Tarocco. "Terminology and Religious Identity: Buddhism and the Genealogy of the Term *Zongjiao*." In *Dynamics in the History of Religions between Asia and Europe: Encounters, Notions, and Comparative Perspectives*, edited by Volkharde Krech and Marion Steineke, 307–19. Leiden and Boston: Brill, 2012.

Bastid-Bruguiere, Marianne. "Liang Qichao and the Question of Religion (Liang Qichao Et Le Problème De La Religion)." In *Liang Qichao, Meiji Riben, Xifang* [Liang Qichao, Meiji Japan and the West], edited by Hazama Naoki, 400–457. Beijing: Shehui kexue wenxian chubanshe, 2001.

Beckford, James A., and N. J. Demerath. *The Sage Handbook of the Sociology of Religion*. Thousand Oaks, Calif.: Sage, 2007.

Bell, Daniel. *East Meets West: Human Rights and Democracy in East Asia*. Princeton: Princeton University Press, 2000.

———. *Beyond Liberal Democracy: Political Thinking for an East Asian Context*. Princeton: Princeton University Press, 2006.

———. *China's New Confucianism: Politics and Everyday Life in a Changing Society*. Princeton: Princeton University Press, 2008.

Bell, Daniel, and Joanne Bauer, eds. *The East Asian Challenge for Human Rights*. New York: Cambridge University Press, 1999.

Bell, Daniel, and Chaibong Hahm. *Confucianism for the Modern World*. New York: Cambridge University Press, 2003.

Bellah, Robert N. *Tokugawa Religion: The Cultural Roots of Modern Japan*. New York: Free Press, 1957.

———. *The Robert Bellah Reader*. Edited by Robert N. Bellah and Steven M. Tipton. Durham, N.C.: Duke University Press, 2006.

———. *Religion in Human Evolution*. Cambridge, Mass.: Harvard University Press, 2011.

Berthrong, John H. *All under Heaven: Transforming Paradigms in Confucian-Christian Dialogue*. Albany: State University of New York Press, 1994.

———. "Review of the Victorian Translation of China." *Journal of Chinese Philosophy* 31, no. 3 (2004): 412–17.

Berthrong, John H., and Evelyn Nagai Berthrong. *Confucianism: A Short Introduction*. Oxford: Oneworld, 2000.Billioud, Sébastien. "Carrying the Confucian Torch to the Masses: The Challenge of Structuring the Confucian Revival in the People's Republic of China." *Oriens Extremus* 49 (2010): 201–24.

———. "Confucian Revival and the Emergence of 'Jiaohua Organizations': A Case Study of the Yidan Xuetang." *Modern China* 37, no. 3 (2011): 286–314.

———. "Revival of Confucianism in the Sphere of the Mores and Reactivation of Civil Religion Debate in China." Paper presented at the City University of Hong Kong Habit of the Heart Conference, December 2011.

Billioud, Sébastien, and Joël Thoraval. "*Lijiao*: The Return of Ceremonies Honouring Confucius in Mainland China." *China Perspectives* 4 (2009): 82–100.

Biondi-Fumasoni, Cardinal Pietro, and Archbishop Celso Constantini. "1939, Dec. 8: The Sacred Congregation for the Propagation of the Faith: Instruction Concerning Certain Ceremonies and the Oath about the Chinese Rites." In Noll, *100 Roman Documents*, Document No. 99, 87–88.

Blair, Tony. "How Will Religion's Growth in China Impact Its Relations with the West?" *Washington Post*, April 11, 2011.

Bloom, Irena, and Wayne L. Proudfoot, eds. *Religious Diversity and Human Rights*. New York: Columbia University Press, 1996.

Bol, Peter. *This Culture of Ours*. Palo Alto, Calif.: Stanford University Press, 1992.

Bosch, Lourens van den. *Friedrich Max Müller: A Life Devoted to Humanities*. Leiden: Brill, 2002.

Bowker, John. *World Religions: The Great Faiths Explored & Explained*. New York: DK, 2006.

Brekke, Torkel. "Conversion in Buddhism?" In *Religious Conversions in India: Modes, Motivations, and Meanings*, edited by Rowena Robinson and Sathianathan Clarke, 181–91. New Delhi: Oxford University Press, 2003.

Brock, M. G., and M. C. Curthoys, eds. *The History of the University of Oxford, Volume VII: Nineteenth-Century Oxford, Part 2*. Oxford: Clarendon, 2000.

Brockey, Liam Matthew. *Journey to the East: The Jesuit Mission to China, 1579–1724*. Cambridge, Mass.: Belknap, 2007.

Cao Zhongjian, ed. *Zhongguo Zongjiaoyanjiu Nianjian, 2001–2002* [Annual of Religious Studies in China, 2001–2002]. Beijing: Chinese Academy of Social Sciences Press, 2003.

Chan, Wing-Tsit. *A Source Book in Chinese Philosophy*. Princeton: Princeton University Press, 1963.

Chau, Adam Yuet. *Miraculous Response: Doing Popular Religion in Contemporary China*. Stanford, Calif.: Stanford University Press, 2006.

Chaudhuri, Nirad C. *Scholar Extraordinary: The Life of Professor the Rt. Hon. Friedrich Max Müller*. London: Chatto & Windus, 1974.

Chen, Hsi-Yuan. "Confucianism Encounters Religion: The Formation of Religious Discourse and the Confucian Movement in China." PhD diss., Harvard University, 1999.

Chen Yongming. "Guojiaji de Doufuzha Gongcheng" [The Federal Project Made of Tofu Dregs: Reflections on the First Volume of *History of Confucianism as a Religion in China*]. 2001. http://www.confucius2000.com/scholar/drjshshyg.htm.

Chin, Ann-ping. *The Authentic Confucius: A Life of Thought and Politics*. New York: Scribner, 2007.

China Confucianism Online. "Zhongguo Rujiao Wang" [China Confucianism Online]. http://www.chinarujiao.net.

Ching, Julia. *Chinese Religions*. Maryknoll, N.Y.: Orbis Books, 1993.

Chow, Kai-wing, Tze-ki Hon, Hung-yok Ip, and Don C. Price, ed. *Beyond the May Fourth Paradigm: In Search of Chinese Modernity*. Lanham, Md.: Lexington Books/Rowman & Littlefield, 2008.

Chung, Edward Y. J. "Confucian *Li* and Family Spirituality: Reflections on the Contemporary Korean Tradition of Ancestral Rites." Paper presented at the annual meeting of the American Academy of Religion, Washington, D.C., 2006.

Collins, Harry M. *Changing Order: Replication and Induction in Scientific Practice*. London: Sage, 1985.

Collins, Randall. *The Sociology of Philosophies: A Global Theory of Intellectual Change*. Cambridge, Mass.: Harvard University Press, 1998.

Company, Robert Ford. "On the Very Idea of Religions (in the Modern West and in Early Medieval China)." *History of Religions* 42, no. 4 (2003): 287–319.

Confucian Ten Scholars. "Zunzhong Zhonghua Wenhua Shengdi, Tingjian Qufu Jejiao Jiaotang" [Respect the Sacred Ground of Chinese Culture, Stop the Building of the Christian Church in Qufu]. 2010. http://www.hxwm.net/viewthread.php?tid=51619.

Confucius Institutes. "About Confucius Institutes." Confucius Institute Headquarters. http://english.hanban.org/node_7716.htm.

"Confucius Stood Here, but Not for Very Long." *New York Times*, April 23, 2011.

Cummins, J. S. *A Question of Rites: Friar Domingo Navarrete and the Jesuits in China*. Aldershot: Scolar Press, 1993.

Cunningham, Adrian. "Religious Studies in the Universities: England." In King, *Turning Points in Religious Studies*, 21–31.

Daston, Lorraine. "The Moral Economy of Science." *Osiris* 10 (1995): 2–24.

Davidman, Lynn. *Tradition in a Rootless World: Women Turn to Orthodox Judaism*. Berkeley: University of California Press, 1993.

de Bary, Wm. Theodore, and Tu Weiming, eds. *Confucianism and Human Rights*. New York: Columbia University Press, 1998.

Defoort, Carine. "Is There Such a Thing as Chinese Philosophy? Arguments of an Implicit Debate." *Philosophy East & West* 51, no. 3 (2001): 393–413.

De Groot, J.J.M. *Religion in China: Universism: A Key to the Study of Taoism and Confucianism*. New York: Putnam, 1912.

Deuchler, Martina. *The Confucian Transformation of Korea: A Study of Society and Ideology*. Cambridge, Mass.: Harvard University Press, 1992.

Duara, Prasenjit. "Religion and Citizenship in China and the Diaspora." In Yang, *Chinese Religiosities*, 43–64.

Duffy, Cathy. *100 Top Picks for Homeschool Curriculum: Choosing the Right Curriculum and Approach for Your Child's Learning Style*. Nashville, Tenn.: Broadman & Holman, 2005.

Ebrey, Patricia B., ed. and trans. *Chu Hsi's Family Rituals*. Albany: State University of New York Press, 1991.

Edkins, Joseph. *The Religious Conditions of the Chinese: With Observations on the Prospectors of Christian Conversion Amongst That People*. London: Routledge, Warnes & Routledge, 1859.

Eliade, Mircea. *The Sacred and the Profane: The Nature of Religion*. 1st American ed. New York: Harcourt, 1959.

Elman, Benjamin A. *A Cultural History of Civil Examinations in Late Imperial China*. Berkeley: University of California Press, 2000.

Elman, Benjamin A., John B. Duncan, and Herman Ooms, eds. *Rethinking Confucianism: Past and Present in China, Japan, Korea, and Vietnam*. Los Angeles: UCLA Asian Pacific Monograph Series, 2002.

Elwell, Walter A., and Robert W. Yarbrough. *Encountering the New Testament: A Historical and Theological Survey*. Encountering Biblical Studies. 2nd ed. Grand Rapids, Mich.: Baker Academic, 2005.

Engelhardt, H. Tristram, and Arthur L. Caplan, eds. *Scientific Controversies: Case Studies in the Resolution and Closure of Disputes in Science and Technology*. Cambridge: Cambridge University Press, 1987.

Eno, Robert. *The Confucian Creation of Heaven: Philosophy and the Defense of Ritual Mastery*. Albany: State University of New York Press, 1990.

Esposito, John L., Darrell J. Fasching, and Todd Lewis. *World Religions Today*. New York: Oxford University Press, 2005.

Feng Youlan [Fung Yu-lan]. *A Short History of Chinese Philosophy*. New York: Macmillan, 1948.

———. *A History of Chinese Philosophy*. Translated by Derk Bodde. Princeton: Princeton University Press, 1952.

Flaix, M. Fournier De. "Development of Statistics of Religion." *Publications of the American Statistical Association* 3, no. 17 (1892): 18–36.

Foucault, Michel. "Truth and Power." In Rabinow, *Foucault Reader*, 51–76.

Furth, Charlotte. "Intellectual Change: From the Reform Movement to the May Fourth Movement, 1895–1920." In *Republican China 1912–1949, Part 1. The Cambridge History of China*, edited by John K. Fairbank, 322–405. Cambridge: Cambridge University Press, 1983.

Gardner, Daniel K. *The Four Books: The Basic Teachings of the Later Confucian Tradition*. Indianapolis: Hackett, 2007.

German Embassy, New Delhi. "Bilateral Cultural Relations." http://www.india .diplo.de/Vertretung/indien/en/13__Culture/Bilaterals/Bilateral__Relations .html.

Gerth, H. H., and C. Wright Mills, eds. *From Max Weber: Essays in Sociology*. New York: Oxford University Press, 1964.

Gieryn, Thomas. "Boundary-Work and the Demarcation of Science from Non-Science: Strains and Interests in Professional Interests of Scientists." *American Sociological Review* 48 (1983): 781–95.

Girardot, Norman J. *The Victorian Translation of China: James Legge's Oriental Pilgrimage*. Berkeley: University of California Press, 2002.

Glossop, Jennifer. *The Kids Book of World Religions*. Tonawanda, N.Y.: Kids Can Press, 2003.

Goossaert, Vincent, and David A. Palmer. *The Religious Question in Modern China*. Chicago: University of Chicago Press, 2011.

"Guo Qiyong: 'Lunyu Benlai Jiushi Jiachuan Husong Zhixue'" [Guo Qiyong: "The *Analects* Is Meant to Be Read in Every Household"]. *Guangming Daily*, April 1, 2008. http://book.people.com.cn/GB/69362/7070134.html.

Guttenplan, D. D. "Critics Worry about Influence of Chinese Institute on U.S. Campuses." *New York Times*, March 4, 2012.

Hacking, Ian. *The Social Construction of What?* Cambridge, Mass.: Harvard University Press, 1999.

Hadot, Pierre. *Philosophy as a Way of Life: Spiritual Exercises from Socrates to Foucault*. Oxford: Blackwell, 1995.

Han Xing. *Rujiao Wenti: Zhengming yu Fansi* [Question of Confucian Religion: Controversies and Reflections]. Shaanxi: Shaanxi People's Publishing House, 2004.

Hardacre, Helen. *Shinto and the State, 1868–1988*. Princeton: Princeton University Press, 1989.

Harpham, Geoffrey Galt. *Language Alone: The Critical Fetish of Modernity*. New York: Routledge, 2002.

Hart, D. G. *The University Gets Religion: Religious Studies in American Higher Education*. Baltimore: Johns Hopkins University Press, 1999.

Hopfe, Lewis, and Mark Woodward. *Religions of the World*. 10th ed. Upper Saddle River, N.J.: Prentice Hall, 2006.

Horne, Charles F., ed. *The Sacred Books and Early Literature of the East. Vol. 12 Medieval China*. New York: Parke, Austin, and Lipscomb, 1917.

Hsu, Cho-Yun. *Ancient China in Transition: An Analysis of Social Mobility, 722–222 B.C*. Stanford, Calif.: Stanford University Press, 1965.

Huang, Chin-shing. *Shengxian yu Shengtu: Lishi yu Zongjiao Lunwenji* [Sages and Saints: Collected Essays on History and Religion]. Taipei: Asian Culture Press, 2001.

Huaxia Fuxing Online. "Yangming Jingshe Huijiang Jianbao" [Yangming Spiritual House Retreat Report]. August 13, 2006. http://www.confucius2000.com/admin/list.asp?id=2574.

Huff, Toby E., and Wolfgang Schluchter, eds. *Max Weber and Islam*. New Brunswick, N.J.: Transaction, 1999.

Hung, Ho-fung. "Orientalism and Area Studies: The Case of Sinology." In *Overcoming the Two Cultures: Science versus the Humanities in the Modern World-System*, edited by Richard E. Lee and Immanuel Wallerstein, 87–104. Boulder, Colo.: Paradigm, 2004.

Israel, Jonathan I. *Enlightenment Contested: Philosophy, Modernity, and the Emancipation of Man, 1670–1752*. Oxford: Oxford University Press, 2008.

Ivanhoe, P. J. *Confucian Moral Self Cultivation*. Indianapolis: Hackett, 2000.

———. "Heaven as a Source for Ethnical Warrant in Early Confucianism." *Dao: A Journal of Comparative Philosophy* 6 (2007): 211–20.

James, William. *The Varieties of Religious Experience*. New York: Penguin, 1982.

Jensen, Lionel M. *Manufacturing Confucianism: Chinese Traditions and Universal Civilization*. Durham, N.C.: Duke University Press, 1998.

Ji Zhe. "Return to Durkheim: Civil Religion and the Moral Reconstruction in China." Paper presented at the Elementary Forms of Religious Life: A Dialogue between the Disciplines workshop, University of Oxford, July 2011.

Jiang Qing. *Zhengzhi Ruxue* [Political Confucianism]. Beijing: Sanlian Shudian, 2004.

———, ed. *Zhonghua Wenhua Jingdian Jichu Jiaoyu Songben* [The Fundamental Texts of Chinese Culture Classics for Reciting]. Beijing: Gaodeng Jiaoyu Chubanshe, 2004.

———. *Wangdao Zhengzhi yu Rujiao Xianzheng: Weilai Zhongguo Zhengzhi Fazhande Ruxuesikao* [The Politics of Kingly Government and Confucian Constitutionalism: Confucian Reflections on the Future Development of Chinese Politics]. Guizhou: Yangming Academy, 2010.

———. *A Confucian Constitutional Order: How China's Ancient Past Can Shape Its Political Future*, edited by Daniel Bell and Ruiping Fan, translated by Edmund Ryden. Princeton: Princeton University Press, 2012.

Jiang Qing and Daniel Bell. "A Confucian Constitution for China." *New York Times*, July 10, 2012.

Jin Ze and Yonghui Qiu. *Zhongguo Zongjiao Baogao 2010* [Annual Report on China's Religions 2010]. Beijing: Social Sciences Academic Press, 2010.

Jing, Jun. *The Temple of Memories: History, Power, and Morality in a Chinese Village*. Stanford, Calif.: Stanford University Press, 1996.

Johnson, Ian. "China Gets Religion!" *New York Review of Books*, December 22, 2011.

Jones, David Martin. *The Image of China in Western Social and Political Thought*. Hampshire: Palgrave, 2001.

Jordan, Louis Henry. *Comparative Religion: Its Genesis and Growth*. New York: Scribner, 1905.

———. *Comparative Religion: Its Method and Scope*. London: Henry Frowde, 1908.

Kang Xiaoguang. *Benevolent Government (Ren Zheng): The Third Path of China's Political Development*. Singapore: World Scientific, 2005.

Kang Youwei. *Kang Youwei Zhenglunji* [Collective Political Writings of Kang Youwei]. Beijing: Zhonghua shuju, 1981.

Kasahara, Kazuo, ed. *A History of Japanese Religion*. Tokyo: Kosei, 2001.

Keenan, Barry C. *Neo-Confucian Self-Cultivation*. Dimensions of Asian Spirituality. Honolulu: University of Hawaii Press, 2011.

Kim, Hongkyung. "A Party for the Spirits: Ritual Practice in Confucianism." In *Religions of Korea in Practice*, edited by Robert E. Buswell Jr., 163–76. Princeton: Princeton University Press, 2007.

King, Ursula, ed. *Turning Points in Religious Studies*. Edinburgh: T&T Clark, 1990.

Kitagawa, Joseph M. "Introduction to the *Essays in the History of Religions* by Joachim Wach." *In Essays in the History of Religions*, edited by Joseph M. Kitagawa and Gregory D. Alles, vii–ix. New York: Macmillan, 1988.

Kitagawa, Joseph M., and John S. Strong. "Friedrich Max Müller and the Comparative Study of Religion." In *Nineteenth Century Religious Thought in the West*, edited by Ninian Smart et al., 179–214. Cambridge: Cambridge University Press, 1985.

Koh, Eunkang. "Gender Issues and Confucian Scriptures: Is Confucianism Incompatible with Gender Equality in South Korea?" *Bulletin of SOAS* 71, no. 2 (2008): 345–62.

Kuah-Pearce, Khun Eng. "Cultural and Network Capitals: Chinese Women and the 'Religious' Industry in South China." In *Chinese Women and Their Cultural and Network Capitals*, edited by Khun Eng Kuah, 121–44. Singapore: Marshall Cavendish Academic, 2004.

Kuhn, Thomas S. *The Structure of Scientific Revolution*. Chicago: University of Chicago Press, 1962.

Kuper, Adam. "Anthropology." In Porter and Ross, *Cambridge History of Science*, 354–78.

Lafraniere, Sharon. "China Might Force Visits to Mom and Dad." *New York Times*, January 29, 2011.

Lamont, Michèle, and Virág Molnár. "The Study of Boundaries in the Social Sciences." *American Sociological Review* 28 (2002): 167–95.

Latour, Bruno. *Science in Action: How to Follow Scientists and Engineers through Society*. Cambridge, Mass.: Harvard University Press, 1987.

———. *The Pasteurization of France*. Cambridge, Mass.: Harvard University Press, 1988.

Legge, James. *The Chinese Classics: With a Translation, Critical and Exegetical Notes, Prolegomena, and Copious Indexes*. London: Trübner, 1861–72.

———. *The Life and Teachings of Confucius, with Explanatory Notes*. Philadelphia: J.B. Lippincott, 1867.

———. *Confucianism in Relation to Christianity: A Paper Read before the Missionary Conference in Shanghai on May 11th, 1877*. Shanghai: Kelly and Walsh, 1877.

———. *The Religions of China: Confucianism and Taoism Described and Compared with Christianity*. London: Hodder and Stoughton, 1880.

———, trans. *The Shu King, or Book of Historical Documents*. Whitefish, Mont.: Kessinger, 2004.

Lewis, Mark. *Sanctioned Violence in Early China*. Albany: State University of New York Press, 1990.

Leys, Simon, trans. *The Analects of Confucius*. New York: Norton, 1997.

Li, Chenyang. *The Sage and the Second Sex: Confucianism, Ethics, and Gender*. Chicago: Open Court, 2000.

Li Shen. "Zhongguo Rujiaoshi Zaokong Zhounianji" [Remarks on the First Anniversary of the Attack on History of Confucianism as a Religion in China], October 16, 2002. http://www.confucius2000.com/confucian/rujiao/zgrjszkznj.htm.

Li Tiangang. *Zhongguo Liyi Zhizheng: Lishi, Wenxian he Yiyi* [Chinese Rites Controversy: History, Documents and Meaning]. Shanghai: Shanghai Guji Chubanshe, 1998.

———. *Kuawenha de Chanshi* [Cross-Cultural Interpretation]. Beijing: New Star Press, 2007.

Liu, Lydia. *Translingual Practice: Literature, National Culture, and Translated Modernity, China 1900–1937*. Stanford, Calif.: Stanford University Press, 1995.

Liu, Xun. *Daoist Modern: Innovation, Lay Practice, and the Community of Inner Alchemy in Republican Shanghai*. Harvard East Asian Monographs. Cambridge, Mass.: Harvard University Asia Center, 2009.

Lloyd, G.E.R. *Disciplines in the Making: Cross-Cultural Perspectives on Elites, Learning, and Innovation*. Oxford: Oxford University Press, 2009.

Long, Arthur J. "The Life and Work of J. Estlin Carpenter." In Smith, *Truth, Liberty, Religion*, 265–89.

Macdonell, Arthur Anthony. "Max Müller, Friedrich 1823–1900." In *The Dictionary of National Biography*, edited by Leslie Stephen and Sidney Lee, 151–57. London: Smith, Elder & Co., 1901.

Macklin, Ruth. "The Forms and Norms of Closure." In Engelhardt and Caplan, *Scientific Controversies*, 615–24.

Madsen, Richard. *Meaning and Modernity: Religion, Polity, and Self.* Berkeley: University of California Press, 2001.

Makeham, John. *Lost Soul: "Confucianism" in Contemporary Chinese Academic Discourse.* Harvard-Yenching Institute Monographs. Cambridge, Mass.: Harvard University Asia Center for the Harvard-Yenching Institute, 2008.

Mann, Susan, and Yu-Yin Cheng. *Under Confucian Eyes: Writings on Gender in Chinese History.* Berkeley: University of California Press, 2001.

Mansson-McGinty, Anna. *Becoming Muslim: Western Women's Conversions to Islam.* New York: Palgrave Macmillan, 2006.

Mao Zedong. "Mao Zedong Tongzhi Guanyu Jiaqiang Zongjiao Wenti Yanjiu de Pishi" [Memo from Comrade Mao Zedong Regarding the Strengthening of Studies of Religions]. December 30, 1963. http://zjwh.qikan.com/ArticleView .aspx?titleid=zjwh20040403.

Martin, Brian. *Scientific Knowledge in Controversy: The Social Dynamics of the Fluoridation Debate.* Albany: State University of New York Press, 1991.

Masini, Federico. *The Formation of Modern Chinese Lexicon and Its Evolution toward a National Language: The Period from 1840 to 1898.* Berkeley: *Journal of Chinese Linguistics* Monograph Series No. 6, 1993.

Masuchika, Glenn. "Review of *The World's Wisdom: Sacred Texts of the World's Religions.*" *Library Journal* (1994). www.libraryjournal.com.

Masuzawa, Tomoko. *The Invention of World Religions: Or, How European Universalism Was Preserved in the Language of Pluralism.* Chicago: University of Chicago Press, 2005.

Max Müller, Friedrich. *Chips from a German Workshop.* New York: Scribner, 1869.

———. *Lectures on the Science of Religion, with a Paper on Buddhist Nihilism, and a Translation of the Dhammapada or "Path of Virtue."* New York: Scribner, 1872.

———. *Lectures on the Origin and Growth of Religion, as Illustrated by the Religions of India 1878, Delivered in the Chapter House, Westminster Abbey, in April, May, and June, 1878.* London: Longmans, Green, and Co., 1878.

———. "Preface." In *Sacred Books of the East,* edited by Friedrich Max Müller, ix–xxxviii. Oxford: Oxford University Press, 1879.

———, ed. *Sacred Books of the East.* Oxford: Oxford University Press, 1879–94.

———. *Natural Religion: The Gifford Lectures Delivered before the University of Glasgow in 1888.* London: Longmans, Green, and Co., 1889.

———. "The Religions of China: Confucianism, Taoism, Buddhism and Christianity." In *Last Essays: Essays on the Science of Religion,* 259–324. New York: Longmans, Green, and Co., 1901.

Max Müller, Friedrich, and Jon R. Stone. *The Essential Max Müller: On Language, Mythology, and Religion.* New York: Palgrave Macmillan, 2002.

Max Müller, Georgina. *The Life and Letters of the Right Honourable Friedrich Max Müller.* London: Longmans, Green, and Co., 1902.

McCannon, John. *How to Prepare for the AP World History.* Hauppauge, N.Y.: Barron's Educational Series, 2005.

McCutcheon, Russell T. *Manufacturing Religion: The Discourse on Sui Generis Religion and the Politics of Nostalgia.* New York: Oxford University Press, 1997.

McGetchin, Douglas T., Peter K. J. Park, and Damodar SarDesai, eds. *Sanskrit and "Orientalism": Indology and Comparative Linguistics in Germany, 1750–1958*. New Delhi: Manohar, 2004.

Minamiki, George. *The Chinese Rites Controversy: From Its Beginning to Modern Times*. Chicago: Loyola University Press, 1985.

"Mind, Faith and Spirit." *Princeton Weekly Bulletin* 88, no. 25 (April 26, 1999).

Molendijk, Arie L. *The Emergence of the Science of Religion in the Netherlands*. Leiden: Brill, 2005.

Molloy, Michael. *Experiencing the World's Religions: Tradition, Challenge, and Change*. 3rd ed. New York: McGraw-Hill, 2004.

———. *Experiencing the World's Religions: Tradition, Challenge, and Change*. 5th ed. New York: McGraw-Hill, 2010.

Moses, Jeffrey. *Oneness: Great Principles Shared by All Religions*. Rev. ed. New York: Ballantine Books, 2002.

Mungello, David E., *Curious Land: Jesuit Accommodation and the Origins of Sinology*. Stuttgart: Franz Steiner Werlag Wiesbaden GMBH, 1985.

———, ed. *The Chinese Rites Controversy: Its History and Meaning*. Nettetal: Steyler Verlag, 1994.

Naquin, Susan. *Peking: Temples and City Life, 1400–1900*. Berkeley: University of California Press, 2000.

Nedostup, Rebecca. *Superstitious Regimes: Religion and the Politics of Chinese Modernity*. Harvard East Asian Monographs. Cambridge, Mass.: Harvard University Asia Center, 2009.

Nelkin, Dorothy, ed. *Controversy: Politics of Technical Decision*. London: Sage, 1979.

Neusner, Jacob, ed. *World Religions in America: An Introduction*. 3rd ed. Grand Rapids, Mich.: Westminster John Knox, 2003.

Neville, Robert C. *Boston Confucianism: Portable Tradition in the Late-Modern World*. Albany: State University of New York Press, 2000.

Nietzsche, Friedrich. *On the Genealogy of Morality*. Translated by Carol Diethe. Cambridge: Cambridge University Press, 1994 (1887).

Noll, Ray R., ed. *100 Roman Documents Concerning the Chinese Rites Controversy (1645–1941)*. San Francisco: Ricci Institute for Chinese-Western Cultural History, University of San Francisco, 1939.

Novak, Philip. *The World's Wisdom: Sacred Texts of the World's Religions*. San Francisco: Harper, 1995.

Nyitray, Vivian-Lee. "Fundamentalism and the Position of Women in Confucianism." In *Fundamentalism and Women in World Religions*, edited by Arvind Sharma and Katherine K. Young, 47–77. New York: T&T Clark, 2007.

Nylan, Michael. *Five "Confucian" Classics*. New Haven: Yale University Press, 2002.

———. "A Problematic Model: The Han 'Orthodox Synthesis,' Then and Now." In *Imagining Boundaries: Changing Confucian Doctrines*, edited by K. Chow, O. Ng, and J. B. Henderson, 17–56. Albany: State University of New York Press, 1999.

Nylan, Michael, and Thomas A. Wilson. *Lives of Confucius: Civilization's Greatest Sage through the Ages*. New York: Doubleday, 2010.

O'Brien, Patrick K., ed. *Atlas of World History*. New York: Oxford University Press, 1999.

Olender, Maurice. *The Language of Paradise: Race, Religion, and Philology in the Nineteenth Century*. Translated by Arthur Goldhammer. Cambridge, Mass.: Harvard University Press, 1992.

Osborne, Mary Pope. *One World, Many Religions: The Ways We Worship* New York: Knopf, 1996.

Overmyer, Daniel L. *Local Religion in North China in the Twentieth Century: The Structure and Organization of Community Rituals and Beliefs*. Handbook of Oriental Studies, Section 4, China. Leiden: Brill, 2009.

Oxford English Dictionary. Oxford: Oxford University Press, 2012.

Pepper, Suzanne. *Radicalism and Education Reform in 20th-Century China: The Search for an Ideal Development Model*. Cambridge: Cambridge University Press, 1996.

Perkins, Franklin. *Leibniz and China: A Commerce of Light*. Cambridge: Cambridge University Press, 2004.

Pluralism Project. "Statistics." Pluralism Project of Harvard University. http://pluralism.org/resources/statistics/.

Poo, Mu-chou. *In Search of Personal Welfare: A View of Ancient Chinese Religion*. Albany: State University of New York Press, 1998.

Pope Benedict. *Truth and Tolerance: Christian Belief and World Religions*. Translated by Henry Taylor. San Francisco: Ignatius Press, 2004.

Pope John Paul II. "In Quest of Dialogue with China." *Fidelio* 10, no. 3 (Fall 2001). http://www.schillerinstitute.org/fid_97-01/013_invite_dialogue_JPII.html.

Porter, Andrew, ed. *The Imperial Horizons of British Protestant Missions, 1880–1914*. Cambridge: Eerdmans, 2003.

Porter, Theodore M., and Dorothy Ross, eds. *The Cambridge History of Science, Vol. 7: The Modern Social Science*. Cambridge: Cambridge University Press, 2003.

———. "Introduction: Writing the History of Social Science." In Porter and Ross, *Cambridge History of Science*, 1–12.

Puett, Michael. *To Become a God: Cosmology, Sacrifice, and Self-Divinization in Early China*. Cambridge, Mass.: Harvard University Press, 2002.

Rabinow, Paul, ed. *The Foucault Reader*. New York: Pantheon Books, 1984.

Rambo, Lewis R. *Understanding Religious Conversion*. New Haven: Yale University Press, 1993.

Rambo, Lewis R., and Charles Farhadian, eds. *Oxford Handbook of Religious Conversion*. Oxford: Oxford University Press, forthcoming.

Raphals, Lisa Ann. *Sharing the Light: Representations of Women and Virtue in Early China*. SUNY Series in Chinese Philosophy and Culture. Albany: State University of New York Press, 1998.

Reader, Ian. *Religion in Contemporary Japan*. Honolulu: University of Hawaii Press, 1991.

"Rectification of Statues." *Economist*, January 20, 2011.

Reischauer, Edwin O. *The Japanese*. Cambridge, Mass.: Harvard University Press, 1977.

Ren Jiyu, ed. *Rujiao Wenti Zhenglun Ji* [Confucianism as a Religion Debate]. Beijing: Religion and Culture Press, 2000.

Reno, R. R. "Best Schools for Theology." *First Things: The Journal of Religion, Culture and Public Life*, August 30, 2006. http://www.firstthings.com/onthesquare/2006/08/reno-best-schools-for-theology/rr-reno.

Robson, James. "Faith in Museums: On the Confluence of Museums and Religious Sites in Asia." *PMLA* 125, no. 1 (2010): 121–28.

Ronan, Charles E., and Bonnie B. C. Oh, eds. *East Meets West: The Jesuits in China, 1582–1773*. Chicago: Loyola University Press, 1988.

Rosenlee, Li-Hsiang Lisa. *Confucianism and Women: A Philosophical Interpretation*. Albany: State University of New York Press, 2006.

Rozman, Gilbert, ed. *The East Asian Region: Confucian Heritage and Its Modern Adaptation*. Princeton: Princeton University Press, 1991.

Said, Edward. *Orientalism*. New York: Vintage, 1979.

Schwartz, Benjamin I. *The World of Thought in Ancient China*. Cambridge, Mass.: Belknap, 1985.

Scott, Janet Lee. *For Gods, Ghosts and Ancestors: The Chinese Tradition of Paper Offerings*. Seattle: University of Washington Press, 2007.

Seager, Richard Hughes. *The World's Parliament of Religions: The East/West Encounter, Chicago 1893*. Bloomington: Indiana University Press, 1995.

Seligman, Adam B., Robert P. Weller, Michael J. Puett, and Bennett Simon. *Ritual and Its Consequences: An Essay on the Limits of Sincerity*. Oxford: Oxford University Press, 2008.

Shapin, Steven. "Here and Everywhere: Sociology of Scientific Knowledge." *Annual Review of Sociology* 21 (1995): 289–321.

Sharpe, Eric J. *Comparative Religion: A History*. London: Duckworth, 1986.

Shih, Fang-long. "Women, Religions, and Feminism." In *The New Blackwell Companion to the Sociology of Religion*, edited by Bryan S. Turner, 221–44. Oxford: Blackwell, 2010.

Shun, Kwong-loi. *Mencius and Early Chinese Thought*. Stanford, Calif.: Stanford University Press, 1997.

Sina News. "Beijing Yibaibashidui Fuqi Zhongqiu Miandui Kongzi Huaxiang Xuanshi Yongbu Lihun" [180 Couples in Beijing Vowing Never to Divorce before the Portrait of Confucius]. September 29, 2004. http://news.sina.com.cn/s/2004-09-29/08543798162s.shtml.

———. "Yu Dan *Zhuangzi Xinde* Baiwan Xiaoshou Jihua Tiqian Wancheng" [Yu Dan's *The Zhuangzi from the Heart* Sold One Million Copies Ahead of Schedule]. March 19, 2007. http://cul.book.sina.com.cn/o/2007-03-19/1025168163.html.

Small, Mario L. "Departmental Conditions and the Emergence of New Disciplines: Two Cases in the Legitimation of African-American Studies." *Theory and Society* 28 (1999): 659–707.

Smith, Barbara, ed. *Truth, Liberty, Religion: Essays Celebrating Two Hundred Years of Manchester College*. Oxford: Manchester College, 1986.

Smith, Christian. *What Is a Person? Rethinking Humanity, Social Life, and the Moral Good from the Person Up*. Chicago: University of Chicago Press, 2010.

Smith, Huston. *The World's Religions: Our Great Wisdom Traditions*. San Francisco: Harper, 1991 (1958).

———. *The Illustrated World's Religions: Guide to Our Wisdom Traditions*. San Francisco: Harper, 1995.

Smith, Jonathan Z. "A Matter of Class: Taxonomies of Religion." *Harvard Theological Review* 89, no. 4 (1996): 387–403.

Smith, Robert. *Ancestor Worship in Contemporary Japan*. Stanford, Calif.: Stanford University Press, 1974.

Smith, Tom W. "Religious Change around the World." NORC/University of Chicago, October 23, 2009.

Smith, Wilfred Cantwell. *The Meaning and End of Religion: A New Approach to the Religious Traditions of Mankind*. New York: Macmillan, 1963.

Spence, Jonathan D. *The Memory Palace of Matteo Ricci*. New York: Penguin, 1985.

———. "Claims and Counter-Claims: The Kangxi Emperor and the Europeans (1661–1722)." In Mungello, *Chinese Rites Controversy*, 15–30.

Spurway, Neil. *Humanity, Environment and God: Glasgow Centenary Gifford Lectures*. Oxford: Blackwell, 1993.

Standaert, Nicolas. "The Jesuits Did Not Manufacture 'Confucianism.'" *East Asian Science, Technology, and Medicine* 16 (1999): 115–32.

Steadman, Lyle B., and Craig T. Palmer. *The Supernatural and Natural Selection: The Evolution of Religion*. Boulder, Colo.: Paradigm, 2008.

Steinfels, Peter. "Globally, Religion Defies Easily Identified Patterns." *New York Times*, October 23, 2009.

Steinmetz, George. *The Devil's Handwriting: Precoloniality and the German Colonial State in Qingdao, Samoa, and Southwest Africa*. Chicago: University of Chicago Press, 2007.

Stocking, George W., Jr. *Victorian Anthropology*. New York: Free Press, 1987.

Stroumsa, Guy G. *A New Science: The Discovery of Religion in the Age of Reason*. Cambridge, Mass.: Harvard University Press, 2010.

Su Shipeng. "Guji Baohu Ying Chuanshi Yu Chutu Bingzhong" [The Preservation of Chinese Classics Should Value Recently Discovered Texts as Well as Received Texts]. *People's Daily*, March 27, 2007.

Sun, Anna. "The Fate of Confucianism as a Religion in Socialist China: Controversies and Paradoxes." In *State, Market, and Religions in Chinese Societies*, edited by Fenggang Yang and Joseph B. Tamney, 229–53. Leiden: Brill, 2005.

———. "Confusions over Confucianism: Controversies over the Religious Nature of Confucianism, 1870–2007." PhD diss., Princeton University, 2008.

———. "The Revival of Confucian Rites in Contemporary China." In *Confucianism and Spiritual Traditions in Modern China and Beyond*, edited by Fenggang Yang and Joseph B. Tamney, 309–28. Leiden: Brill, 2012.

———. "To Become a Confucian." In Rambo and Farhadian, *Oxford Handbook of Religious Conversion*. Oxford: Oxford University Press, forthcoming.

Sutcliffe, Peter. *The Oxford University Press: An Informal History*. Oxford: Oxford University Press, 1978.

Swidler, Ann. "Culture in Action: Symbols and Strategies." *American Sociological Review* 51 (1986): 273–86.

Swyngedouw, Jan. "Religion in Contemporary Japanese Society." In *Religion and Society in Modern Japan*, edited by Mark R. Mullins, Shimazono Susumu, and Paul L. Swanson, 49–80. Berkeley, Calif.: Asian Humanities Press, 1993.

Tamney, Joseph B., and Linda Hsueh-Ling Chiang. *Modernization, Globalization, and Confucianism in Chinese Societies*. Westport, Conn.: Praeger, 2002.

Taylor, Rodney Leon. *The Cultivation of Sagehood as a Religious Goal in Neo-Confucianism*. Missoula, Mont.: Scholars Press, 1978.

———. *The Way of Heaven: An Introduction to the Confucian Religious Life*. Leiden: Brill, 1986.

———. *The Religious Dimensions of Confucianism*. Albany: State University of New York Press, 1990.

Teiser, Stephen F. "Introduction: The Spirits of Chinese Religion." In *Religions of China in Practice*, edited by Donald Lopez, Jr., 3–37. Princeton: Princeton University Press, 1996.

Thal, Sarah. "A Religion That Was Not a Religion: The Creation of Modern Shinto in Nineteenth-Century Japan." In *The Invention of Religion: Rethinking Belief in Politics and History*, edited by Derek R. Peterson and Darren R. Walhof, 100–114. New Brunswick, N.J.: Rutgers University Press, 2002.

Tiele, C. P. *Outline of the History of Religion to the Spread of Universal Religions*. Translated by J. Estlin Carpenter. London: Kegan Paul, Trench, Trübner, 1877.

Tillman, Hoyt Cleveland. "The Use of Neo-Confucianism, Revisited: A Reply to Professor de Bary." *Philosophy East and West* 44, no. 1 (1944): 135–42.

Toropov, Brandon, and Father Luke Buckles. *The Complete Idiot's Guide to World Religions*. 3rd ed. New York: Alpha Books, 2004.

Treadgold, Donald W. *The West in Russia and China: Religious and Secular Thought in Modern Times, Volume 2: China, 1582–1949*. Cambridge: Cambridge University Press, 1973.

Tu Weiming. *Centrality and Commonality: An Essay on Chung-Yung*. Honolulu: University Press of Hawaii, 1976.

———. *Humanity and Self-Cultivation*. Berkeley: University of California Press, 1979.

———. *Confucian Thought: Selfhood as Creative Transformation*. Albany: State University of New York Press, 1985.

———, ed. *The Triadic Chord: Confucian Ethics, Industrial East Asia, and Max Weber: Proceedings of the 1987 Singapore Conference on Confucian Ethics and the Modernization of Industrial East Asia*. Singapore: Institute of East Asian Philosophies, 1991.

———. *Confucian Traditions in East Asian Modernity: Moral Education and Economic Culture in Japan and the Four Mini-Dragons*. Cambridge, Mass.: Harvard University Press, 1996.

———. *Lunruxue de Zongjiaoxing: Dui Zhongyong de Xiandai Chanshi* [The Religiosity of Confucianism: Modern Interpretation of Zhongyong]. Wuhan: Wuhan University Press, 1999.

Tucker, Mary Evelyn, and John H. Berthrong. *Confucianism and Ecology: The Interrelation of Heaven, Earth, and Humans*. Religions of the World and

Ecology. Cambridge, Mass.: Harvard University Center for the Study of World Religions, 1998.

Tucker, Mary Evelyn, and Tu Weiming, eds. *Confucian Spirituality*. New York: Crossroad, 2003–4.

Turner, Bryan S. *Weber and Islam*. London: Routledge Kegan Paul, 1978.

United Nations Educational, Scientific, and Cultural Organization. "Literature and Translation." http://portal.unesco.org/culture/en/ev.php-URL_ID=1523&URL_DO=DO_TOPIC&URL_SECTION=201.html.

Vatican Holy Office. "1704, Nov. 20: Rome's Evaluation of Maigrot's 1693 Edict." In Noll, *100 Roman Documents*, Document No. 6, 8–24.

Veyne, Paul. *Did the Greeks Believe in Their Myths? An Essay on the Constitutive Imagination*. Chicago: University of Chicago Press, 1988.

von Falkenhausen, Lothar. *Chinese Society in the Age of Confucius (1000–250 BC): The Archaeological Evidence*. Los Angeles: Cotsen Institute of Archaeology, University of California, Los Angeles, 2006.

Walls, Andrew F. "The Eighteenth-Century Protestant Missionary Awakening in Its European Context." In *Christian Missions and the Enlightenment*, edited by Brian Stanley, 22–45. Surrey: Curzon Press, 2001.

Wang Dasan. "Dalu Xin Rujia Yu Xiandai Xin Rujia" [Mainland China New Confucians and Modern New Confucians]. September 29, 2009. http://www.xici.net/d31196763.htm.

Watts, Ruth. "Manchester College and Education, 1786–1853." In Smith, *Truth, Liberty, Religion*, 76–110.

Weber, Max. *The Religion of China: Confucianism and Taoism*. Translated by Hans H. Gerth and Don Martindale. New York: Free Press, 1951 (1915).

———. *Ancient Judaism*. Translated by Hans H. Gerth and Don Martindale. New York: Free Press, 1952 (1917–19).

———. *The Religion of India: The Sociology of Hinduism and Buddhism*. Translated by Hans H. Gerth and Don Martindale. New York: Free Press, 1958 (1916–17).

———. *The Protestant Ethic and the Spirit of Capitalism*. Translated by Talcott Parsons, introduction by Anthony Giddens. New York: Routledge, 2001 (1904–5).

Wen Li. "Guanyu Rujiao yu Zongjiao de Taolun" [Confucianism and Religion Debate]. *Zhongguo zhexue shi* [The History of Chinese Philosophy] 2 (2002): 63–75.

Whitney, William Dwight. "Müller's Rig-Veda and Commentary." *The New Englander* 35 (1876): 772–91.

Widmer, Ellen, and Kang-i Sun Chang. *Writing Women in Late Imperial China*. Stanford, Calif.: Stanford University Press, 1997.

Wiebe, Donald. *The Politics of Religious Studies: The Continuing Conflict with Theology in the Academy*. New York: St. Martin's, 1999.

Wilson, Epiphanius. *Sacred Books of the East*. Rev. ed. New York: Colonial Press, 1900.

Wilson, Thomas A. *Genealogy of the Way: The Construction and Use of the Confucian Tradition in Late Imperial China*. Stanford, Calif.: Stanford University Press, 1995.

———. "The Ritual Formation of Confucian Orthodoxy and the Descendants of the Sage." *Journal of Asian Studies* 55, no. 3 (1996): 559–84.

———. *On Sacred Grounds: Culture, Society, Politics, and the Formation of the Cult of Confucius.* Harvard East Asian Monographs. Cambridge, Mass.: Harvard University Asia Center, 2002.

World Values Survey. "World Values Survey: China." http://www.worldvaluessurvey .org/index_surveys.

Wuthnow, Robert. *Communities of Discourse: Ideology and Social Structure in the Reformation, the Enlightenment, and European Socialism.* Cambridge, Mass.: Harvard University Press, 1989.

Xiao, Yang. "Ethical Thought in China." In *The Routledge Companion to Ethics*, edited by John Skorupsi, 3–20. London and New York: Routledge, 2010.

Xinhua News Agency. "Qufu Kongmiao Juxing Dadian Jikongzi 2,555 Sui" [Grand Ceremony Venerating Confucius on His 2,555th Birthday Took Place in the Confucius Temple in Qufu]. September 28, 2004. http://news.xinhuanet .com/photo/2004-09/28/content_2034695.htm.

———. "Quanqiu Jiangban Baisuo Kongzi Xueyuan" [There Will Be 100 Confucius Institutes All over the World]. November 21, 2004. http://news.xinhuanet .com/newscenter/2004-11/16/content_2222750.htm.

———. "07 Zhongguo Zuojia Fuhaobang Jiexiao" [The 2007 List of Wealthiest Chinese Writers]. November 6, 2007. http://news.xinhuanet.com/book/2007 -11/06/content_7018276.htm.

———. "Jesus to Join Confucius as Qufu Plans Church." *China Daily*, December 12, 2010. http://www.chinadaily.com.cn/china/2010-12/13/content_11695800 .htm.

———. "Statue Moved Inside." *China Daily*, April 22, 2011. http://www.china daily.com.cn/cndy/2011-04/22/content_12373866.htm.

Xue Yong. "Zouxiang Mengmei de Wenhua Baoshou Zhuyi—Chi Dangdai 'Daru' Jiang Qing" [Blind Cultural Conservativism: Refuting the So-Called "Confucian Master" Jiang Qing]. http://www.people.com.cn/GB/wenhua/27296/2627986 .html.

Yamane, David, and Sarah MacMillen. *Real Stories of Christian Initiation: Lessons for and from the RCIA.* Collegeville, Minn.: Liturgical Press, 2006.

Yang, C. K. *Religion in Chinese Society: A Study of Contemporary Social Functions of Religion and Some of Their Historical Factors.* Berkeley: University of California Press, 1961.

Yang, Fenggang. "Between Secularist Ideology and Desecularizing Reality: The Birth and Growth of Religious Research in Communist China." *Sociology of Religion* 65, no. 2 (2004): 101–19.

———. "A Sociological Perspective on Confucianism as Religion." *Journal of Lanzhou University (Social Sciences)* 36, no. 2 (2008): 2–8.

———. "Confucianism as Civil Religion." Paper presented at the City University of Hong Kong Habit of the Heart Conference, December 2011.

———. *Religion in China: Survival and Revival under Communist Rule.* Oxford: Oxford University Press, 2011.

Yang, Fenggang, and Joseph B. Tamney, eds. *State, Market, and Religions in Chinese Societies.* Leiden: Brill, 2005.

———, eds. *Confucianism and Spiritual Traditions in Modern China and Beyond*. Leiden: Brill, 2012.

Yang, Fenggang, Victor Yuan, Anna Sun, Lu Yengfang, Rodney Stark, Byron Johnson, Eric Liu, Carson Mencken, and Chiu Heu-Yuan. *Spiritual Life Study of Chinese Residents*. University Park, Pa.: Association of Religion Data Archives, 2007.

Yang, Mayfair Mei-hui, ed. *Chinese Religiosities: Afflictions of Modernity and State Formation*. Berkeley: University of California Press, 2008.

Yu Dan. *The* Analects *from the Heart*. Beijing: Zhonghua Shuju, 2006.

———. *Lunyu Xinde* [Confucius from the Heart]. Beijing: Zhonghua, 2006.

Yu Dan, and Esther Tyldesley. *Confucius from the Heart*. New York: Atria Books, 2009.

Yu Ying-Shih. *Rujia Lunli yu Shangren Jingshen* [The Spirit of Confucian Ethics and the Merchant]. Guilin: Guangxi Normal University Press, 2004.

Zhang Wei-Bo. *Minguo Chuqi Zunkong Sichao Yanjiu* [Study of Confucianity Thoughts in Early Republic China]. Beijing: Renmin Chubanshe, 2006.

Zhou Beichen. *Rujiao Yaoyi* [The Essentials of Confucian Religions]. Hong Kong: China International Culture Press, 2009.

Index

Lightning Source UK Ltd.
Milton Keynes UK
UKHW012002220123
415737UK00003B/108